MENTORING
TEACHERS
TOWARD
EXCELLENCE

MENTORING TEACHERS TOWARD EXCELLENCE

Supporting and Developing Highly Qualified Teachers

Judith H. Shulman and
Mistilina Sato, Editors

Foreword by Sharon Feiman-Nemser

WestEd Published in
Partnership with WestEd

JOSSEY-BASS
A Wiley Imprint
www.josseybass.com

Published by Jossey-Bass
A Wiley Imprint
989 Market Street, San Francisco, CA 94103-1741   www.josseybass.com

Jossey-Bass books and products are available through most bookstores. To contact Jossey-Bass directly call our Customer Care Department within the U.S. at 800-956-7739, outside the U.S. at 317-572-3986, or fax 317-572-4002.

Jossey-Bass also publishes its books in a variety of electronic formats. Some content that appears in print may not be available in electronic books.

Library of Congress Cataloging-in-Publication Data
Mentoring teachers toward excellence : supporting and developing highly
qualified teachers / Judith H. Shulman and Mistilina Sato, editors ;
foreword by Sharon Feiman-Nemser.—1st ed.
    p. cm. — (Jossey-Bass education series)
  Includes bibliographical references and index.
  ISBN-13: 978-0-7879-8434-2
  ISBN-10: 0-7879-8434-5
  1. Mentoring in education—United States. 2. Teachers—In-service
training—United States. 3. Teachers—Certification—Standards—United
States. I. Shulman, Judith. II. Sato, Mistilina.
  LB1731.4.M473 2006
  371.2'03–dc22   2006001255

Printed in the United States of America
FIRST EDITION
HB Printing 10 9 8 7 6 5 4 3 2 1

Jossey-Bass Education Series

CONTENTS

FOREWORD

Judy Shulman and Misty Sato have assembled an intriguing collection of cases and case commentaries about the mentoring of candidates applying for certification by the National Board for Professional Teaching Standards (NBPTS). In these cases, experienced teachers who have already earned National Board Certification and other experienced educators write about the challenges and dilemmas of helping colleagues prepare for this rigorous, standards-based assessment. In particular, they describe their efforts to help teachers understand, enact, and document the vision of accomplished teaching embodied in the Board's professional teaching standards. The cases raise important questions about the role of the mentor, the pedagogy of mentoring, and the culture of teaching.

In calling these "cases of mentoring," the editors highlight two characteristics: the hierarchical nature of the mentoring relationship and its educative purposes. The first characteristic flows from the term *mentor*, which denotes someone with more experience and expertise helping someone with less experience and expertise. In principle, the mentoring relationship is symmetrical in terms of respect and asymmetrical in terms of expertise. The latter distinction sits uneasily in a field like teaching, where teachers are differentiated by years of experience, not levels of expertise, and there is no strong tradition of peer mentoring and review. Many of the cases in this book show teacher-mentors struggling to exercise their authority as stewards of standards and the profession, especially in situations where teachers' practice does not reflect the spirit of the standards formulated by the National Board.

The second element reminds us that serious mentoring is a form of individualized professional development, a mini-apprenticeship in "critical colleagueship" (Lord, 1994). The cases provide vivid images of mentors trying to help teachers develop the analytical skills needed to study their practice and determine how well it aligns with the vision of good teaching reflected in national teaching standards. This is not the conventional image of mentoring, which we generally associate with veteran teachers assisting new teachers during their early years on the job. Too often such mentoring takes the form of technical assistance and emotional support. In my own studies of mentoring, I discovered that the most thoughtful mentors had a clear vision of good teaching to guide their work and a repertoire of strategies for helping teachers develop a principled and reflective practice (Feiman-Nemser and Parker, 1993; Feiman-Nemser, 1998). Borrowing from Dewey, I coined the phrase "educative mentoring" to refer to standards-based, development-oriented mentoring and to distinguish it from what Ellen Moir, director of the New Teacher Center at the University of California, Santa Cruz, likes to call "feel good support." The cases here help fill out our images of educative mentoring.

They also reveal how educative mentoring challenges prevailing norms of interaction among teachers and calls for skills and dispositions that most teachers have little opportunity to develop. Reading this book, I was reminded of a peer mentoring project in which two teachers with greater expertise but fewer years of teaching experience mentored a veteran of twenty years who was struggling to align her teaching with new math and reading standards. The teachers who participated in this project, which took place in a professional development school affiliated with Michigan State University, had to overcome the risk of sharing their teaching with others and develop new ways of talking and working together (Beasley, Corbin, Feiman-Nemser, and Shank, 1996, 1997).

At the time, I had been leading a school-based study group for mentor teachers working with teacher-interns. In addition to developing new roles and practices as mentors, the teachers were experimenting with new teaching roles and practices reflected in recently published national standards in their own classrooms. One dedicated veteran teacher, Carole, was attracted to these new ideas about teaching and learning but struggled to enact them. Although she had a vision of the kind of classroom learning community she wanted to create, she did not know how to make it happen. Her grade-level colleagues, Kathy and Debi, who had previously worked together in a student teaching relationship, were well aware of Carole's struggle and its impact on her students and interns. Constrained by the culture of teaching that inhibits teachers from offering (or seeking) help, they hesitated to talk with Carole about what was going on in her classroom even though the three teachers ate lunch together every day.

With some prodding on my part, Kathy and Debi gingerly broached the subject that everyone was avoiding. Eventually they agreed to mentor Carole, using the tools of observation, critical conversation, and writing that they had been developing in our mentor study group. The journals that the teachers kept over the three years of the project detail the evolution of new norms and a new kind of professional discourse. Kathy and Debi found the courage to show Carole their field notes, ask her for reasons and evidence, and give her direct feedback. Carole overcame her sense of vulnerability and her reluctance to let others see her problems firsthand. She actively sought opportunities to observe her colleagues and be observed by them, and she came to welcome their questions and feedback.

This case of peer mentoring, like the cases in this book, underscores the ways in which serious mentoring challenges the culture of teaching, placing both mentors and mentees in unfamiliar, often uncomfortable roles. While some schools promote active collaboration among teachers, such interactions are the exception, not the rule. For the most part, teaching is regarded as a highly personal activity. Teachers work alone in their classrooms protected by norms of privacy and noninterference. Norms of politeness and the desire for harmony create additional barriers to productive mentoring interactions. Teachers are unaccustomed to questioning a colleague's practice, asking for evidence, offering a different interpretation. The desire to maintain cordial relations works against serious professional discourse. Without shared standards, a common vocabulary, and analytical skills, talk among teachers tends to be anecdotal and laden with jargon.

This book reminds us that just as teachers must learn how to participate in the systematic study of teaching and learning, so too must mentors learn how to facilitate such professional work. Fortunately, the case writers did participate over several years in a professional network where they talked about the challenges and successes in helping teachers prepare for the National Board assessments. Yet even with portfolio guidelines that served as a kind of mentoring curriculum and professional standards and supplied a common language and framework, the mentors still needed to develop a sophisticated mentoring practice, a repertoire of strategies to use with the wide range of teachers who presented themselves as candidates for National Board Certification, and the professional judgment to manage difficult dilemmas.

A final issue concerns the mentor's responsibility in situations where the teacher's practice does not meet the National Board's ambitious teaching standards. Several cases and commentaries deal with this complicated issue, raising questions about whether the mentor is obligated to do everything in her power to help the teacher pass, or whether she is responsible for making visible the discrepancy between the vision of equitable and engaged teaching embodied in the National Board's professional teaching standards and the teacher's pedagogy. This is an area where mentors need clearer guidelines. A parallel problem faces mentor teachers working in induction programs that define the mentor's role as providing confidential and unconditional support. This works when new teachers make acceptable progress, but it does not work when new teachers' practice borders on the unacceptable (for a discussion of this problem, see Carver and Katz, 2004). In thinking about this dilemma, I have been aided by Peter Elbow's argument (1986) that teachers (and mentors) must find ways to embrace contrary obligations, upholding high standards so that grades and certificates have meaning and helping learners realize and represent such standards in their work.

Mentoring Teachers Toward Excellence: Supporting and Developing Highly Qualified Teachers helps open up an important discussion about the pedagogy of educative mentoring. It reminds us that mentoring is not only a social role but also a complex professional practice aimed at teacher growth. It gives us a picture of how teachers can learn to challenge one another to reach standards of excellence in their work and what kind of professional leadership that entails.

March 2006   Sharon Feiman-Nemser
                                                  Brandeis University

References

Beasley, K., Corbin, D., Feiman-Nemser, S., and Shank, C. "'Making It Happen': Teachers Mentoring One Another." *Theory into Practice,* 1996, *35*(3), 158–164.

Beasley, K., Corbin, D., Feiman-Nemser, S., and Shank, C. "'Making It Happen': Creating a Subculture of Mentoring in a Professional Development School." In M. Levine and R. Trachtman (eds.), *Making Professional Development Schools Work.* New York: Teachers College Press, 1997.

Carver, C. L., and Katz, D. "Teaching at the Boundary of Acceptable Practice: What Is a New Teacher Mentor to Do?" *Journal of Teacher Education,* 2004, *55*(5), 449–462.

Elbow, P. *Embracing Contraries: Explorations in Teaching and Learning.* New York: Oxford University Press, 1986.

Feiman-Nemser, S. "Teachers as Teacher Educators." *European Journal of Teacher Education,* 1998, *21*(1), 63–74.

Feiman-Nemser, S., and Parker, M. "Mentoring in Context: A Comparison of Two U.S. Programs for Beginning Teachers." *International Journal of Educational Research,* 1993, pp. 699–718.

Lord, B. "Teachers' Professional Development: Critical Colleagueship and the Role of Professional Communities." In N. Cobb (ed.), *The Future of Education: Perspectives on National Standards in America.* New York: College Board, 1994.

PREFACE

When Odysseus went off to fight in the Trojan Wars, he left his household under the protection of his valued adviser and friend, Mentor. So trusted was this remarkable counselor that when the goddess Athena wished to advise Telemachus, the son of Odysseus, she disguised herself as Mentor. This character left such a powerful impression on later generations that we now use the term *mentor* as both noun and verb to describe an unusually effective and trusted adviser and the act of guiding and counseling itself. Today we tend to think of mentors as operating within organizations or professions as they nurture future leaders. They thus carry a double burden: they support and teach the newcomers even as they retain responsibility for the integrity and quality of the organization or profession they represent. They are stewards in the deepest sense, providing much-needed help to the newcomers while also sustaining high standards for the profession and protecting the well-being of clients. It is a delicate balance to sustain.

When the National Board for Professional Teaching Standards was created, it mirrored the twin missions of all mentors. It was a rigorous and demanding assessment that incorporated the highest standards of the education profession. Indeed, its teaching standards reflected a high bar of accomplishment toward which all teachers might strive. The creators of the Board envisioned preparation for the board assessments as itself a demanding form of professional learning and development. Since it is difficult to achieve such standards in isolation, the Board encouraged candidates to work together with mentors to raise their levels of performance. At the same time, mentors were expected to help candidates demonstrate their full potential legitimately, not create the illusion that they were better educators than they really were. In this sense, the work of mentors for National Board candidates exemplifies the universal challenges of guiding, supporting, and counseling both students and professionals. Although the particular cases in this book are all taken from the experiences of National Board support providers, their narratives are cases of the general dilemmas of mentoring. Like Mentor's counsel to Telemachus, all good cases must be particular and local. The lessons learned from the cases are generalizable to many contexts.

This book is the legacy of a network of National Board candidate support providers who met regularly over a five-year period at WestEd, a nonprofit research, development, and service agency that works with education and other communities to promote excellence, equity, and improved learning for children, youth, and adults. Participants shared experiences, received technical assistance, and discussed the celebrations and challenges of mentoring veteran teachers toward a high-stakes, standards-based assessment. (The term *support provider* will be used interchangeably in this book with *mentor, coach,* and *facilitator.*) Participants in this learning community included teacher educators, staff developers, administrators, and National Board Certified Teachers (NBCTs), as they increasingly began to assume mentoring roles for novices and veterans in their schools districts. Misty Sato, director of the National Board Resource Center at Stanford University, was one of the most active members of the network. As we all worked together, we became convinced that the candidate process, enriched within support groups and guided by skillful facilitators, represented one of the most powerful professional development mechanisms for strengthening teaching, the teaching workforce, and student learning. We also realized that the practical and moral challenges that we confronted as support providers were complex and pervasive, and demanded continued collaborative analysis and revisiting as new challenges arose in the network and newcomers joined the network. This book, supported by grants from The William and Flora Hewlett Foundation and The Stuart Foundation, focuses directly on these challenges. It is geared toward all educators who take seriously the complexity that accompanies constructive, principled, and ethical mentoring of teachers.

Written by veteran support providers, these narratives and their commentaries fill a gap in the case literature, as they portray the challenges associated with helping teachers risk making their teaching public—through sharing videos of their teaching, curriculum materials, and student work with other teachers—and facilitating the kind of collaborative feedback that enables them to analyze and reflect on their practice according to a set of teaching standards. While all the cases were written in the context of supporting National Board candidates, teacher preparation and induction programs are increasingly requiring similar kinds of educative experiences. These programs demand a paradigm shift from traditional modes of mentoring teachers one-on-one and specific kinds of pedagogical skills when facilitating support groups. Themes that continued to be thorny during conversations at network meetings are represented in this volume. They include:

- Enabling teachers to analyze and reflect on their practice according to a set of teaching standards
- Using a vision of accomplished teaching that can be demonstrated in a variety of ways as the basis for collaborative conversations
- Balancing professional development and assessment support
- Determining the appropriate role of the mentor for a high-stakes assessment
- Supporting teachers who do not have appropriate content and pedagogical content knowledge
- Recognizing personal biases about teaching when providing critique to others
- Meeting the needs of challenging mentees
- Setting personal boundaries in the mentoring relationship
- Creating a supportive climate for teachers to risk making their teaching public with colleagues through videos, samples of student work, and lesson plans
- Dealing with the complexities of individual mentoring
- Structuring and sustaining group process
- Mentoring colleagues at a school site
- Attending to issues of student diversity and educational equity

We have tried to sequence the cases to highlight these dilemmas. But since cases are usually cases of many things, they often do not fit neatly in any one section. An analysis that examines how the dilemmas are portrayed across the cases is presented in Table I.1 in the Introduction.

DEFINING AND USING CASES

The cases in this book are not simply stories that a teacher might tell. They are crafted into compelling narratives that, as Jerome Bruner (1986) has observed, are accounts of "the vicissitudes of human intention"—a plan that has gone awry, an intention unfulfilled, or some surprise that disrupts the expected scenario and requires the teacher to reflect on and modify her plans in some way. Our cases include the thoughts and feelings of the teacher-writers as they describe the set of events and are rich with detail and dialogue about the challenges encountered. They also include reflective comments by the author that raise questions about what they might do differently in the future.

But good stories do not necessarily make educative cases. To call something a case is to make a theoretical claim that it is a "case of something" or an instance of a larger class (Shulman, 1986, p. 11). This is not to say that all cases illustrate, exemplify, or teach a theoretical principle. To be valuable as a case, however, the narrative should be representative of a class or type of dilemma, problem, or quandary that arises with some frequency in teaching situations. It has to be worthy of spending time reflecting on it and learning from it for both the author and future users. Read on one's own, cases offer the vicarious experience of walking in another's shoes and engaging in self-reflection. In group discussion, cases are especially powerful, eliciting differing points of view to be aired and examined. For that reason, our cases are consciously designed to provoke discussion that is engaging, demanding, and intellectually exciting.

All of the cases have gone through a series of iterative drafts and have been field-tested with new and veteran support providers from a variety of contexts. The insights we gained from these experiences are compiled in a set of teaching notes that follow each case in this book.

GETTING STARTED

Each case in this book has three parts: (1) the narrative, (2) one or two commentaries that analyze the case from different perspectives, and (3) a teaching note designed to help individual readers or discussion facilitators analyze the case. As you read the narratives, you may want to ask yourself questions such as: How did the mentor frame the problems he or she encountered? In what other ways could the problem have been framed? What did this mentor actually do, and why? With what result? What alternative strategies might have been tried? At what risk? With what consequences? What were other teachers thinking and feeling when the support was facilitated in groups? How did they try to communicate this to the mentor? How does this mentor's story parallel experiences of your own? How might this case (or case discussion) lead you to think of different ways of dealing with these dilemmas? What principles of teaching and learning can be generated from your analysis?

The commentaries that follow each case add information and insights that participants might otherwise not have. Written by both practitioners and academics, they view the case from multiple lenses and are meant to enrich an analysis, not to provide the "right" answer. They can be read simultaneously with each case or used as the basis of a second-stage analysis. We have heard from the field that teacher educators often ask their students to write their own commentaries to the cases. We welcome you to do the same.

If you are planning on using the cases in professional development or teacher education programs, you may also want to refer to Chapter Seven. Our experience and research suggest that case discussions, guided by skillful facilitators, can help discussants bridge theory and practice, frame problems in ambiguous situations, interpret situations from multiple perspectives, identify crucial decision points and possibilities for action, and recognize benefits and potential risks inherent in any course of action. In short, case discussions enable participants to make the familiar strange and learn to think like a mentor.

If you are interested in additional reading about mentoring or creating your own cases, we have included an annotated bibliography of selected references and a methodological note that describes our case development process in the Appendix. Feel free to adapt any of the methods. We hope that this book will provide you and your colleagues a useful supplement to other readings about mentoring and a tool for professional development.

Judith H. Shulman
Mistilina Sato

References

Bruner, J. S. *Actual Minds, Possible Worlds.* Cambridge, Mass.: Harvard University Press, 1986.

Shulman, L. S. "Paradigms and Research Programs for the Study of Teaching." In M. C. Wittrock (ed.), *Handbook of Research on Teaching* (3rd ed.). New York: Macmillan, 1986.

ACKNOWLEDGMENTS

We are grateful to many people for their contributions to this book. First, we acknowledge The Stuart Foundation and The William and Flora Hewlett Foundation for their continued financial support of this project. We feel fortunate to have had the wisdom and guidance of two special program officers, Ellen Hershey and Ray Bacchetti. They had the vision of how National Board Certification could help improve the quality of teaching in our schools and the teaching profession and often asked tough questions that helped us clarify our goals for the project. We were also inspired by the leadership of the National Board for Professional Teaching Standards—in particular, Joe Aguerrebere and Nancy Schwartz—who work tirelessly to sustain the Board's mission.

The guidelines for the cases were influenced by discussions among National Board candidate support providers at WestEd and the National Board Resource Center at Stanford University; many of the participants in these deliberations are case authors in this book. We thank all of the participants for their honest and frank contributions, many of which dealt with the delicate issues embedded in the cases. We are particularly grateful to the teachers, teacher educators, and researchers who contributed both cases and commentaries to this book; often the writing took much longer than they had originally anticipated.

During the development of this project, there were times when delicate and challenging issues surfaced. We were fortunate to be able to look to a remarkable group of educators who provided guidance when needed. They included Lee Shulman, Lloyd Bond, and Ann Colby from the Carnegie Foundation for the Advancement of Teaching; Sam Wineburg and Linda Darling-Hammond from Stanford University; and Gary Fenstermacher and Virginia Richardson from the University of Michigan. We thank them for their astute insights and understanding of the challenges we faced. We are also indebted to the many teachers, teacher educators, staff developers, and administrators who participated in field tests of case discussions and provided valuable feedback; we often made revisions to the narratives as a result of their comments.

Finally, we acknowledge a group of people without whose assistance we could never have finished this book: Gloria Miller, who compiled and wrote the annotated bibliography; Jim Johnson, who skillfully edited the cases; Rosemary De La Torre, who kept track of and proofread this book as well as other books that we have published in previous years; and Lesley Iura from Jossey-Bass whose insights helped us refine the manuscript.

THE SPONSOR

WestEd

WestEd is a nonprofit research, development, and service agency that works with education and other communities to promote excellence, achieve equity, and improve learning for children, youth, and adults. The agency focuses on what goes on not just in school but also in early childhood; in children's homes, afterschool programs, and communities; in the training and development of those who teach and guide children; and in legislatures and other decision-making bodies whose policies touch all of these. WestEd's headquarters are in San Francisco, with offices in Oakland and other cities in California and in Arizona, Massachusetts, and Washington, D.C.

THE EDITORS

Judith H. Shulman is director of the Institute for Case Development and the National Board Support Network at WestEd, where she develops materials and resources designed to improve teachers' capacity for instruction. Her research focuses on the professional development of teachers, approaches to engaging in the scholarship of teaching of one's practice, and the development of cases and their impact on teacher learning. Her publications include *Case Methods in Teacher Education,* several edited casebooks and facilitators' guides, and numerous chapters and articles in professional journals such as *Educational Researcher, Teaching and Teacher Education, Journal of Teacher Education, Teacher Education Quarterly,* and *Educational Leadership.* Shulman is currently involved in a study of mentoring in the context of supporting candidates for National Board Certification and in several activities that assist National Board support providers and organizations that develop new candidate programs. Before joining WestEd, she served as an instructor in the School of Education at Michigan State University and as an elementary school teacher. She received a B.S. in elementary education from Northwestern University and an M.A. in education from Michigan State University.

Mistilina Sato is an assistant professor of teacher development and science education at the University of Minnesota, Twin Cities. Sato holds a Ph.D. from Stanford University in curriculum and teacher education, with a specialty in science education. She began her career in education as a middle school science teacher in Plainsboro, New Jersey, and as an instructional team leader at the Merck Institute for Science Education in Rahway, New Jersey.

While coediting this book, Sato was the director of the National Board Resource Center at Stanford University, where she developed and directed a regional National Board support program for practicing teachers in the San Francisco Bay Area. Through this program, she worked with several hundred teachers who were pursuing National Board Certification, developed standards-based professional development curriculum materials, and coached support providers in her program and for district-based support programs. Sato's research has focused on teacher leadership, teacher learning related to National Board Certification, and the personal nature of teacher professional development and change, especially related to everyday classroom assessment practices. She coauthored the book *Designing Everyday Assessment in the Science Classroom* and has published articles in *New Educator, Curriculum Journal,* and *Teacher Development.*

The Contributors

Dawne Ashton, NBCT Early Adolescence Through Young Adulthood World Languages Other than English, teaches Spanish in a Bay Area school district.

Vicki Baker, NBCT Early Adolescence Science, is a science teacher at Alvarado Middle School in the New Haven Unified School District, in Union City, California.

Carne Barnett-Clarke is the project director of the Math Case Methods Project at WestEd in San Francisco.

Diane Barone is a professor of literacy studies at the University of Nevada, Reno, and director of the National Board support program on campus.

George Bunch is an assistant professor of education at University of California, Santa Cruz.

Myriam Casimir is a research associate in the Teacher Professional Development Program at WestEd in San Francisco.

LaRie Colosimo, NBCT Early Childhood Generalist, is the regional director of the Beginning Teacher Support and Assessment program, Claremont Unified School District, in Claremont, California.

Sandra Dean, NBCT Early Childhood Generalist, is a first-grade teacher at Shepherd Elementary School in the Hayward Unified School District in Hayward, California.

William Dean, NBCT Adolescence and Young Adulthood English/ Language Arts, is a humanities teacher at East Palo Alto High School, in East Palo Alto, California.

Yvonne Divans-Hutchinson, NBCT Early Adolescence English/ Language Arts, is an English teacher at the King-Drew Medical Magnet School in the Los Angeles Unified School District.

Susan Elko is an education consultant and teacher educator at West Chester University in West Chester, Pennsylvania.

Lynn Gaddis, NBCT Middle Childhood Generalist, is codirector of the National Board Resource Center at Illinois State University in Normal, Illinois.

Diane Garfield, NBCT Middle Childhood Generalist, is a fifth-grade teacher at Clarendon Elementary School in the San Francisco Unified School District and a lecturer at San Francisco State University.

Wendy Hacke, NBCT Early Childhood Generalist, is a kindergarten teacher at the Cesar Chavez Elementary School in the Alum Rock Union School District in San Jose, California, and head of the Child Development Emphasis at National Hispanic University.

Kay Hones, NBCT Early Childhood Through Young Adulthood Library Media, is a librarian at O'Connell High School in the San Francisco Unified School District.

Maria Hyler, NBCT Adolescence and Young Adulthood English/ Language Arts, is a doctoral candidate at the Stanford University School of Education and a program associate with the National Board Resource Center at Stanford University.

Ann Ifekwunigwe, NBCT Early Childhood Generalist, is a second- and third-grade teacher at the Carthay Center Elementary School in the Los Angeles Unified School District and codirector of the National Board Project at the University of California, Los Angeles.

Gloria Ladson-Billings is the Kellner Family Chair in Urban Education at the University of Wisconsin in Madison.

Hector Viveros Lee, NBCT Early Childhood Generalist, is an instructional reform facilitator at the Leonard R. Flynn Elementary School in the San Francisco Unified School District.

Amber Lewis-Francis, NBCT Middle Childhood Generalist, is a fifth-grade teacher at Clarendon Elementary School in the San Francisco Unified School District.

Rachel A. Lotan is the director of the Stanford Teacher Education Program at Stanford University.

Pat Kemeny Macias, NBCT Early Adolescence Through Young Adulthood Art, teaches art at Piedmont High School in the Piedmont Unified School District, Piedmont, California.

Adrienne Mack-Kirschner, NBCT Early Adolescence English/Language Arts, is an education consultant in the Los Angeles area.

Elizabeth Matchett is the site director for the Bay Area Foreign Language Program at Stanford University and teaches Spanish at Gunn High School in the Palo Alto Unified School District in Palo Alto, California.

Gloria I. Miller is a doctoral candidate at the Stanford University School of Education.

Joan Peterson is a senior program associate at WestEd in San Francisco.

Jerome Shaw is an assistant professor of education at the University of California, Santa Cruz.

Lee S. Shulman is president of the Carnegie Foundation for the Advancement of Teaching and the Charles E. Ducommun Professor of Education Emeritus at Stanford University.

Rose Vilchez, NBCT Early and Middle Childhood English as a New Language, is a graduate student at the University of California, Berkeley; the lead facilitator for the Oakland National Board support program; and a research associate in the Teacher Professional Development Program at WestEd in San Francisco.

Ann-Marie Wiese is a research associate in the Teacher Professional Development Program at WestEd in San Francisco.

Rae Jeane Williams is a faculty adviser in the Graduate School of Education and Information Studies at the University of California, Los Angeles, and codirector of the National Board Project at the University of California, Los Angeles.

Introduction: Mentoring Practitioners Toward Standards of Excellence

Mistilina Sato

The idea of mentoring in education typically evokes the image of an experienced or veteran teacher guiding a novice during the first year or two of teaching. Such formal mentoring relationships among teachers are often organized and governed by programs designed to assist new teachers' transitions into the teaching profession. The particular roles that a mentor teacher plays vary depending on the particularities of the mentor program and its expectations, the experience of the mentor teacher, and the norms of the working context of the teachers. The variety of potential roles for mentors has been summarized as (1) serving as a local guide who familiarize new teachers with their teaching assignments and context, (2) being educational companions who assist novices in examining their practice and developing plans of action, and (3) working as agents of change who build networks and challenge the norms of traditional isolation of teachers (Feiman-Nemser and Parker, 1992).

The cases in this book represent the notion of mentoring more broadly than the novice-expert relationship during induction by focusing on the relationships between teachers who would consider themselves peers or colleagues, and between professional developers and experienced classroom teachers. As the Selected Annotated Bibliography on mentoring at the end of this book points out, these relationships among peers or near-peers are also known as coach–teacher, critical friends, community of learners, support network, collaboration, and study groups in the literature

1

on teacher development. We have chosen to cast the dilemmas in this book as cases of mentoring because the hierarchy between the experienced one and the lesser-experienced one brings focus to the purposefulness of these relationships—that is, to mentor practitioners toward standards of excellence in teaching.

Standards of Excellence in Teaching

Teaching and teacher education have entered an era of standards-based teaching. Three agencies have worked together to create a compatible set of performance-based standards for teacher preparation and licensing, authentic assessments for teachers as they enter the profession, and a certification program to recognize accomplished teaching (Darling-Hammond, 1996). As the accrediting agency for teacher education institutions, the National Council for Accreditation of Teacher Education (NCATE) developed a set of accreditation standards for colleges of education that range from criteria for admission to the teacher education programs to establishing a curriculum based on current understanding of sound professional practice (Wise, 1994). Since 2001 NCATE has required education schools to provide evidence that their graduates can successfully teach using their teaching standards as the performance measure. The Interstate New Teacher Assessment and Support Consortium (INTASC) created a set of model performance-based licensing standards for new teacher licensing. These standards were developed by a consortium of more than thirty states and professional organizations and are designed to define the knowledge, dispositions, and performances essential for all beginning teachers (Darling-Hammond, 1999; Weiss and Weiss, 1998). Both of these agencies worked to align their standards with the teaching standards established by the National Board for Professional Teaching Standards (NBPTS), which has been certifying experienced teachers based on its standards-based performance assessment since 1994. The standards developed by these three organizations create a cohesive professional vision for what teachers should know and be able to do at the various stages of their professional development. Supporting teachers to meet these performance standards has challenged the repertoires of experienced professional developers, and calls for developing mentoring practices that support standards-based teaching.

The cases in this book are situated in the context of supporting and mentoring teachers toward meeting the teaching standards identified by the NBPTS. The NBPTS was created in 1987 with the mission to "establish high and rigorous standards for what accomplished teachers should know and be able to do, to develop and operate a voluntary national system to assess and certify teachers who meet those standards, and to advance related education reforms—all with the purpose of improving student learning." Its teaching standards identify essential aspects of teaching—such as a firm grounding in content knowledge, establishing and maintaining supportive learning environments, assessment practices, and equitable and fair treatment of all students, to name just a few examples of teaching standards—without specifying or delineating specific practices. The standards are based on current and relevant research, are grounded in specific subject matter areas, and focus on specific age groups of children.

Teachers attempt to demonstrate that their teaching practice embodies and exemplifies the teaching standards of the NBPTS through a performance assessment that includes both a classroom-based portfolio and a set of examination questions. For the portfolio portion of the assessment, teachers submit videotapes of their classroom teaching, student work samples, and extensive commentary that describes the teaching context and planning process, analyzes the instructional processes, and reflects on the success of the instruction based on student learning. If they demonstrate the standards in practice through the assessment, the teachers are identified as National Board Certified Teachers (NBCTs). While engaged in this year-long assessment process, many teachers seek the guidance and assistance of others more experienced with both the teaching standards and the performance expectations of the assessment. Teachers who have already achieved National Board Certification often mentor other teachers toward the NBPTS standards, thus supporting those teachers toward achievement of this certification. Mentoring can take place through formal program arrangements or informally among colleagues, and in one-on-one relationships or in small groups. The cases and commentaries in this book illustrate how the teaching standards form the cornerstone of the mentoring process by focusing the conversations among teachers on essential questions about their teaching practices.

CHANGING THE PROFESSIONAL CONVERSATION IN MENTORING PRACTICES

Wang and O'Dell (2002) critically examined common conceptions of mentoring new teachers in an era of educational reform that promotes establishing rigorous standards for both what students should learn and how teachers should teach. They conclude that "although reformers encourage mentoring for standards-based teaching, the assumptions underlying mentoring programs are often focused not on standards but on emotional and technical support" (p. 481). While supporting and mentoring teachers engaged in the National Board assessment process has important emotional and technical issues to attend to, the cases in this book provide a detailed look at attempts to bring greater focus to conversations about teaching by aligning with a set of rigorous standards for teaching.

As more teachers become involved in the National Board Certification process (as of the 2004–2005 assessment cycle, more than forty-seven thousand teachers have achieved National Board Certification nationwide), new opportunities are arising for teachers to coach one another in analyzing teaching practices using the NBPTS teaching standards. With new opportunities to work together and talk about practice in a reflective, critical, and forward-thinking manner, discussions among teachers are taking on new dimensions as they use the standards as a framework for analyzing and reflecting on their own teaching and discussing the practices of other teachers. Researchers who have studied case-based professional development indicate that professional knowledge building is nurtured and stimulated by professional dialogue (Barnett and Ramirez, 1996; Ingvarson and Marrett, 1997; Schifter and Fosnot, 1993; Shulman, 1996). Candidates for National Board Certification echo this conclusion by consistently identifying collegial interaction during National Board candidacy as essential (Chittenden and Jones, 1997; Rotberg, Futrell, and Lieberman, 1998; Sato, 2000). The National Board standards provide teachers with "something to be collegial about" (Ingvarson, 1998, p. 137)—a vision of accomplished practice and a professional language for articulating aspects of teaching and learning. The essence of teaching is captured in the standards, explicating the essential stances toward students and learning process, the importance of subject matter ideas, and the central values of equity and caring. Examining the processes of engaging in standards-based analysis of practice in the National Board candidate context can help the field of mentoring develop the practices and approaches for working with teachers using other sets of teaching standards and techniques for analyzing practice.

CHALLENGES AND ISSUES FACED IN MENTORING

As the cases in this book demonstrate, mentoring toward standards of excellence poses many challenges to both mentors and mentees. Table I.1 highlights some of the key areas of focus for the cases in this book. Nine of the thirteen cases address the issue of standards-based analysis of practice in both one-on-one and small-group environments. This is new territory for most teachers and mentors. The cases raise questions such as how to help a group align its vision of accomplished teaching with the standards, how to provide feedback and raise questions for a teacher whose teaching is not aligned with the standards, and how to help a teacher peel back the assumptions embedded in his or her beliefs about learning in order to better align practice with the standards.

Recognizing that the mentoring dilemmas in the cases are situated in a high-stakes assessment for teachers, the cases also address how to find the balance between helping teachers with the logistics and technicalities of the assessment process and the more enduring aspects of learning the analytical and reflective stance toward practice that provide greater opportunities for professional growth. Similar to mentoring new teachers, the emotional and technical support cannot be ignored when these needs are immediate. Yet the long-term outlook of the development of the practice and instilling a reflective stance must be an ongoing part of the mentoring conversation. These cases raise questions such as how to help teachers get over an initial sense of failure if they do

Table I.1. Cross-Cutting Issues

	Standards-based Analysis of Practice	Balancing the Focus on Professional Development and a High-Stakes Assessment	Roles and Responsibilities of the Mentor	Recognizing Personal and Professional Bias	Meeting the Needs of Challenging Mentees
Case 1	X	X	X		
Case 2	X		X	X	
Case 3	X	X	X		X
Case 4	X				X
Case 5	X			X	
Case 6	X	X	X	X	X
Case 7			X		X
Case 8		X	X		X
Case 9				X	
Case 10	X	X	X		X
Case 11		X	X	X	X
Case 12	X				X
Case 13	X	X			

Setting Personal Boundaries	Risk of Making Teaching Public	Complexities of Individual Mentoring	Structuring and Sustaining Group Process	Mentoring Colleagues at a School Site	Attention to Issues of Equity and Diversity
			X		
	X		X		X
		X			X
			X		
		X		X	X
X	X	X			X
	X		X		
			X		
X	X	X			
X		X		X	
	X		X	X	
			X	X	

Note: The X's characterize the key issues represented in each case.

not achieve certification and focus instead on identifying the aspects of practice in need of professional development, how to help teachers maintain momentum in the assessment process while continually probing on their practice, and how to situate the mentoring of teachers toward standards of excellence within a political context that seeks success over development.

All of the cases recognize that mentoring is a complex process with many dimensions of support, assistance, and guidance that depend a great deal on the relationship between the mentor and mentee (Bey and Holmes, 1992). The complexities of the mentoring process and the associated relationships are highlighted through attention to key issues such as the roles and responsibilities of the mentor, recognizing personal and professional bias in mentoring, meeting the needs of challenging mentees, and setting personal boundaries. Mentors in the cases explore their roles as they try to enable their mentees to become more self-reliant and autonomous, seek appropriate strategies to use with individuals, and consider how far their influence as mentors can go given the relationship they have created with mentees. Some mentors confront their own biases and preferences for what constitutes "good" teaching and struggle with how to honor their own beliefs and values while trying to understand and appreciate alternative beliefs and values about teaching presented by their mentees. For some mentors, an individual mentee poses a particular challenge or need, and they must address whether they can meet those needs given their own skills and expertise, the competing needs within a group setting, the extremeness of the needs of the mentee, or the nature of the relationship they have with the mentee. Mentors also face the ongoing question of how much of themselves they can give to another: Where are their boundaries, how do they set them, and how do they maintain them?

A focus on standards for teaching requires taking a critical look at practice and assessing how the practice is and is not aligned with the expectations set out in the teaching standards. This examination of practice requires teachers to take the risk of making teaching public by opening their classroom door (even if it is through showing a videotape to peers) and allowing others to see what they do. For most, this exposure (whether it is to only the mentor or to a small support group) is a new experience. Mentors must learn how to assist others in overcoming their anxiety about making their practice public and how to engage mentees in productive conversations that will enable them to see their teaching practice analytically in light of the expectations of the standards.

Whether working with an individual or working in small-group settings, mentors face a variety of process issues in structuring and sustaining their interactions with mentees. Much of what happens in mentoring relationships goes undocumented, and the need for better images of how these conversations and relationships unfold is needed (Wang and O'Dell, 2002). These cases provide an insider's perspective on a variety of processes and procedures for analyzing videotapes of teaching practices, organizing groups for collegial interactions, appropriately framing questions for reflection and analysis, recognizing one's own biases about teaching and learning, and centering conversations on the teaching standards. Some cases focus particularly on mentoring school site colleagues, where existing relationships are in place and teaching context is an important feature of the mentoring process.

Throughout the cases, mentors face moral and ethical issues of mentoring in different contexts: What is my role? What is right for the children in the classrooms of teachers I mentor? What biases do I bring to teaching? These issues are especially highlighted in cases with attention to issues of equity and diversity. In these accounts, mentors face faulty assumptions that some teachers have about children's capacity to learn and struggle with both how to address them with the teacher and how to refine their own thinking and articulation of their beliefs about all children's capacity to meet high expectations for learning.

Helping Mentors Develop Their Practice

The cases in this book serve as pedagogical tools to assist new and experienced mentors in analyzing others' practice and developing and improving their own skills as mentors. They illustrate how mentors navigate complex relationships, sometimes successfully and sometimes with a stumble. They illustrate the skills and dispositions of mentors who choose to work with colleagues and peers in a professional relationship aimed at improving practice. And they highlight the role that beliefs and values play in close working relationships around issues of teaching and learning. All of these features of mentoring are complex; no single approach will answer the difficult question of how to mentor the right way. Developing as a mentor is a process of learning through personal and others' experiences. Through the descriptions of the mentors' experiences in this book, their careful reflection on how the events unfolded, what decisions they saw before them, and the choices they made, these cases provide both new and experienced mentors with a variety of nubby issues to consider in light of their own developing practice.

References

Bey, T. M., and Holmes, C. T. (eds.). *Mentoring: Contemporary Principles and Issues.* Reston, Va.: Association of Teacher Educators, and Athens, Ga.: University of Georgia, 1992.

Barnett, C., and Ramirez, A. "Fostering Critical Analysis and Reflection Through Mathematics Case Discussions." In J. A. Colbert, P. Desberg, and K. Trimble (eds.), *The Case for Education: Contemporary Approaches for Using Case Methods.* Needham Heights, Mass.: Allyn & Bacon, 1996.

Chittenden, E., and Jones, J. "An Observational Study of National Board Candidates as They Progress Through the Certification Process." Paper presented at the annual meeting of the American Educational Research Association, Chicago, Apr. 1997.

Darling-Hammond, L. "The Quiet Revolution: Rethinking Teacher Development." *Educational Leadership,* 1996, *53*(6), 4–10.

Darling-Hammond, L. *Reshaping Teaching Policy, Preparation, and Practice: Influences of the National Board for Professional Teaching Standards.* Washington, D.C.: American Association of Colleges for Teacher Education, 1999.

Feiman-Nemser, S., and Parker, M. B. *Mentoring in Context: A Comparison of Two U.S. Programs for Beginning Teachers.* East Lansing: National Center for Research on Teacher Learning, Michigan State University, 1992.

Ingvarson, L. (1998). Professional development as the pursuit of professional standards: The standards-based professional development system. *Teaching and Teacher Education, 14*(1), 127–140.

Ingvarson, L., and Marrett, M. "Building Professional Community and Supporting Teachers as Learners: The Potential of Case Methods." In L. Logan and J. Sachs (eds.), *Meeting the Challenge of Primary Schooling for the 1990s.* London: Routledge, 1997.

Rotberg, I. C., Futrell, M. H., and Lieberman, J. M. "National Board Certification: Increasing Participation and Assessing Impacts." *Phi Delta Kappan,* 1998, *79*(6), 462–466.

Sato, M. "The National Board for Professional Teaching Standards: Teacher Learning Through the Assessment Process." Paper presented at the annual meeting of the American Educational Research Association, New Orleans, La., Apr. 2000.

Schifter, D., and Fosnot, C. T. *Reconstructing Mathematics Education: Stories of Teachers Meeting the Challenge of Reform.* New York: Teachers College Press, 1993.

Shulman, J. H. "Tender Feelings, Hidden Thoughts: Confronting Bias, Innocence, and Racism Through Case Discussions." In J. Colbert, P. Desberg, and K. Trimble (eds.), *The Case for Education: Contemporary Approaches for Using Case Methods.* Needham Heights, Mass.: Allyn & Bacon, 1996.

Wang, J., and O'Dell, S. "Mentored Learning to Teach According to Standards-Based Reform: A Critical Review." *Review of Educational Research,* 2002, *72*(3), 481–546.

Weiss, E. M., and Weiss, S. G. "New Directions in Teacher Evaluation." *ERIC Digest,* 1998, *97*(9), 1–2.

Wise, A. E. "Teaching the Teachers." *American School Board Journal,* 1994, *181*(5), 22–25.

PART ONE

THE ROLE OF THE MENTOR

CHAPTER ONE

THE CONFLICTING ROLES OF A SUPPORT PROVIDER

Where does a mentor's loyalty lie? To the teachers you support, or to the district that pays your salary? What do you do when the goals of these parties are at odds with each other and with your own vision of professional development? This case takes up the issue of accountability and the unexpected conflicts of interest that arise when working in a high-stakes, high-profile environment.

CASE

CASE BY ADRIENNE MACK-KIRSCHNER

National Board Certification (NBC), a voluntary assessment of highly accomplished teaching, has attracted individual teachers seeking to improve and validate their practice against the rigorous standards established by the National Board. But what happens to the voluntary nature of NBC when a school district selects this process as its primary professional development vehicle, pays the candidate fees, provides release days for candidates and a highly qualified facilitator, and rewards teachers who attain certification with a substantial annual stipend? And what are the implications for candidates and support providers in such a high-profile district?

Pseudonyms have been used to maintain the confidentiality of people and places in the case.

I have been an education consultant working with schools and districts in all areas around teacher professional development for twelve years. I began as a National Board support provider working with teachers in year-long candidate support groups throughout our large county. For the first several years, candidates mostly came alone, usually the sole maverick teacher from his or her site. As the single candidate, these teachers frequently had to combat the lack of administrative support; even colleagues who did not understand the National Board process frequently criticized them for doing so much work for so little reward. Once certified, these same teachers often returned to a school environment feeling more isolated than they had before.

Dissatisfied with this experience, I shifted my program from countywide support to school or small district support. This allows teacher candidates from a single site, or close cluster of school sites, to work together supporting one another throughout the year. The model also allows me to educate their site administrators and secure additional support for them in the form of fee assistance, release days, salary stipends, videotaping assistance, and encouragement. When the cohorts return to their schools, they do so as leadership groups equipped and motivated to effect school-wide change.

Typically my program begins in the spring with a three-session series of workshops that examine in depth the five core propositions of the National Board for Professional Teaching Standards:

1. Teachers are committed to students and their learning.
2. Teachers know the subjects they teach and how to teach those subjects to students.
3. Teachers are responsible for managing and monitoring student learning.
4. Teachers think systematically about their practice and learn from experience.
5. Teachers are members of learning communities.

Some candidates determine, after the spring workshops, that they are not ready to pursue certification. Either they need to spend more time developing their teaching practice or the overall time commitment is too much at this point in their lives. The remaining teachers attend a five-day summer workshop in which we delve deeply into the certificate standards, completing personal inventory profiles to determine what evidence of accomplishment already exists in their teaching practice. Throughout the week, my facilitators and I model best teaching practices, including effective group work, Socratic seminars, searching for meaning in texts, and other practices directly related to the National Board process. Because I know that many of the teachers will choose to not pursue certification, I conduct the week as a professional development institute so everyone benefits. During the year, we meet monthly with the teachers who remain as candidates to continue working on best practices and provide support as they complete the National Board portfolio entries.

In one school district where I work, the superintendent proclaimed his intent on having the highest ratio of National Board Certified Teachers (NBCTs) to students of any district in the state. As a result of this mandate, the administrative staff actively recruited all qualified teachers to apply for candidacy. The board of education supported the superintendent's actions with a commitment to pay all related fees and provide release days, money for supplies, a high-quality support program, and a substantial annual stipend for teachers who certify. Even the union supported the new policy of differentiated pay for teachers because NBC was seen as a more valid assessment than one developed within the district. This was unprecedented since historically, unions have opposed differentiated pay due to concerns about how salary bonuses were assigned and whether they were politically motivated—the "principal's pet" syndrome.

When I was asked to become the official candidate support facilitator in January of that school year, I was thrilled at being part of a districtwide effort to improve teacher quality. I looked forward to working with teacher cohorts from a single site and from several sites within this school district. Teachers throughout the district, I reasoned, could collaborate during the certification process and would also be able to continue working together as colleagues in their own learning community after the certification process was complete. Working in cohort groups would eliminate some of the isolation that is inherent in teaching. Together, teacher candidates and NBCTs would create and sustain programs and policies that could reform their schools, involve more parents and community partners, and boost achievement for all students. Furthermore, as collaborative groups, they could raise the teaching standards at their sites and be mentors and teacher-leaders for novice and experienced teachers, thereby fostering a school culture that supports high-quality teaching and learning. Over 40 of the 630 teachers in the district applied for certification the first year of this comprehensive support effort.

Coming into the district in mid-school year, I was able to provide only minimum support to the first cohort of teachers, responding to questions about the portfolio entries, conducting group meetings, and fielding candidate concerns; I didn't critique any portfolio entries. But I encouraged the teachers to open their classroom doors, share their lessons, and examine each other's student work—in other words, to be team players working smarter together, not working harder alone. Although this first group began the process late in the year, my initial impression was that most were highly accomplished teachers.

While these teachers were working on their portfolios, others talked excitedly about when they would participate. In the spring, we began the precandidate workshops for the second cohort. Although I was not a district employee, everyone from the district-level offices to the school sites knew I was there to support teachers as they worked toward National Board Certification. Our work was valued and highly visible. I had never worked in such an ideal setting. The certification process was seen as a long-term, districtwide commitment supported by every level of district administration, the teachers, and the union.

By June, the second cohort was already up and running. Twenty-five candidates participated in the five-day summer workshop, and another fifteen signed up soon after the fall semester began. I don't know how many came urged on by the desire to deepen their teaching practice and also earn the high annual stipend, or how many were lured by the expectation of a monetary reward. I know that at one school, nearly the entire faculty came at least partly due to peer and principal pressure and their desire to be part of the district's team of NBCTs. The district and I welcomed everyone's participation, even the latecomers. I attempted to bring the newcomers current by starting them on their portfolio entries. Although I asked them to complete the personal inventory against the National Board standards as a self-assessment of readiness, not everyone chose to do this exercise. Through observation, reading their preliminary drafts, and discussing their practice, goals for students, and strategies they regularly employ, it didn't take long to suspect some teachers were woefully unprepared.

In November, before the first cohort candidates' scores were released, the superintendent applauded their efforts at a wine and cheese party at the district office. He emphasized the strength of the process, not the certification. Everyone heard what the superintendent said, but since every teacher expected to achieve certification, I don't think his words registered. When it was my turn to speak, I reiterated how proud they should feel about completing this rigorous process: only 2 percent of the teachers nationally had even attempted certification, and the National Board considered this a two- or even three-year program, as teachers who do not certify in their first assessment can continue as candidates for two subsequent years. Teachers left the meeting thanking me for my help during the year but not expecting to see me again. Their anticipation was palpable; they all expected to certify on their first attempt. But I knew that wouldn't happen and had already arranged for an after-school workshop for those who didn't certify.

And then the National Board scores for the first group were released. The district's certification rate was a whopping 67 percent of candidates who submitted portfolios and assessments, which was much higher than the 40 percent national certification rate that year. In spite of the astounding success, I soon began to understand the effects of this highly visible, high-stakes certification process on teachers who attempt but don't achieve certification. There is no way to quietly hide. The names of certified teachers were posted on the district Web site; by omission, everyone knew who didn't certify. The superintendent personally called each participating teacher to congratulate him or her or to encourage continued work; fee and candidate support would continue to be available. But candidates who did not certify were embarrassed. Colleagues didn't know what to say to them. Those who certified were reluctant to shout about their success. Current candidates looked nervously at one another, noting that if teachers they considered outstanding had not certified, what chance would they have? Second-year cohort candidates began to drop out.

I arranged to meet those who didn't certify as a group to examine their scores and discuss how to determine what portfolio entries or assessments to retake. Only six teachers replied but a dozen came—nearly all of the advanced candidates in the district. I was at least as nervous as they were. They arrived one at a time, tentatively entering the computer lab where I was meeting them. Then one of the candidates looked around and said, "I'm in really good company." That broke the ice. I led a discussion about disappointment and the public nature of their status. We went to the National Board Web site and examined together one candidate's scores after I encouraged someone to volunteer. We talked about what the ten scores on the combined portfolio and assessment center represented, where her strengths were, and where she needed to improve. I had deliberately selected a candidate whose score, I already knew, fell only twelve points short of the certification cutoff score. I did a think-aloud, talking to myself as if I were the candidate, considering all of the options I had. It was a highly productive two hours, with most candidates committed to continuing the process.

Jackie hung back at the end. She had the lowest score in the group. We waited until everyone had left before going online to her candidate file. All of her scores were low. She needed to redo nearly all parts of the assessment. Her teaching practice was not yet at the accomplished level, and we both knew it. I had first met Jackie at her school with five candidates. Four were veteran teachers, excited and enthusiastic about the program and eager to have my support. Jackie had expressed concern about her own readiness since she had been teaching for only four years; she was the junior teacher of the group. Nevertheless, her colleagues had urged her to participate and assured her they would help. She reluctantly continued despite her own doubt.

The reality is that it is very difficult to know much about what is happening in another teacher's classroom beyond that person's classroom management. While it is easy to know if the students are out of control, it's more difficult to know if they are progressing as learners. Faced with the standards and the portfolio guiding questions, the individual teacher is the best judge of her own accomplishment. Jackie knew she was not accomplished yet. Just as National Board Certification does not create accomplished teachers—it merely identifies them—the process only identified her weaknesses; it did not create them. While her colleagues' assistance might have helped move her toward higher accomplishment, they could not guarantee her certification.

I wondered what my role as a support provider should have been in this situation. Should I have been more proactive during support sessions by speaking with her privately, discussing her readiness, examining the standards, and helping her do a personal inventory against those standards? Based on our limited conversation, I had suspected she was not ready, but I kept silent. I believe so strongly in the process and how it improves everyone's practice that I remained silent in favor of her making her own decision. She has since decided to wait a year, to work on her teaching practice, and then to return as an advanced candidate for certification.

Gary, another teacher who did not certify, requested a private audience. We arranged for him to come to my house where we could view the videos in question and read his entries without interruption. He was embarrassed about not achieving certification and adamantly believed that the board had erred; most of his scores were quite high, and he had missed the cut-off score by only one point. But the scores for his two video entries were quite low. He was one of the most senior teachers in the district. A highly acclaimed professional respected for his innovative practice working with a dual-immersion program, Gary refused to accept that anything he had done or failed to do on the portfolio or in the assessment center deserved an insufficient score. He wanted to appeal and asked my opinion. I asked him to hold off until we had reviewed his entries and videos; he agreed.

When we read the instructions for the early childhood small-group and whole-group entries together, examined his responses, and viewed the videos, it was immediately evident why his scores were so low: he had not followed the instructions. For example, instead of describing how he planned a lesson and why he chose his instructional strategies, he painted a broad picture of the lesson using general education jargon in his written commentary. And rather than provide evidence of how he interacted with students in small groups, his video showed groups of students engaged in the lessons and impressively working well together, but they were working without him. So it appeared to me that although he may have exhibited excellent teaching, he simply had not presented what the Board had asked for. There were technical problems as well; the children's voices could not be understood on the videotape. When I pointed out what was lacking based on the instructions, he understood immediately and left convinced that he could redo the two portfolio entries and raise his scores accordingly.

These two experiences and the stories of other advanced candidates left me with many questions about my ideal district-level support model when NBC becomes such a high-profile program. Now in the middle of my second year supporting candidates in this district, I wonder if the district can do anything to diminish the pressure on candidates. About a third of this year's cohort have dropped out. Sometimes teachers feel they are not ready as they get deeper into the candidate process. This might be appropriate for those who decided to become candidates merely because of the financial incentives or peer pressure. But I fear that some excellent teachers may have dropped out after seeing outstanding teachers fail to certify. Is there a way to maintain the excellent professional experience that National Board candidacy offers without putting so much pressure on candidates to achieve?

I also have questions about my role as support provider in this district. Given my personal commitment to using National Board candidacy as a tool for professional development, how do I balance this goal with the candidates' need to focus on their individual portfolios? Should I preview every entry and raise questions when I don't see evidence of standards? Should I voice my opinion when I see gaps? Should I provide more proactive support, like demonstrating model lessons and assisting with their written commentaries? Or should candidates be dependent on their cohort group and the support provider remain hands off? If that's more desirable, what should I do when the cohort group falls apart or members drop out?

Finally, I question my responsibilities to the district; after all, they pay me to support candidates. I want districts to use the National Board Certification process as they focus on teacher quality. But how should they evaluate me? Will district administrators believe that I have failed if some candidates don't certify?

COMMENTARIES

COMMENTARY BY LYNN GADDIS

Just like the consultant in this case, I worked with a supportive administration and the newly named National Board for Professional Teaching Standards (NBPTS) coordinator in a large urban district to begin a candidate support program. We identified similar issues and solutions based on the premise that large percentages of candidates participating in the professional development of the NBPTS process would have a positive impact on school improvement and student learning. I will speak to four of these key issues.

CANDIDATE PREPAREDNESS

In the quest to recruit numbers of candidates in a short amount of time, administrators at awareness sessions motivated teachers to apply for National Board Certification by also offering financial and recertification incentives. Thus, many teachers decided to participate in the NBC process without fully understanding the requirements. Because so many were unprepared and the achievement rate after the first year was low, we decided to develop precandidacy sessions and an application process for the support program. The precandidacy course was similar to the one in this case in that teachers examined their own practice against the NBPTS five core propositions and standards. We chose to design this three-day experience to enable teachers to complete an application to the support program aligned with Charlotte Danielson's *Enhancing Professional Practice: A Framework for Teaching* (1996). We did not want participants writing a full National Board portfolio entry, but wanted them to experience conversations and a writing task required to show evidence of practice in thinking through the NBPTS "Architecture of Teaching." In this architecture, teachers are asked to first consider who their students are as learners, what worthwhile learning goals they have set for their particular students, how their instructional design aligns with the goals they have set, what assessments they will need to have to determine how the students are progressing toward those learning goals, and, finally, how they will set new learning goals for the students based on the assessments they have made. We continually questioned ourselves as to whether we should determine who may participate in the support program, the validity of the application we designed for selecting participants, and whether the in-depth writing was too difficult or redundant for what teachers should do to prepare for National Board candidacy.

QUALITY OF MENTORS

For the first few years, we had few mentors for the large numbers of candidates in the support program, with only four NBCTs for 150 candidates; only two had supported candidates before. We tried to arrange readers, facilitators at sessions, and certificate-alike mentors through any means possible. The administration hired experienced district professional development providers to serve as one-on-one mentors to candidates and delivered a three-day training session to help them understand the NBPTS process. It became apparent within a few weeks of working with the candidates that the mentors would not be able to give in-depth support. We scrambled to arrange for NBCTs in neighboring suburban districts to mentor National Board candidates. Teacher education faculty from my university conducted workshops on content identified by candidates in the weekly session. As year two began, we still did not have many district NBCTs and asked candidates from the previous year who had not yet received their assessment scores to support the new candidates. Once notification of who had (or had not) achieved certification occurred, some of the teachers who had not achieved certification withdrew from mentoring, and some newly identified NBCTs volunteered. Most of the NBCT mentors did not have the knowledge, skills, and experience to mentor candidates. Questions arose for us about how to link candidates with mentors. Who has the knowledge about NBC and is available to support candidates? Who has the skill to mentor candidates so the process remains a professional development experience? How can we train NBCTs as mentors at the same time they are mentoring candidates and continuing to teach their students without burning them out? What comes first: the NBCTs or the candidates? How does a district build the capacity to develop an effective learning community of NBCTs and candidates?

POLITICS OF PASS RATES

Our program experienced the dilemma of believing NBPTS was a professional development experience that may take three years while answering to a public that wanted immediate results. The school district, a philanthropic foundation, and a state agency offered funds for application fees, incentives for completion and passing, and the implementation of the candidate support program. Policymakers expected pass rates that were higher than the national average because other support programs publicly acknowledged their pass rates of over 60 percent. We empathized with the affective consequences many advanced candidates experienced internally and externally, and we questioned the accountability and responsibility of the mentors to the policymakers. It was difficult to help candidates, teachers, administrators, and policymakers understand that the process was a three-year professional development experience, since release of the names of new NBCTs was highly publicized. In one school, only two of six teachers achieved certification. The principal sent a memo to the staff congratulating all six on participating in a rigorous certification process, noting that two had completed the process and achieved certification and offering support to the four teachers who were continuing as candidates. We shared this letter with mentors so they could understand that completing the process meant exhausting the three years of professional development opportunity available. The question remains as to how we build this perception and community of teachers at all stages of the assessment and certification process.

SUPPORTING ADVANCED CANDIDATES

Like the district in this case, the district I was working in organized a celebration prior to the announcement of results, and the district coordinator held a meeting to support advanced candidates. About fifty advanced candidates attended the latter meeting and expressed anger, embarrassment, frustration, and confusion to the whole group and to the coordinator, myself, and the newly named NBCTs who were now mentors in the program. We determined that to be more effective the following year, we should interview and survey advanced candidates to learn more about their needs. As a result, we designed support for advanced candidates with fewer meetings than for first-time candidates and more one-on-one mentoring, NBCTs who had been advanced candidates speaking at all meetings, training for NBCTs to mentor advanced candidates, and workshops on topics identified by advanced candidates. We also continued to address the emotional aspects of not achieving certification on the first or second attempt. How can a support program respect the candidates' unique responses and needs in continuing their professional learning through retaking entries and assessment center exercises? How does a support program design a system that addresses the different issues for first-time and advanced candidates? How can school or district programs communicate the message that National Board Certification is a three-year process of learning?

COMMENTARY BY ROSE VILCHEZ

District support programs offer unique opportunities that may benefit candidates, their schools, the school district, and ultimately their students. Adrienne Mack-Kirschner attributes these kinds of opportunities to the sustained and collaborative nature of her year-long program. Her National Board support program encourages cohorts of candidates from multiple school sites to embark on the certification process as learning communities. Furthermore, Adrienne views the certification process as a professional development tool that creates a space for teachers to delve further into their instructional practice while demonstrating accomplished teaching for the purpose of certification. Her vision for this district's support program is admirable, but this case also presents tensions that arise when a highly visible program represents the multiple agendas belonging to Adrienne, the candidates, and the school district. Whether the agendas are aligned or at cross-purposes, tensions arise because the players share neither the same perspectives nor consequences with regard to accomplishing or not accomplishing National Board Certification.

And so Adrienne is left wondering what her role should be in responding to the differing candidate and district needs and expectations to which she answers as the district's support provider. How can she hold true to *her* vision of an ideal support program while remaining true to those she has been hired to support? I will respond to Adrienne's questions by building on my own experiences when developing an equally visible support program with other NBCTs within a large urban school district.

The heart of Adrienne's questions focus on her dual role of supporting candidates to complete the certification process successfully while also using the National Board process as a professional development experience. I too have asked myself this question as I purposefully attempted to develop a professional development frame for the process. My method was using the core propositions globally to make critical inquiries into instructional practices beyond the scope of a single certificate entry. Yet I found that many candidates had more pressing needs directly related to the high-stakes assessment to which they had committed. While I had a long-term agenda of improving practice through examination, inquiry, and reflection over time, my candidates were embroiled in an anxiety-inducing process with a portfolio due date looming on the horizon. Clearly the professional development was *my* agenda; *their* agenda was, not mistakenly, to compose written commentaries that met the rubric expectations. Varying motivations must be acknowledged, taken into account, and made explicit among those who design and participate in the support program. Understanding the individual goals and agendas will allow co-construction of a vision for the support program that may allow for more than one voice. My hope is that candidates will come to see the additional benefits of the National Board process as complementary to their own professional and personal goals and motivations for engaging in it.

These conversations must be ongoing throughout the support process because candidates' understanding of what they have chosen to undertake changes and transforms over time as they become more mindful and aware of their instructional practices. As support providers, it behooves us to explicitly acknowledge our personal and professional goals and agendas and to make clear what the vision and goals are of the support program we are offering.

That means that the program designer must have a vision, as Adrienne does, of what an ideal program can and will offer its participants. It is far too easy to focus on the portfolio and assessment exercises with a mechanistic and rote approach to "passing the test." This is the true loss of opportunity for creating a rich learning experience for candidates. And I propose these suggestions not because I have managed to balance these roles successfully, but because I had difficulty doing so; my suggestions are based on what I think I would have done next in my role as a support program designer.

The third player in this agenda-setting process is the school district. A district's agenda, as Adrienne shares, is certainly well intentioned. The goal of recruiting, retaining, and developing as many quality teachers as possible is admirable. This goal is purposeful when it is viewed as a long-term process with ongoing support, as in the district in which Adrienne worked. To reach this goal, the district invests in the support provider, the support program, and the purpose and agenda of that program. Ultimately the district's investment, even over a three-year period, is in the candidates' ability to demonstrate accomplished teaching through certification. And so we find Adrienne asking herself, "How should I be evaluated? Will I be viewed by some as having failed when candidates do not certify?" Again, I return to the importance of the purpose, goals, and agenda of the support program, especially as it is situated within the district's priorities. Goals that focus on increasing the number of NBCTs are different from goals that aim to improve the quality of teaching through a standards-based assessment process. Defining the goals of the program also requires defining the means by which progress toward those goals will be measured.

Adrienne wonders if she should preview every entry in order to ensure that candidates address gaps between their practice and the National Board teaching standards. This is not only impossible for one individual to accomplish, but does not build sustained effort or independence among the candidates. If certification is to be a true professional development tool, shouldn't candidates in groups be acquiring constructive critical stances toward their own and their colleagues' teaching practices? How do the candidates benefit when Adrienne is, or for that matter, NBCT coaches, are solely responsible for providing all the support through model lessons and assistance with written commentaries?

It is too easy for us to label National Board Certification as a professional development tool. It is a tool, but only when it is used purposefully. The purposeful implementation of certification as deep and rigorous professional development requires us to take more time in stating and describing what our vision for professional development is; we must know our agendas. We must extract and make explicit the processes of taking critical stances, self-evaluation, and reflection to coaches and candidates in order to truly use certification as professional development. These processes create a foundation for approaching the National Board portfolio and assessment exercises.

Reference

Danielson, C. *Enhancing Professional Practice: A Framework for Teaching.* Alexandria, Va.: Association for Supervision and Curriculum Development, 1996.

TEACHING NOTE

Adrienne, an experienced education consultant and National Board Certified Teacher, works in a school district that chooses National Board Certification as a focus for teacher professional development and school reform. As the support provider for this districtwide program that is well supported financially and politically, Adrienne initially thinks she has helped create an ideal setting for teachers pursuing certification. When some teachers do not achieve certification, Adrienne comes to understand that the high profile National Board Certification receives in the district can be both a blessing and a curse.

This case helps us understand some of the nuances of why some teachers choose to pursue National Board Certification. Adrienne also questions her role as support provider and where her accountability lies—to her own vision of support, to the teachers she serves, or to the district that pays her salary. The commentaries take up the issue of mentoring in high-stakes, high-profile programs and how such programs can sometimes operate with competing agendas.

ISSUES AND QUESTIONS

What Are the Stakes for Teachers in Mentoring Programs?

Mentoring teachers in programs that are highly visible in a district can be a double-edged sword. On the one hand, the district is supportive in providing the necessary funds and resources for the mentoring. On the other hand, when the district provides such visible support, the participating teachers are well known to their colleagues. In such cases, the teacher's performance becomes public knowledge—to be celebrated when successful and questioned when unsuccessful. As mentors in such programs, how do you think the participation of teachers should be handled publicly?

Accountability of the Support Provider

Adrienne questions her role as a support provider in this district program. She has a vision of the structure of support that she believes to be beneficial to teachers in broader terms of professional development, and she knows her limitations of how much of the teachers' work she can read and respond to. She wonders, though, if her vision is enough for the teachers and if she is adequately meeting their needs. She also wonders by what standards she should be (or will be) evaluated by the district. Does the district see her responsibilities as making the certification process a productive professional experience for teachers, as she does, or is their main concern a high pass rate so that they can meet their targeted numbers in the program? The commentaries by Lynn Gaddis and Rose Vilchez, who both worked in similar district-supported programs, raise this issue as well. Lynn discusses the "politics of the pass rate," and Rose explores the competing agendas of the various stakeholders in such programs.

Tension Between High-Stakes Assessment Process and Professional Development

Adrienne believes that the National Board Certification process offers teachers a professional development opportunity, not solely an opportunity to showcase their best work and to be validated by a certifying agency. Her program design for supporting teachers as candidates reflects this belief, as do the programs designed by the two commentators to this case. In other words, Adrienne does not view her program as a preparation program for National Board Certification. How is Adrienne's program structured to support the professional development of the teachers who participate?

Given this view of candidate support, Adrienne did not initially see her role as reading every portfolio entry of the candidates to check their quality and give feedback. After reviewing entries that did not meet the National Board's benchmark scores for passing, she questions whether a little intervention from her would have helped some of the teachers better meet the requirements, potentially saving them and the school district time and money. This leads Adrienne to wonder if she has given her candidates enough support. Is it enough for her to equip the teachers with a set of tools for analysis and thorough grounding in the teaching standards, or should she act as a screener of candidate entries before she allows them to send their portfolios off to the National Board? What would you do in her position?

CHAPTER TWO

FACILITATING FROM THE SIDELINES

Balancing Group Collaboration and Facilitator Expertise

How do you encourage group discussion that is honest, focused, and constructive? Should you intervene if discussion moves in directions that are not especially useful or appropriate? And what can you do to facilitate the discussion without upsetting the dynamics of the group? These are among the challenges presented in this case of a support provider working with a group of teachers who are discussing each other's classroom teaching videos.

CASE

CASE BY VICKI BAKER

As a support provider for National Board candidates in science, the ideal I strive toward is that the members of the group I work with will support each other so well in examining their teaching that I become almost unnecessary as a facilitator. But in reality, it is difficult to determine how to help bring a group to this point and to

---

Pseudonyms have been used to maintain the confidentiality of people and places in the case.

know when they are ready to provide honest and rigorous feedback to each other without direct and ongoing guidance from the facilitator. This tension between the need to lead and the desire to step back caused me to react badly in an unfortunate situation.

My cofacilitator, Sandra, and I worked hard to develop within our group this trust, self-sufficiency, and the necessary skills to discuss teaching practices in constructive and supportive ways. In one of our first meetings, we showed a video of classroom teaching from someone who was not part of the group to give the candidates practice in looking for evidence of standards and to encourage them to bring tapes of their own work. After suggesting that the group pretend the candidate was in the room and think about what they would say to her, we viewed some of the tape. I explained that we would go around the table twice: first to share a standard that we saw in evidence, and then to ask a question that was raised by the video. We never got to the second part because the group almost immediately began to criticize the lesson. Finally, the last candidate, Cheryl, sensed our frustration, and said, "Sandra, I'm going to pretend that you're the candidate and talk directly to you." She then proceeded to make several positive comments and ask a few questions aimed at helping the candidate clarify a problem she saw in the tape. "Sandra," she said, "I noticed that you set up this lesson as a competition, in which students were encouraged to try to beat each other. Why did you choose to do the lesson that way instead of as a cooperative experience?" We were thrilled with Cheryl's example, and it inspired Sandra to write a page of prompts entitled "Constructive Criticism: How to Help and Not Hinder." We presented it to the group at the third session, stating more strongly how important it is to support each other by asking questions that might lead the candidate to a better understanding of his or her practice. Some of the question starters on the handout included:

- Tell me/us more about . . .
- Can you describe more about . . .
- What made you decide to . . .
- What was your rationale for . . .

After reviewing Sandra's document, we began watching videos from the candidates. On this Saturday morning, there were ten of us in the small, darkened conference room. I was in my second year of offering support to National Board Science candidates since achieving my Early Adolescence Science certificate in 2000. Our group consisted of both Early Adolescence and Adolescence and Young Adult Science candidates. Although there are differences in portfolios and assessment center questions for these two certificate areas, our standards are nearly identical.

As usual, we were gathered around the long table, and I was sitting at the head. The first video belonged to Kelly, who was clearly nervous about showing it. As candidates often do, she had spent several minutes explaining why the tape was not perfect before popping it into the VCR. The video showed a small high school class discussing a local issue that pitted business against environmentalists. Students were generally engaged, and though I felt that Kelly sided too obviously with the environmentalists, I thought she effectively moderated the discussion. I especially noticed that she made sure students included the subject matter they had previously learned when contributing to the discussion. I hoped that the group would notice these things and also be sensitive to Kelly's nervousness.

At the end of the video, I asked for comments. The group was positive, and everyone had feedback, some in the form of praise, some as questions, such as: "I am wondering why you seated the students the way you did." No one mentioned Kelly's one-sidedness, including me. Experience had taught me that my criticism could carry more weight than I intended it to. I didn't want Kelly to forget all the positive comments from the group. Also, they had come up with some excellent questions for Kelly to address in her written analysis if she chose to use the tape for her National Board portfolio. After everyone had had a chance to comment, I looked at Kelly. She was clearly pleased with the feedback, and no doubt happy to have shown her first video to peers without wanting to run out of the room in tears.

This discussion also helped me to get a sense of the teachers I was working with this year. Although all were white, the group was diverse in other ways. The ages spanned from mid-twenties to around sixty. There were men and women, teaching grades from 6 to 12, in settings ranging from inner-city urban to upper-middle-class suburbs. They also varied in motivations and attitudes. Some were there for the challenge; some had set out to prove something; some wanted the state monetary incentives.

The second video was from Cheryl, a physics teacher, who had only one question: "The sound is pretty bad. Do you think it's worth working on?" She put the video on, and we sat back and watched. Cheryl was trying to teach some trigonometry that would help students with a lab on trajectory motion. It was clear in just a few minutes that the sound was too poor to submit to the National Board. Several candidates had positive comments about what they could see in the video, but they had some questions as well. I hoped that these questions would help Cheryl reflect on her practice while planning the next taping.

As we prepared to watch the third video, I felt satisfied that the group was beginning to think about the standards and show empathy at the same time. Sandra and I have struggled with our role as support providers, trying to bring candidates to the point where they support each other rather than looking to us for advice and knowledge. Most of our colleagues who are support providers are National Board Certified Teachers, but some are candidates waiting to hear if they have passed or candidates who are redoing some of their portfolio entries. I think I am not speaking only for myself when I say that we do not consider ourselves experts and strive to create a collaborative atmosphere in our support groups. I now shifted my position from the head of the table to the outskirts of the group, as a signal encouraging members to continue the conversation whether I was leading it or not.

Robert, the teacher in the third video, was a quiet man in his late twenties. I still did not feel that I understood his motivation for pursuing certification or his teaching situation. It was getting close to the end of our session, but I wanted to get a sense of his teaching context and his style. The video showed a large, bright classroom, with students sitting in groups. The previous two tapes had shown classes of twenty-five or fewer students. This class had more than thirty students. Although Kelly taught in an urban setting, the class she taped was an upper-level elective science class. Cheryl taught at an urban magnet school, and her ethnically diverse students were also in an elective college preparatory class. The students in Robert's urban class appeared to be about fourteen years old, primarily Hispanic, and from a low socioeconomic group. Unlike the other two classes we had viewed, the students had to be there: this was a required class.

This portfolio entry was supposed to show the teacher helping students grasp a concept at the beginning of a unit. I soon recognized that familiar sinking feeling I get when a video shows poor teaching. The students looked bored, and I could see why. A large packet of worksheets lay in front of the students. There was no evidence of lab equipment or manipulatives of any kind, nor was Robert using a demonstration or any visual aid. The lesson was about cells, and this teacher actually videotaped himself going over the worksheet. All I saw for ten minutes were interactions like this:

> *Teacher:* I see you've left number 3 blank.
> *Student:* Yeah. I don't know the answer.
> *Teacher:* An animal cell is surrounded by a . . . [teacher waits for answer].
> *Student:* I don't know [you can see her girlfriends smiling].
> *Teacher:* Membrane [the girls write it down].

This kind of exchange was repeated a few times. The students, even this early in the school year, had clearly learned that they could get answers without putting forth much effort. The smiles between the girls made this clear to me. Robert's voice betrayed irritation with the students. After talking to a couple of small groups, he switched to going over the worksheet with the whole class. That was the entire lesson: filling out a worksheet.

Every once in a while, I see a video that makes me want to jump in and save the class, and this was one of them. At the same time, I felt sorry for the teacher. I know how hard it is to bring a video in and expose yourself to the judgment of peers. Emotions are raw, and teachers are very vulnerable. I hoped that the candidates would be kind in their criticism. My job would be to make sure the group was constructive and to help Robert see where he could improve.

When the tape ended, I opened my mouth to ask what standards were evident, to begin on a positive note. But before I could say a word, the group started talking:

"That was good."

"Yes. I saw that you were dealing with some learned helplessness."

"It's a tough class."

"That was probably a good lesson for *that* population."

These kinds of comments continued for a while. I was stunned. Why was the group so positive? What evidence did they see that this was a tough class? I saw few behavior problems. Had we put too much emphasis on being positive? Were they just being kind, or did they think there was something good about the lesson? At this point, it was almost time to end the session, but I said, "Does anyone have any questions for Robert?" I thought this might elicit a discussion of some of the poor teaching in the video, but there were no questions. The session ended, and I was very troubled.

By encouraging the candidates to use helpful language, did we unknowingly discourage criticism of any kind?

The most troubling part, which continues to gnaw at me, was the mention of "that population." What was the speaker referring to? Hispanics? Poor kids? The teacher who made this statement worked in an upper-middle-class suburban setting, but several candidates, representing all teaching settings, nodded in agreement at this remark. I wanted to say something, but I began to have doubts. My gut feeling is that bad teaching is bad teaching, no matter the population. I like to think that good teaching crosses all cultural and economic boundaries. But when there was so much consensus in the room, I questioned my own beliefs. I have spent my entire teaching career in the same suburban, middle-class school, and I began to wonder if these teachers knew some truth that I didn't. Was this an example of "the racism of low expectations," or was this an example of doing the right thing for "these students in this setting at this time"?

One thing I did not notice at the time is that the group's comments were not about standards. They were not helpful comments at all. How did I miss that the first time? Was it too soon to expect the group to have any comfort with standards-based discussions? Should we have modeled how to have a discussion following a poorly done lesson? Should I have brought the incident up at the next meeting? Maybe someone else was troubled and would have liked to discuss it.

In hindsight, I realize that by not saying anything, I was giving my silent consent to the remarks. I still am not sure what I should have said. I wonder whether I should have remained at the head of the table and become a much more active member of the group. Should support providers truly see themselves as members of a group who are just one step ahead (due to having gone through the process), or should we see ourselves as having some important expertise?

After discussing this incident with other support providers, I have learned that the attitudes I encountered that day are not unusual. Should there be a discussion of fairness and equity for students at the first session? Robert never returned to the group after that day. Although the video showed poor teaching, National Board candidacy is about transforming yourself. Maybe some standards-based questions would have helped Robert begin a long journey.

COMMENTARIES

COMMENTARY BY CARNE BARNETT-CLARKE

This case reminds me how difficult it is to give and receive constructive criticism. It also points out the added layer of helping others learn how to give and receive constructive criticism. Learning the art of reflecting on and critiquing our teaching is essential to improving it, and such experiences are core to the National Board assessment.

What role does the facilitator serve in supporting the process of conducting a critique? There are many possible responses to this question. Vicki describes the tension she feels between the need to lead and the desire to step back. She and her cofacilitator had worked hard to develop trust, self-sufficiency, and skills for offering constructive feedback. Yet when faced with the touchy situation of critiquing a videotape that did not conform to the Board's quality teaching standards, the teachers in the group gave only positive comments. Perhaps they were being honest, but I doubt if their comments rang true with Robert, the teacher in the videotape, since he never returned to the group.

So what might the facilitator have done in this situation to have a more honest and constructive discussion? Although the facilitator might have taken a more active role in asking the group to comment on the evidence of standards, my guess is that the teachers jumped in with unrelated positive comments *because* they didn't see any evidence of the standards. They wanted to say something—anything—positive to support their colleague. In thinking about how the situation might be handled differently, I found myself thinking about how the whole process, as well as the role of facilitator, might be adjusted to bring about more honest and rigorous discussions.

For example, I wonder if it might help to have the page of prompts that Sandra had written titled, "Constructive Criticism: How to Help and Not Hinder," posted on the wall or at each member's fingertips during each session. Perhaps at the end of each session, the group could refer to the prompts to reflect on how to reframe their question. They might also discuss how well they balanced positive comments and constructive criticism. The facilitator might ask them to discuss why a session that has only positive comments or only critical comments would not be productive.

Perhaps we can draw from what has been learned in the National Writing Project, which has developed a process that successfully fosters thoughtful critiques of one another's writing. Jim Gray (2000), the former director of that project, suggests several ideas about the process that might be helpful in this case. First, teachers in the Writing Project are given time to formulate and write down their critiques before sharing them with the group. Having time to write privately about Robert's teaching example might have led to better ways of formulating questions and comments that would bring about productive discussion. It is difficult to be asked to comment on the spot, especially when there is an element that creates discomfort. The comments are likely to be more thoughtful and responsive to sensitive issues when the commenter is given time to think.

Also, in the National Writing Project, teachers are asked to volunteer to present their work for critique, allowing less confident or competent members of the group time to learn from other colleagues before putting their own teaching up for criticism. Perhaps if Robert had participated in several critiquing sessions, he would have improved his instruction before having to present his work to the group.

Another idea drawn from the Writing Project is asking the teacher in the video to comment before turning to the other members of the group. This allows the person to describe his intentions, provide some background about what standards he is working on, and present his point of view about how he met or did not meet his goals. After all, the goal is to improve no matter where we are starting from, and who knows whether Robert had a particular standard in mind for that lesson. Perhaps after watching his own video, he realized that doing worksheets was not likely to be conducive to providing evidence for the National Board standards. The group could discuss why and think about what kinds of tasks would work better and why.

I find it difficult to learn how to frame comments and questions in ways that are less judgmental. Yet it is important to do so for several reasons. First, I want teachers to appreciate that any teaching strategy, style, or decision has both benefits and drawbacks. One way we learn to improve our teaching is by weighing benefits and drawbacks, using our beliefs and standards as measuring sticks. For example, in this case, Cheryl posed the question, "I noticed that you set up this lesson as a competition in which students were encouraged to try to beat each other. Why did you choose to do the lesson that way instead of as a cooperative experience?" If I were the teacher in the video, this question would possibly put me in a defensive mode instead of a more open, analytical mode. As a facilitator, I have seen teachers clam up, and even cry, feeling that they are put on the spot with questions such as this. Over time, I have found that it helps if the facilitator can teach the group to frame questions in less challenging ways. For example, a gentler question might be, "What are the possible benefits and drawbacks of setting up a lesson as competition?" Making the question a little less personal and opening it up for looking at the consequences for students, both positive and negative, helps make the discussion more conducive to healthy, honest criticism and keeps members of the group from feeling alienated.

The facilitator wears many hats and must take on the roles of leading, teaching, challenging, and supporting, as this case illustrates. It may be just as important to design the process carefully and teach members of the group how to participate respectfully, thoughtfully, and productively as it is to orchestrate the discussion.

Reference

Gray, J. *Teachers at the Center: Early Years of the National Writing Project.* Berkeley, Calif.: National Writing Project, 2000.

COMMENTARY BY YVONNE DIVANS-HUTCHINSON

This case, that of National Board candidates making "nice" and maybe racist concessions when commenting on an obviously inept videotaped teaching performance by a colleague and the facilitator's reluctance to intervene, nay, take charge, made me wish for the little kid whose childishly uninhibited impulse gave vent to the open and honest response: "The emperor has no clothes." This case raises three issues. First, how strong a role should the facilitator play during the discussion of the candidates' work? Second, how does the group balance the need to give positive strokes against the need to be honest and fair, especially if it means pointing out blatant deficiencies? Third, and most urgent, are there different criteria for judging the teaching and learning of poor and Latino children ("that population," as they were referred to in the case)?

As a support provider for National Board candidates, I understand the need to make the process as collegial as possible. I agree that critiques should not be handled as if one is handing down answers from on high. As facilitators, we strive to help the candidates—who are, for the most part, exemplary teachers—to make discoveries about their process—to reflect, to gain insight about what they do, how they do it, and how it benefits their students. However, this was one time when the facilitator should have intervened as the expert and guided the group of candidates around the minefields and pitfalls, such as this obvious misstep: the group's cosigning of poor teaching. Was it shock or disbelief at the blatant inadequacy of the lesson that prevented the cofacilitator from asking the group and the teacher himself to look at the lesson through the lens of the standards? The facilitator's first instinct, "that bad teaching is just bad teaching, no matter where it is found," was correct.

Her dilemma of not wanting to usurp the collaborative process of the group balanced against the need to point out obvious shortcomings of the candidate's video was a tough one. However, confronting the preconceived notion that lowered expectations were acceptable because these students were poor and Latino should have been the first priority. Allowing such prejudicial notions to stand renders a disservice to the students in question. It sends the wrong message that poor teaching is acceptable practice among a certain segment of the student population and that there exists a double standard: one for a National Board candidate whose misfortune it is to have poor Latino children and another for those who have academically advanced students. In this case, it seemed that the teacher's classroom video garnered positive marks simply because of his "dumbing down" his instruction or just plain ineptitude.

The patent racism in that comment is staggering. The facilitator questions the lack of tough criticism on the part of the group;

despite the conviction that "good teaching crosses all cultural and economic boundaries," she allowed herself to be swayed by the consensus of the members of her support group and the acquiescence of her cofacilitator. She agonizes, "Was this an example of the 'racism of low expectations' or was this an example of doing the right thing for 'these students in this setting at this time'?"

I would answer that question by asking one. In terms of National Board standards, or any other standards for that matter, what makes inferior teaching "good enough"? Public schools have a long history of institutional racism and failing to meet the needs of poor children and children of color in urban schools. Given that this is the case, National Board Certified Teachers should be extraordinarily skilled at recognizing and rejecting poor teaching no matter where it occurs. Among National Board support groups, exemplary teaching and sensitivity to the needs of children should be the norm rather than the exception. By definition, NBCTs are among the children's strongest advocates. Consequently, they should speak up, as did the child in the fairy tale, and be the first to point out that the emperor has no clothes—that is, to call poor teaching what it is: unacceptable for all children.

TEACHING NOTE

Vicki portrays the tensions that existed when she attempted to wean herself away from the facilitator role with a group of teachers. The context is a support group of Early Adolescence and Adolescence and Young Adulthood Science candidates. We see how Vicki tries to prepare group members to give appropriate feedback to one another's videos and then steps back from that role when she was satisfied that candidates were starting to generate appropriate questions for each other. But when the teachers provided inappropriate feedback to a candidate, she did not know how to intervene and chose to remain silent.

The case focuses directly on the role of a mentor. Vicki questions her own expertise and wonders what her role is in the context of the National Board support group and as a mentor in general. It also deals with the challenges of how to give and receive constructive criticism, and what to do when teachers' biases appear to be misguiding their collaborative feedback.

ISSUES AND QUESTIONS

Preparing for Honest and Constructive Feedback in a Learning Community

Like many other accounts in this book, this case is embedded in the challenges of developing a learning community of teachers. It begins with a description of the facilitator's disappointing attempt to scaffold the skills required of a critical friend, who looks for evidence of teaching standards and asks questions that help teachers analyze and reflect on their practice. Examine the strategies that Vicki and her cofacilitator used before showing the first video. Can you think of others that might have made it more likely that the teachers' comments would focus more on evidence of standards or clarifying questions than on criticisms? Some people who discussed this case suggested that the facilitators and participants develop consensus on ground rules or protocols for examining one another's practice. What might be some examples of appropriate ground rules for collaborative feedback? What are the risks and benefits of this approach?

Carne Barnett-Clarke's commentary focuses on the difficulty of giving constructive criticism and provides some suggestions for developing processes that foster thoughtful critique. She also examines the importance of how questions are phrased, which either opens or closes analyses of practice. For example, Carne points to Cheryl's question in the second paragraph of the case that attempts to help clarify a problem: "I noticed that you set up this lesson as a competition in which students were encouraged to try to beat each other. Why did you choose to do the lesson that way, instead of as a cooperative experience?" Although the teachers in Vicki's group "were thrilled with this example," Carne suggests that it would have made her feel defensive and she offers other ways of phrasing it that would make it less personal and more open to honest critique. How did you feel about the question?

Examine the series of question prompts that Sandra developed to help candidates frame constructive feedback questions. Her goal was to help candidates create a balance between descriptive, analytical, and reflective questions. Can you add any prompts? Carne suggests posting the list on the wall and using it to debrief how well teachers balanced positive and constructive questions. What do you think about this approach?

Delegating Authority

Vicki writes that the "ideal that [she] strives toward is that the members of the group will support each other so well in examining their teaching that she becomes unnecessary as a facilitator." But her plan backfired. After stepping back and essentially delegating authority to the group when she felt the teachers were ready, she was uncertain how to intervene when she disagreed with the feedback given. This raises an interesting question: When facilitating a group during which participants are supposed to give feedback on one another's practice, is it ever desirable to relinquish control of the discussion? If yes, under what circumstances?

Trusting Your Judgment

When Vicki saw that group members gave positive feedback to Robert's video, she questioned her "gut feeling" that this was bad teaching and chose to remain silent instead of pursuing with probing questions. It is not uncommon for mentors to question their expertise. What would you do or say if you are not sure about the quality of teaching represented in a video? What kind of message does silence communicate?

Addressing Bias

As depicted in the feedback to Robert's video, some teachers had stereotypically low expectations about what his students are capable of learning. Look in the case for examples of biased statements and opinions rather than comments and questions that address evidence of standards. Yvonne Divans-Hutchinson's commentary poignantly addresses the ramifications of these kinds of expectations. How would you handle this situation? What would you say if you heard teachers express similar misconceptions? What are the advantages and disadvantages of each of your suggestions?

Some veteran mentors who discussed this case noted that they anticipate this kind of bias when they work with groups of teachers, so they examine the standard on equity, fairness, and diversity and come to a consensus on what comprises evidence of good teaching in all contexts before asking teachers to share their videos. This strategy, they suggest, provides a vision of teaching that helps candidates scaffold their analyses and prevent bias from appearing when they share their own videos. What do you think of this approach?

PART TWO

VISION OF ACCOMPLISHED TEACHING

CHAPTER THREE

WHAT TO DO ABOUT JAKE

*One of the most difficult challenges for any mentor
or supervisor is what to do with the teacher who
lacks the basic knowledge and skills needed for
accomplished teaching. Furthermore, what do you
do if that teacher doesn't realize there is a problem?
Can the process of certification along with
additional professional development make up for
serious deficiencies in a teacher's preparation?*

CASE

CASE BY ANN IFEKWUNIGWE

It was early December, and the teacher candidates in our National
Board support project had recently learned the outcome of their
efforts to become National Board Certified Teachers (NBCTs). As
in previous years, we notified our candidates that we would be
holding a meeting for those who had not certified and asked them
to bring copies of their portfolio entries, portfolio instructions, and
score reports. (Candidates who do not certify can "bank scores,"
which means they can save scores from entries that reached the
benchmark score and retake those that did not reach the benchmark. Candidates have three years to certify, and each "retake"
attempt costs three hundred dollars per entry at the time this case

---

Pseudonyms have been used to maintain the confidentiality of people and places
in the case.

was written.) After several years of supporting candidates both informally and as part of a structured support group, I had discovered that it was essential to begin this part of the National Board Certification process with sharing. The teachers needed time to communicate their feelings about not attaining certification, come to terms with the results of their assessments, and be reassured that there was nothing wrong with them because they had not certified on their first attempt. This emotional venting was a critical component of the process, especially if the teachers were planning to resubmit unsuccessful portions of the assessment.

Although sadness and disappointment were part of the sharing sessions, bitterness and anger always prevailed. Angry at the outcome, teachers found that questioning the policies and wisdom of the National Board took the onus off themselves. Whether twenty-year veterans or novices with only a few years in the classroom, all believed they were accomplished teachers and felt demoralized that the National Board had suggested otherwise. The caliber of the teachers who typically pursued certification made it easy for me to be genuine as I reassured them that they were accomplished educators and that we would work together to identify which areas of their practice needed to be strengthened.

After giving the candidates ample time to express their feelings, I guided them in carefully analyzing their work for evidence of accomplished teaching. It was at this point that the teachers generally took one of two paths: they continued to assert that they were accomplished teachers and the National Board's assessments were flawed, or they came to acknowledge that they had not provided clear, consistent, and convincing evidence that they were accomplished teachers, and began to reflect on their teaching practices with a more honestly critical eye.

It was at one of these meetings that I met Jake. A young man with a bright smile and a soothing voice, Jake had been teaching for three years, the minimum required by the National Board, when he began his candidacy. During the sharing session, he had expressed much more disappointment and confusion than anger. He was nonplussed that his submitted work had received such low scores and did not understand what was lacking in his teaching. He asked me if I would be willing to watch one of his videos after the meeting. He said he was particularly proud of his integrated science math video and was not convinced that it merited a score of 0.75 on the scale of 0.75 to 4.25 used by the Board.

After the other candidates had departed, I asked Jake to provide the context for me before beginning the video. He began by telling me that the students in his first-grade class were very poor, many were being raised by a single mother, some had an incarcerated parent, and it was a daily struggle for him to keep some of his students' attention focused on their lessons. Although he demonstrated knowledge of his students, I found it odd that Jake provided so much more information about their lives outside school rather than sharing information about their interests and abilities as learners inside his classroom. I asked if he could provide some background about the math/science lesson he had taught. He said he did not usually teach science; his day was primarily dedicated to teaching the language arts and math programs mandated by his school district, and felt he had no time for science instruction. He continued by saying that he had found a science activity workbook at a bookstore and had used some of the material from the book in his videotaped lesson. I asked what kind of feedback he had received from his colleagues in the support group. He replied that although he had attended the support project's summer institute, he had not made time to attend the monthly Support Academy meetings held by our candidate support program. Consequently, no one had provided feedback on his videotaped lessons or his written commentaries.

The video began with Jake standing in front of the class. For a first-grade classroom, the room seemed rather stark: the walls were bare, the desks haphazardly arranged, and little in the room felt warm and inviting. The students were predominantly African American and Latino, they sat at their desks facing the teacher, and all appeared ready to learn. "Today we're going to do science," Jake began. "We're going to learn all about water. The video camera is recording, so you have to be on your best behavior. If you're not on your best behavior, I'm going to show the video to the principal." I resisted the urge to question this class management technique and tried to watch with an open mind.

The video continued, "I need a helper to pass out the papers we're going to use today." Mayhem broke out as all the students vied for the opportunity to be the helper. Jake was allowed to submit only a fifteen-minute lesson, and he was wasting valuable minutes as materials that could have already been at students' desks were distributed. It then took several more minutes for Jake to recapture the students' attention. Two of the children who had not been chosen to pass out papers glared at Jake with arms crossed and faces scowling. When I asked him why he had chosen to include this section in the video he submitted, he said he thought it showed that his students were eager and enthusiastic learners. I added this to my growing list of concerns I would address at the end of the video.

I found little in the remainder of the taped lesson that demonstrated highly accomplished teaching. In this video, through which Jake was expected to "help students acquire important science and mathematics knowledge . . . understand a 'big idea' in science . . . engage students in the discovery, exploration, and implementation of these science and mathematics concepts, procedures, and processes by integrating these two disciplinary areas," he demonstrated quite convincingly that he would need much assistance and guidance in doing any of the above. The video showed Jake directing students to complete a dot-to-dot worksheet of a water faucet, color a picture of an oversized water droplet, complete a count-the-raindrops activity page (there were twelve raindrops in all), and copy sentences from the board about water: "Water is wet. Without water we would die. Pipes bring water to our homes. Drink 8 glasses of water every day!"

I was stunned. Since I had been supporting candidates for several years, I had encountered a fair number of teachers who would have benefited from professional development in various areas. Some of these teachers had good instincts and were skilled in the delivery of information but needed to develop their content knowledge; some had a wealth of content knowledge but needed support in pedagogy; others needed help understanding how to align their instruction with the state's content standards. Jake appeared to lack critical content knowledge for his grade level, seemed to lack skill in delivering that content knowledge, and was apparently unaware that his state had developed and adopted content standards for math and science instruction.

Jake's teaching was far from reaching the high levels set by the standards of the National Board. I carefully considered what to do. Should I tell this young man that he was not yet an accomplished teacher and that National Board Certification might be something for him to consider later in his teaching career? Or should I encourage him to continue pursuing certification with the hope that it would make him a better teacher? I realized I needed more information about Jake and the choices he had made in his video-taped lesson, so I decided to move forward with a discussion of his video.

When working with National Board candidates, I strive to begin feedback sessions with positive comments about what teachers have done well. I was able to point out one or two features of Jake's videotaped lesson that reflected the National Board's Early Childhood Generalist Standards: he did a good job of circulating among the students and was quite generous with praise for his children as they worked on their tasks. In doing so, Jake demonstrated his understanding that "accomplished teachers are systematic and insightful observers of young children at work" and they "know the importance of motivation in the learning process, and use a variety of means to encourage children to do their best."

In discussing the many concerns I had with Jake, I tried to be as objective as possible. I found our ensuing conversation about the serious pedagogical and content-related issues in his work both unnerving and encouraging. First, we discussed Jake's classroom management strategies and the fact that the workbook he purchased had been created for students much younger than those in his class. The activities were developmentally inappropriate and did little to challenge his students' developing brains with more complex ideas, concepts, and information. Second, if the state's science content standards for first-grade physical science included exploration of states of matter and the properties of those states of matter, I queried why Jake's lesson had not included inquiry-based experiments to help students discover that "solids, liquids, and gases have different properties, and that the properties of substances can change when the substances are mixed, cooled, or heated." Third, I wanted to understand why Jake had chosen not to use hands-on science in a lesson on water. Hands-on activities through which students could explore water's various states and properties would help his children construct deeper knowledge and understanding of the concepts. Finally, I wanted Jake to help me understand his choices for the math activities and explain why his integration of math and science had been so minimal. Why did he believe that having the students color worksheets, count raindrops, and copy sentences from the board stimulated active discovery, exploration, and application of critical math and science concepts?

Initially I was disturbed that Jake was so unaware that his teaching was less than accomplished. However, in the course of our conversation, Jake acknowledged that he was not prepared to teach certain subjects. Hired on an emergency credential, his first day of work was the first time he had been in a classroom since his own days as a student. Jake's status was like that of many other teachers in this large urban district, where the demand for credentialed teachers far exceeds the supply. He was taking classes at a local college to earn a teaching credential but was often so drained by the time he arrived at his evening and weekend classes, he felt he actually learned very little that would improve his teaching. His interest in National Board Certification was driven by financial incentives offered by his district in the form of a salary increase and by his state in the form of a stipend, as well as by a genuine desire to be a better teacher. Jake's video demonstrated that he needed intensive, focused professional development to help augment his skills and improve his practice. I was encouraged when he admitted that he didn't know enough about science and should have asked for help in planning his lessons. It would have been wonderful if I could have paired Jake with an accomplished mentor teacher at his school site, but that did not happen, and I did my best to assist him. Jake was grateful for the mini-workshop I conducted for him on the water cycle, he appreciated the set of grade-level standards I provided, and he welcomed the developmentally appropriate science materials and accompanying literature I let him borrow from my classroom. Jake was surprised when I told him that our school district had math, science, and technology centers staffed by instructional experts, full of teaching resources available for teacher checkout, and offering ongoing professional development classes free of charge. I told him that I used the center extensively, especially when I began teaching, and encouraged him to contact his local center for information about available resources and classes. Jake was excited about using the centers and assured me he would call the next day.

In working with Jake, I found myself in a disturbing quandary. The National Board for Professional Teaching Standards "believes strongly in the power of National Board Certification as a professional growth experience that improves individual teachers and strengthens the teaching profession." My initial observations of Jake's teaching led me to believe that he might strengthen the teaching profession most by leaving the classroom. I had expected the candidates in our support group to have already achieved a certain level of proficiency and was surprised to encounter a teacher in need of so much professional development in the most fundamental aspects of teaching. Rather than supporting an already accomplished teacher through advanced certification, I found myself working with a beginning teacher whose basic preparation was woefully inadequate to meet the needs of his students.

Fortunately, Jake was willing to reflect honestly on his teaching and proved to be an enthusiastic learner. He was open to suggestions and eager to improve his practice. But was zest for learning enough? As a National Board Certified Teacher who is steadfastly "committed to students and their learning," I continued to worry about the children in Jake's class. My work with him left me with some deeply troubling questions. What should support providers do when they encounter teachers who are not qualified to teach? What systemic flaws allowed Jake to be in the classroom in the first place? Why didn't he receive the support he so desperately needed from his school or his school district? I wanted to provide Jake with all the skills, resources, and materials he would need to help all of his students excel, but my limited time, energy, and resources precluded that degree of support. I often wonder whether I did enough. What more could I have done to help Jake become a better teacher for his students, who deserved so much more than their teacher was able to provide?

COMMENTARIES

COMMENTARY BY MYRIAM CASIMIR

This case presents fundamental dilemmas for National Board support providers and, more broadly, for educators concerned with teacher quality. First, how do we communicate high standards for teaching to teachers who are not aware that their standards are low? Second, how do we support such individuals in moving toward accomplished teaching practices? In my commentary, I identify some central ideas relating to these dilemmas from macro- to microlevel viewpoints.

From a macrolevel perspective, at the societal level, I found that the case of Jake reiterated discourses on public school teaching and on the education of poor and minority children. In the twentieth and early twenty-first centuries, one of the prevailing views of public school teaching in the United States has been that it is an easy profession. Teachers, some believe, "get to go home at 3:00 P.M. and have summers off." Teachers, some believe, need only demonstrate basic content knowledge through a multiple-choice test in order to be qualified to teach subjects. (In other words, "If you speak English, you can teach English; if you can count, you can teach math.") And a prevailing view about poor and minority children is that schooling can serve to teach them the "more civil" customs and knowledge base of mainstream society.

For many years, teachers on emergency credentials could basically walk off the street and end up responsible for the literacy and content knowledge development of some of the most educationally needy children. These children, chronically underserved by the public education system, have typically been handed the least prepared teachers, many of whom focus on having them be "enthusiastic" or "respectful" learners rather than competent, or excellent, learners.

Jake's perspective toward the National Board assessment made me think of this structural dysfunction relating to the way many members of the public consider public education. Somehow Jake got the idea that teaching was easy, and that in his National Board assessment he need only show happy children in a classroom in order to certify. I read incredulously as Ann described Jake's 0.75 entry and his rationalization of that entry. At the same time, I understood how, given the societal context, Jake could in fact be a real teacher (not just a caricature) with low standards for himself and his students. As a former teacher who routinely worked late into the night to prepare for students' learning, I also reacted negatively to Jake's lackadaisical attitude toward teaching. Although most of the teachers I know are diametrically opposed to Jake in their engagement in their profession, I thought, annoyed, "It is the Jakes of the world who give teaching a bad name." That is, it is the individuals whose practices mirror the negative stereotypes about teaching that make it difficult for the societal views on public school teacher quality to be changed.

At the institutional level, I wondered what structures existed to make Jake think that he could become an NBCT when he knew well that his teacher preparation was incomplete and that he was deficient in the teaching of a major core curriculum area: science. What were teacher expectations like in his school? Were teacher evaluations in his district meaningful? What standards for accomplished teaching were articulated and discussed at the state level? Were these considered seriously by teachers, or were they considered to be just hoops to jump through? What role did the state's financial incentives for NBCTs working in low-performing schools play in his decision to seek certification at this early point in his career?

From time to time, I have run into teachers who are in my estimation not yet accomplished in their practice or highly reflective but who attempt certification in order to receive the incentives. While I have found that many of those individuals do not become certified, reading the case of Jake made me think that the state's financial incentive ought to be accompanied with a clear statement of purpose of what, as NBPTS puts it, "accomplished teachers should know and be able to do." This statement should be related not only to test scores but to the competencies, dispositions, content, pedagogical knowledge, and knowledge of students that accomplished teachers are expected to possess. This message would need to be taken seriously at all levels and incorporated into institutional practices, so that it would be accepted as a professional expectation.

Unfortunately, when systems are dysfunctional at the less visible macro- and mesolevels (societal and institutional, respectively), gaps and difficulties become most apparent at the microlevel—at the level of one-to-one interactions and of individuals' understanding of themselves. It was interesting to note that Jake avoided peers' examinations of his National Board portfolio videos and writings. What kind of self-image must he have to keep his practice that private, even while going through an assessment process designed to make his teaching public? What was his identity as a teacher of undereducated children—his beliefs and his standards? And how was he inducted into the profession so that he considered it professionally responsible never to get any feedback from colleagues? I wondered whether Jake had had any honest interactions about his teaching with fellow educators prior to his meeting with Ann. Was Ann the first person to bring up the issue of quality teaching and the meeting of National Board standards? Not likely, considering Jake had undergone an entire year of candidacy before going to Ann's meeting.

In my experience supporting candidates who are private with their practices, I have found that while they do learn about their teaching through listening to and viewing others' work, the windows of opportunity for discussing their own practice are few and far between. Like Ann, I am never sure how to address this type of individual. Fortunately, with her careful and honest approach, she was able to engage Jake in what seemed to be one of the few conversations he had ever had about his preparedness to teach to high standards. Ann is to be commended for meeting Jake at his level and working to move him up regardless of the glaring evidence that he was not yet prepared to become an NBCT. Given the same circumstances, I would have done the same: pointed out areas where Jake was not meeting the standards, enriching his knowledge of content and pedagogy, helping him to articulate why his standards for his students were not high, and mapping out next steps for his professional development.

Still, it seems to me that Ann was left to clean up after other people's messes. Societal factors and institutional factors conspired to create a situation where this teacher thought he could become recognized as highly effective without actually being highly effective. I empathized with Ann as she found herself face to face with an individual who was a product of a dysfunctional teacher education and induction system. Her strategies for working with Jake were admirable, particularly considering the situation she inherited. When all else fails (at the macro and meso scales), it takes competent individuals to engage in the difficult work of interacting with colleagues to establish not only high standards but also paths toward achieving those standards. Still, for Ann, acting as this type of microlevel Band-Aid and knowing that she would have little or no impact on the systems that caused this challenge must have been very frustrating.

COMMENTARY BY LARIE COLOSIMO

Jake has fallen between the professional development cracks, and Ann is faced with the job of pulling him out and helping him find the professional growth track that will support and assist his attainment of the knowledge and skills he needs to become a proficient teacher and apply them in his classroom so that he can have a positive impact on student learning.

We enter this case study at the conclusion of a series of missed opportunities to support Jake's professional growth with these questions:

- Where is the breakdown in a system (district, site, somewhere else) that allows an inexperienced, underprepared, beginning teacher to invest time and money in professional growth that is obviously developmentally inappropriate for him?
- Where was the breakdown in this facilitated National Board candidacy support program that allowed such a novice to progress through orientation, portfolio development, and submission only to discover, finally on receipt of scores, that he had not yet attained even a beginning skill level?
- What is the responsibility of a facilitator to counsel a teacher out of candidacy?

The National Board Certification (NBC) experience is powerful, advanced professional development. For many teachers, it advances them in their progression across what California calls the "Learning to Teach Continuum." This multitiered continuum charts professional growth across a teacher's career, beginning with preservice teacher education, through the preliminary credential and induction supported by the state Beginning Teacher Support and Assessment (BTSA) program, to a clear credential. Relevant and meaningful professional development in each of these phases is inquiry based, job embedded, linked to evidence of practice, and measured against standards. Following the induction phase, teachers self-select professional development opportunities that have the same characteristics and are developmentally appropriate as they move from novice to experienced and, finally, accomplished status. Many districts have begun to build systems that support this continuum, with trained instructional leaders in administrative positions to provide systematic advice and counsel based on observation and other assessment measures to teachers as they progress through the continuum. As an NBC support provider and BTSA regional director since 1999, I will address each of the questions posed above based on my experience in working with teachers across this professional continuum.

DEVELOPMENTALLY APPROPRIATE PROFESSIONAL DEVELOPMENT FOR TEACHERS

First, where is the breakdown in a system that finds a brand-new teacher with an emergency credential enrolled in a professional growth program for accomplished teachers? We know that beginning teachers at the lowest end of the pay scale often seek additional duties that provide stipends to augment their income. Generally, however, programs that are supported by district funds have some level of screening of candidates before allowing them to take on duties or otherwise participate. Clearly this advice was not available or heeded by this candidate. But as Ann may have learned, the onus often falls on the facilitator to create a screening mechanism to ensure that candidates are participating in the professional growth program that is developmentally appropriate for them.

Facilitators of National Board candidate support may want to ask their candidates about the access they have to professional development. What local system of support do these teachers have access to that informs their professional growth choices? Have they been thoughtfully and carefully screened and informed as to the nature of the NBC process at the system level? Are there other professional growth opportunities within the system that support teacher development across the continuum? This is critical contextual information a facilitator needs before beginning to work with candidates in order to inform their work.

In addition, they might ask what entices each candidate in the group to accept the National Board challenge. Knowing why candidates have chosen to pursue certification may inform us about the nature of their commitment and the pressures they may be under, and provide understanding that may guide the advice and assistance they will need as they progress through the process. My experience has been that candidates who answer the question with "for the money" often manifest significantly different facilitation challenges than do those motivated by other rationales, including pride, challenge, or curiosity.

As facilitators, we are rarely responsible for these systemic breakdowns, and we are not empowered to repair them. But when we miss the opportunity to understand a candidate's professional development context, we limit our ability to be attuned to the possible pressures and challenges candidates may face as they navigate the certification process and to apply our own pressure to candidates who seem to have found themselves in the wrong Learning to Teach phase.

ENGAGING TEACHERS DEEPLY IN DIALOGUE ABOUT PRACTICE

The second question relates more directly to our sphere of influence as facilitators: How did Jake manage to participate in the summer institute without gleaning the extent to which he was underprepared for the certification process? Assuming that the workshops or seminars included dialogue, inquiry, examination of the standards, and analysis of student work relative to the portfolio experience, it seems doubtful that Jake could have participated in the dialogue to the extent that his lack of preparation and experience would not have become transparent. So where is the breakdown that allowed Jake not only to complete the institute but progress through the portfolio unaware that he was working on a developmentally inappropriate project? This brings us to Ann's query about the value of the process as professional development and the possibility that Jake may have learned something from the experience in spite of his novice status. If we were to apply the same question to our work with students, the answer would probably be negative. Perhaps if Jake had attended the ongoing support network groups to share his work and learn from other candidates, he may have gained the vocabulary and perspective that would help him reflect on his skills and strategies, but working in isolation as he apparently did, that opportunity was missed as well.

How do we facilitate deep, meaningful dialogue about classroom practice and student assessment and learning that allow them to build shared understanding of what accomplished teachers should know and be able to do? Workshops focused on bringing the standards to life allow candidates to reflect on their practice and compare their practice to others and to the standards. This facilitates inquiry and helps the candidate build perspective. We can also design video-sharing experiences to engage candidates in observing for evidence of and comparison to standards. Beginning the certification process by analyzing numerous snippets of teaching videos in a shared context enables participants to focus on themes: teaching strategies that meet the standards, student engagement, and evidence of for portfolio use. In this way, Jake would have been able to view many accomplished and not-so-accomplished teachers and participated in the analysis of their teaching, giving him a way to compare his own practice with those being discussed. Perhaps an opportunity like this would have allowed Jake to admit his frustrations early on to Ann, in which case he might have been able to invest his time and effort in professional development activities that would have been more meaningful for him.

We may even question how we structure our support in such a way as to first place emphasis on the National Board standards and how they look in our classrooms rather than the building of candidates' portfolios. While we do not have information about the institute in this case study, my experience working with candidates is that to start with the portfolio rather than the standards places the importance on the product instead of the process and dilutes the professional growth possibilities inherent in the process.

I have worked with many candidates who were inexperienced and underprepared. Most of them find that they cannot maintain a level of dialogue comparable to their colleagues. At that point, they provide entry point for me to engage in the hard conversation about readiness. Facilitators who are knowledgeable about other professional development opportunities in candidates' districts are poised to gently assist the teachers in finding the right fit for their assessed growth areas. This cannot wait until the watching-of-the-videos phase of the workshop. It must be done from the first dialogue point where risk is low and investment is limited.

COUNSELING CANDIDATES ABOUT THEIR READINESS FOR NATIONAL BOARD CERTIFICATION

Finally, Ann wonders, along with all of us, should we counsel candidates out of the process (or the profession) and if so, how? I can respond only with an opinion. Although I would not feel responsible for directly advising a teacher that he or she is not ready for the NBC process, I do feel quite comfortable doing so in an indirect manner. A dialogue-rich environment, where teachers have many opportunities to share best practice, compare it to standards, discuss alternatives, analyze teaching moments, and reflect on teaching and learning allows candidates and facilitators to get a sense of their level of readiness. Asking the hard questions about one's practice gets to the answers of level of practice. Assessing the developmental level of the candidate pool is a critical first responsibility for a facilitator, just as it is in the classroom with students.

National Board Certification is powerful professional development because it is grounded in formative inquiry and self-assessment. It is ultimately the role of the district and site administrators to evaluate the performance level of teachers, even when the system lacks the capacity to do it well. A facilitator's job is to hold the mirror; the standards suggest what the candidate should be looking for. We have the power to ask deep, probing questions when we do not see the evidence of the standards in practice, but the power to dissuade is indirect—it must be the candidate's decision. Developmentally appropriate professional growth, based on one's current level of practice and experience, is critical if we want teachers to be able to make meaningful adjustments that will truly engage students in the kind of classroom learning experiences they deserve.

TEACHING NOTE

Ann encounters a teacher who has pursued National Board Certification and did not achieve certification. When he asks her to look at his video of teaching an integrated math and science lesson to a group of first graders, she sees a startling example of teaching that is "far from reaching the very high levels set by the standards of the National Board." Ann was not sure how to proceed in working with the teacher and describes the approach she took in tuning into his current practice and trying to move him forward.

This case identifies some of the challenges of mentoring teachers toward a vision of accomplished practice when the teacher's current vision is limited. The case also explores questions of how educational systems allow teachers who are underprepared into classrooms and the moral implications this has for the education of children.

ISSUES AND QUESTIONS

Mentoring Toward a Standards-Based Vision of Teaching

When Ann views Jake's classroom videotape, she sees a teacher she believes is underprepared for teaching. Ann's experience with National Board candidates who typically have stronger pedagogical skills and knowledge of the standards for teaching than Jake demonstrates did not prepare her for responding to him. Ann has many questions about Jake's practice—about his knowledge of his students as learners, about how he has established a supportive learning environment for his students, and about his understanding of the math and science teaching standards and curricular resources. She carefully considers how to begin her feedback to Jake. A typical mentoring strategy is to ask questions to promote reflective thinking on the part of the teacher. But if the teacher's practice is at a novice level, with limited experience and knowledge, the teacher may not have a basis on which to reflect productively. How did Ann approach her feedback and discussion with Jake? Do you think her approach was reasonable? What else could have been done as a mentor with Jake? What would you have done?

What Is the Role of the Mentor in a High-Stakes Assessment Environment?

Ann questions if she should be counseling Jake out of the certification process given that his practice seems to be so far from meeting the teaching standards. Many mentoring situations have a high-stakes component to them: recommending teaching candidates for a teaching credential, supervising new teachers toward their full credential or tenure, and advising students into college or graduate school, to name just a few. How far should a mentor go in advice and counseling in such situations? Is the mentor's role to raise questions for the mentee-candidate to consider? To help screen out lesser-prepared candidates from the process? To support the candidate regardless of his or her preparation? What are your views on the role the mentor should play in such high-stakes situations?

Mentor Support from Programs and Educational Systems

Jake entered the classroom on an emergency credential with no formal teacher preparation. His teaching on his National Board video suggests that at least in the area of science, he lacks sufficient preparation or new teacher support to help him learn to teach his students effectively. The commentary by LaRie Colosimo speaks to the kind of support a new teacher should be getting in Jake's state. Jake's case calls the system of support that he had into question. Myriam Casimir's commentary speaks to the moral imperative to ensure students are assigned competent teachers. What kind of new teacher support would have helped Jake develop his skills as an elementary teacher? What is the support system's responsibility to Jake? What is the support system's responsibility to the students in Jake's classroom?

Jake chose to pursue the National Board Certification process as a fourth-year teacher. He attended introductory sessions that helped him learn about the certification process and get started. For reasons that only Jake knows, he did not participate regularly in a candidate support program, choosing to complete the certification process on his own with little to no feedback from colleagues. While National Board Certification is a voluntary process, there remains a question as to why a teacher would choose to pursue this certification when his or her teaching practice is currently far from the teaching standards. What kind of information do teachers need prior to pursuing National Board Certification that will help them make the best decision about their readiness to attempt the certification process?

CHAPTER FOUR

GETTING A SMALL GROUP ON BOARD WITH THE STANDARDS

*Can you effectively support teachers who don't share
your vision of teaching? Does it matter if you don't
share the same content area expertise? In this case,
a support provider struggles to engage a group of
teachers in a process they question and toward a
goal they do not fully support.*

CASE

CASE BY WILLIAM DEAN

After achieving National Board Certification in Adolescence and
Young Adulthood/English Language Arts (AYA/ELA), I became
a support provider for other AYA/ELA teacher candidates. The
training I had received prepared me to provide the same guidance
and encouragement to others going through the process. When a
local support program asked me to work with four librarians applying for the new Library Media certificate, I didn't hesitate to agree.
I felt prepared to tackle the assignment, although it was out of my
certification area. Little did I imagine the challenge these four
librarians would pose as I strove to guide them through the standards and the assessment process.

Pseudonyms have been used to maintain the confidentiality of people and places
in the case.

Each monthly meeting began with a large group session that provided general guidance for all of the candidates. We then broke into certificate area groups. In the large sessions, there was much shared energy and information about the process to spill over to the certificate area meetings. I anticipated that my group would follow up on the same topics and I would offer some specific guidance based on my experience as a candidate. I did not sense any hint of anxiety about the process among the four librarians when I first met them in the large group, so I assumed our coming together would be positive, productive, and pleasant. To my surprise, our small group sessions began with their disgruntled reaction to the teaching standards and the expectations of the portfolio entries. In their initial conversations, they could not seem to relate their current teaching practices to the expectations for accomplished library media specialists set out by the National Board, and they chose to spend our time together complaining about their working conditions and the certification process.

I had to reconsider my role with this group. Instead of just facilitating a continuation of the large group's focus, I thought I would have to focus on convincing them that the standards made good professional sense for them as librarians and that the portfolio tasks were reasonable. The standards say that accomplished library media specialists:

- Have knowledge of learning styles and of human growth and development.

- Know the principles of teaching and learning that contribute to an active learning environment.

- Know the principles of library and information studies needed to create effective, integrated library media programs.

- Integrate information literacy through collaboration, planning, implementation, and assessment of learning.

- Lead in providing equitable access to and effective use of technologies and innovations.

- Plan, develop, implement, manage, and evaluate library media programs to ensure that students and staff use ideas and information effectively.

- Engage in reflective practice to increase their effectiveness.

- Model a strong commitment to lifelong learning and to their profession.

- Uphold professional ethics and promote equity and diversity.

- Advocate for the library media program, involving the greater community.

At first, facilitating conversations about the vision of the standards was challenging for me since I am not a librarian. I could not completely relate to their experiences at their school sites and was just getting familiar with their standards myself. But I had faith in the National Board, and as I read the standards I could see the vision of accomplished practice more clearly. The work of the librarian is more than clerical and more than knowing a lot about books. Librarians work with the children and teachers in the school. As accomplished education professionals, they should know about child development and be able to design learning activities that are engaging and supportive of deep understanding. They should have active and collaborative relationships with the classroom teachers in the school so they are working in partnership. But my group's perspective on their role in the school was quite different. They did not see themselves as teachers of students, and their situations often made it difficult to collaborate meaningfully with classroom teachers.

Much questioning of the standards and doubting comments ensued in the group discussions, and I went back and forth with them to keep the standards and vision of accomplished teaching at the forefront. This resistance was evident while we were examining the standard on integrating information literacy through collaboration, planning, implementation, and assessment of learning.

"Well," said Katherine, "we don't plan that way. We just find the books for the teachers."

"Are you sure you are not doing this?" I asked. "Let's look at this statement more closely to see what is being addressed."

"Listen," Maureen interjected. "I spend all my time bar-coding books and policing students who come into the library. I don't have time to teach a class; it's not expected of me."

"See here," I replied. "Doesn't this standard say that you are possibly already doing that? What about this one too? Doesn't it specifically speak to your issue?"

Janet asked, "What does the National Board mean by this? Have they been into a school lately?"

I responded, "Don't forget that librarians like yourselves designed and wrote these standards."

These standards made sense to me. I thought my candidates needed to reexamine what they were claiming as their role at their school sites and find ways to connect their work to the professional expectations described in the standards. How was I to get this group of librarians to understand that they were teachers even though they did not have a group of assigned students to their classroom? How was I to get them to understand and accept the National Board standards for a library media specialist? I began to feel a little perplexed. It was hard to believe that a group of educators who wanted to receive recognition of accomplishment in their field were unwilling, to some degree, to embrace the tenets that would enable them to become accomplished.

The portfolio tasks also raised many issues for the group. Tightly connected to the standards, the portfolio tasks often asked the librarians to demonstrate their instructional practices. One portfolio task, for example, required librarians to demonstrate their ability to collaborate with others in their instructional community to create, plan, and implement learning experiences. The group was skeptical about demonstrating this task because they maintained that they did not work directly with other teachers' curriculum planning.

With a focus on the standards and portfolio tasks, I was determined to keep the four of them concentrating on the National Board's vision of accomplished practice and help them find ways to better align their practice with this vision. I knew I needed to communicate with them in a nonjudgmental and neutral way so they would not feel belittled or criticized. I also wanted them to take ownership of the process so that they would develop their practice while completing the portfolio. And with a little help from one of them, I figured out how to do some of this.

That help came from James, who was the only man in the group and who doubted the vision of the standards the least. I saw early on that James would be a positive force within the group since he came to the sessions with a greater focus on the standards and seemed to connect them to his practice more easily than the others. In discussing the portfolio entry on collaboration with other teachers in the school, James offered encouraging responses.

Maureen complained, "I have no idea how to get somebody else's students to do this lesson."

James replied, "Have you tried talking with one of the teachers who is always bringing their students to the library?"

"How can I get them to work with me?" asked Katherine.

"What I did," said James, "was to invite a teacher to discuss how I could help with part of her curriculum from a library perspective. I even suggested that we plan a lesson together."

James regularly brought his work on the portfolio to the group meetings and talked about his teaching and his students' learning. He also communicated through e-mail to us when he had an idea or resource for the others. I got very excited when he started using the language of the standards while talking with the other members of our group. At one meeting, he showed us his video on collaboration in teaching a group of students with a classroom teacher. The video provided evidence of how he established a setting and opportunity for students to engage in learning when they were in the library and he talked about the evidence he saw that related to his knowledge of teaching and learning, library and information studies, and integrating instruction. James's practice on tape provided an authentic model for the rest of the group, and I think it encouraged them to work further on their own portfolios.

I began to emphasize James's work in the group discussions, drawing on his examples to show the others the possibilities for their own practice. He became my resource, assisting me in my support role, without any cooked-up conspiracy between us. When I started to direct the group's attention to James's commentaries and videos, without in any way implying that he was better than they, the others began to respond to his work by talking about the standards and brainstorming what they might do for their own portfolio entries.

I continued to showcase James's efforts in a subtle way that would not offend but motivate the others to see things differently so they could move forward in the process. For example, when

James brought in another video or entry, I led a discussion focused on evidence of the standards, reminding them that they too needed to show the same kind of evidence in their practice. They listened and responded to me and each other, but never completely abandoned their discontent with the standards.

To some degree, each of the members began to assume some type of ownership of the process, although their complaining and skepticism did not stop. The others began to bring in entries for us to read, and a couple of them shared their videos. Some of their work did not show they had a solid understanding of the standards and how to connect them to their sequence of instruction for the classroom-based entries. It was clear that their entries needed revision, but they were making efforts to engage in the portfolio work. One member of the group never showed any videotapes or commentaries to the group, causing me to wonder why she still would not share with the group after James had shared so much with us.

Ultimately they all submitted portfolios to the National Board, but I was left with many lingering questions about my effectiveness as a support provider for this group. Was my approach of trying to convince them that the standards made sense the right thing to do? Was using James's work as a model appropriate?

I also felt dissatisfied with the amount of time the group spent complaining about their working situations and their lack of support at their school sites. Maybe I should have focused on each one as an individual instead of as a group with a common energy to complain. The reality for the teachers was not only that they did not fully see the vision of the National Board, but that they also did not have the school site support to make the shift in their practice that would help them realize that vision. How does a support provider shut down the doubt and lack of confidence in the group to move on to the real business of the process? How much complaining about their working conditions is okay? Is it necessary to spend time on their immediate emotional needs before we can begin the work of analyzing teaching practice? Should I have been more open-minded to ways to balance people's anxieties and professionalism? Although we all completed the journey to submit their work, I felt unsettled about how much they had accomplished.

My dilemma is not over for me, although my being a support provider for the librarians is. I am still looking for answers to what

I should have done differently. I am wondering whether their going through the process provided some positive, informative, and revelatory experiences to bring about change in their thinking and practicing as library media specialists. I hope my guidance and support facilitated their becoming accomplished teachers, realizing that only they can make that happen.

COMMENTARY

COMMENTARY BY KAY HONES

When I heard that the National Board Library Media Certification was finally available, I sent for the materials and shared them with twenty-five to thirty school librarians at our monthly district meeting. No one else was interested, and I put the idea on the back burner until I got an e-mail from a professional listserv about a regional support program that I could attend. I went to the first meeting in September to find out more details about the process. Based on the information at that meeting and the opportunity to collaborate with other librarians on the process, I applied to be a candidate.

I met the three other school library candidates and our support provider, William, at the October meeting. William was certified in English/Language Arts and was an experienced support provider. Since this was the first year that the library media certification was offered and our portfolio instructions would not be ready until December, he initially guided us to read and discuss the standards and to work on two areas that were the same in all portfolios: the context description of our schools and portfolio Entry 4, in which we would document our professional accomplishments that related to student learning.

When I read William's description of our group in his case, I was surprised that he felt we were disgruntled and complaining. I think this may be because our work situations as school librarians are at best dire. Perhaps in reflecting on our school library programs, we tend to have gallows humor. We have little or no administrative support from sites or districts. My principal's one and only comment when I said I was going to work on National Board Certification was, "That's nice." School libraries in our district have no clerical support and are underfunded. Most teachers are unaware that the position requires not only a school library credential but a curriculum credential as well. For several years, I had worked with other librarians to write district information literacy standards, exemplars, and sample lessons based on the national standards developed by the American Library Association (ALA); currently there are no published state library standards.

So while I was familiar with the intent of the National Board teaching standards, I had a hard time with their practical application. My library program was inadequately funded and understaffed, and it had a marginal collection. ALA national standards require a minimum of twenty books per student; I had fewer than eight. On a daily basis, I had to prioritize what essential work to do, always leaving something undone. William's reminder, "Don't forget that librarians like yourselves designed and wrote these standards," helped me focus on the standards and the requirements of the portfolio entries. Although it was difficult to envision the teaching standards in action with our very substandard working conditions, the reminder motivated me to respond and dig into the process.

William was helpful in so many ways. When we began our work together, he guided us to read and reread the standards and asked each of us to explain them and give examples from our practice. During our work with portfolio Entry 4, in which we were expected to document the impact on student learning that our accomplishments as leaders, learners, and collaborators outside our classroom had, we gave several examples of activities. Often he pointed out, "Hey, that sounds as if it fits in this area," and then asked us how we could demonstrate the "impact on student learning." At each session, he encouraged us to set goals: "When will you finish each component?" "What can you bring to share next month?" And when we began to show videos to one another in January, he helped us get beyond careful comments like, "That's interesting," and to focus on whether the video showed evidence of the standards and student learning required by the portfolio expectations and teaching standards. It was good to get constructive feedback and not just positive comments.

One thing that William could not help with, however, was figuring out whether we were on the right track. Since he was not a librarian, he could not help us with some models of what accomplished practice looked like. Then I found a listserv for school librarians working on National Board Certification, which was helpful for the more esoteric questions specifically about the librarian certificate that were not part of his expertise.

In general, we had to embark on radical changes—not only our way of thinking about our practice but also our way of expressing ourselves. We had to move from being implicit about what we knew, to being clearly and concisely explicit, always making sure to show an impact on student learning. I learned a tremendous amount from this process. For instance, I developed a tool to guide the student research process. It was a print pathfinder template that guided students to resources such as books and encyclopedias, electronic databases, and media sources such as videos and DVDs for researching specific topics. I knew this was a good tool, but when I had to reflect on why I chose this method and explain my rationale, I realized I was responding to second-language students' need for print as well as oral scaffolding. I have continued to use this tool with students and refined it based on their feedback.

In hindsight, I often found the portfolio commentary writing arduous, artificial, and awful, and I had to develop a "just do it" attitude. I was thankful for the critique and comments by William and my fellow librarians and am very glad that he gently pushed us to complete certain things for every meeting. Even when I felt what I was bringing to the meeting was not the quality that I hoped for, it helped to get the feedback and ideas from the group.

TEACHING NOTE

William is a National Board Certified Teacher with experience supporting candidates in his field of English/Language Arts. When he agrees to work with a group of librarians who are pursuing a newly released certificate from the National Board, he anticipates that he will be able to draw on his general knowledge of the certification process to support them as candidates. He is surprised to encounter several members of the group who find a disconnect between the vision of teaching in the National Board standards and their current practices as library media specialists. At first, William struggles with his new task of helping this group better understand how they might enact the vision of accomplished practice. He tries a few strategies and in the end continues to question his effectiveness at helping them develop a vision of their practice that is better aligned with the teaching standards of the National Board.

This case explores the complex territory of helping teachers develop a vision of accomplished teaching as well as enacting that vision in practice. It also touches on the issue of mentoring peers in a different content area specialty.

ISSUES AND QUESTIONS

Mentoring Toward a Standards-Based Vision of Teaching
When William encountered the skepticism that the group of librarians had with regard to the scope of responsibilities described in the National Board teaching standards and portfolio instructions, he was not sure what to do. Although the Library Media standards were new to him given that this was not his field of expertise, he resonated more strongly to the expectations in the standards and the portfolio than did his group of mentees. He could imagine the professional role of the Library Media Specialist including a focus on teaching and learning in addition to the specialized knowledge, the resources, and the technological expertise that librarians must have. He struggled with how to help the librarians shift their thinking from a "we can't/don't do this in our libraries" to an attitude of how they might be able to incorporate these ideas into their

practice. Examine the case to see how William approaches this charge. What does he do to help the librarians embrace the National Board standards? What does he do to encourage his group members to try to enact this vision in their practice? What else might he have done to help them better envision the possibilities of enacting the standards in their practice? What are the advantages and disadvantages of these suggestions?

Using Models of Practice in a Group

James, one of the teachers in William's group, has a much different attitude toward the teaching standards from those of the other librarians and begins to produce video and written commentary from his practice earlier than the other members of the group. When William sees that James's practice is aligned with the teaching standards, he begins to draw on James as an example for the others to see the standards in practice. William notes that he uses James's work "not to offend but to motivate the others to see things differently so they could move forward in the process." What do you think of this strategy as a means of motivating the group in the process? What are the advantages and disadvantages of using models to demonstrate what is possible?

Seeing the Case from the Librarians' Perspective

William discusses how much time and energy the group spent "complaining about their working situations and their lack of support at their school sites." He feels frustrated that so much time was taken up by this kind of conversation and wonders if this kind of venting or commiserating is a necessary part of the group bonding process. Then we see the commentary by Kay Hones, one of the librarians in William's group. She provides a description of some of the realities that librarians face in their working conditions and clues us into the fact that while she understood the intent of the standards, enacting them in her context was difficult. As a mentor, how much do we let the working context of the teacher shape our mentoring approach? If a science teacher has thirty-five to forty students in a classroom with no running water and limited teaching supplies, do we still coach that teacher to do scientific inquiry-centered instruction? Do you think the time spent sharing the trials and frustrations of workplace conditions helps build community among the group? If you think this is wasting time, how do you curb that kind of discussion among the group? What are the alternatives?

Mentoring Outside Your Content Area

William describes that he feels initially out of sync with the group because he is not a librarian and does not share their expertise and workplace conditions. He seems to feel that he overcomes this limitation after he has had the opportunity to read and digest the teaching standards and the portfolio expectations. His experience with the National Board Certification process enables him to grasp the big picture of the standards and portfolio expectations quickly, even though he is not a content area expert. Kay reminds us that William was able to give the group feedback on their portfolio entries, but that she turned to an electronic group of librarians for her specialized questions about library media issues or more specific models of accomplished practice in her field. Mentors view the need to share the content area specialty with their mentees differently. Some think that knowing general principles of good teaching practice and being able to ask reflective questions of the mentee is sufficient for effective coaching or mentoring. Others think that pedagogy is linked to the discipline, and the content area focus of the teaching needs special attention. Put another way, how can one judge the accuracy and integrity of a unit plan without understanding the content? Where do you come down on this issue? What role does content area expertise play in the process of mentoring?

PART THREE

COMPLEXITIES OF EFFECTIVE MENTORING

CHAPTER FIVE

WHAT DO YOU DO
WHEN BIAS SNEAKS IN?

*Can you effectively mentor someone whose teaching
methods and philosophy differ from your own?
How do you keep your professional biases from
coloring your analysis of their performance?
In this case, a veteran support provider works
with someone whose instructional strategies
reflect a more traditional approach to teaching.*

CASE

CASE BY PAT KEMENY MACIAS

I have been teaching art for thirty years and received my National
Board Certification in 1996. For the past five years, I have been
working with a university-based support program helping National
Board Art candidates, meeting monthly with the group on Saturday mornings. My typical approach is to encourage the candidates
to regularly share their progress on their National Board portfolios
with each other and to help them develop ways to give each other
feedback on their videos and commentaries by using both the
National Board teaching standards and by raising questions to help
them develop their portfolio entries.

Pseudonyms have been used to maintain the confidentiality of people and places
in the case.

83

I know from my experience as a support provider that I am not supposed to let my own bias about teaching guide my comments and suggestions to candidates about their National Board portfolio work. One experience with my candidate group revealed to me just how difficult it is to leave my professional biases and classroom experience checked at the door when viewing candidates' practice.

At this particular meeting during my fourth year as a support provider, my group of four art candidates planned to look at their video entries. Before this meeting, we had discussed the advantages and challenges of videotaping their classroom teaching. I had shown the group the video that I submitted with my National Board portfolio to discuss both the technical side of videotaping and the quality of teaching as it related to the teaching standards. We used a handout that the support program had distributed, "Tips for Videotaping," to critique my video example for technical strengths and weaknesses. We also used the National Board standards to discuss the group's analysis of the teaching they saw in the video.

Since this was the first time we were looking at these candidates' videos together, I reminded the group that both the students and the teacher need to be at ease with the camera in the room and that sometimes the videotaped lesson does not work the first time.

I handed out comment response sheets to the group while the teacher who volunteered to go first loaded her video into the VCR. These response sheets had a place for the candidates to note particular teaching standards to be addressed and a place for noting evidence of those standards in the video's example of teaching. This format was one way to remind us of the National Board teaching standards for this portfolio entry while we searched for evidence in the teaching. We were also prepared to offer our insights about the evidence of standards and give any constructive comments or questions we thought would help the candidate develop the written commentary and reflection. Before we watched the video, we reviewed the specific instructions and expectations for the entry, and the teacher gave a brief description of the lesson on drawing that we were going to see. She pressed Play, and we settled back to observe.

Soon after the video started, I found myself thinking that the teaching I saw was an example of really bad art teaching. In my experience as a support provider, I had seen teaching practice that I thought was very different from mine, but these were mainly because the class sizes were different, the classroom setup was different, the particular content or projects were different, or the students looked different from mine. In this case, I just did not like the overall approach this teacher was taking and my gut reaction was this approach was not right in some universal sense.

The students in the classroom were seated at tables, all facing forward, and they were offered no opportunity to move around. The teacher was leading the students through a structured, step-by-step drawing process. The students were expected to follow the teacher's moves exactly, doing each step together with her. All of the students' work in the end looked almost identical. The teacher asked questions and repeatedly called on the same students to respond but never walked around the room to check in or give feedback. At times, she interrupted the students' answers, and she did not follow up with any of the students about their responses. Several thoughts ran through my mind during the first few minutes of the video:

"This looks nothing like my art classes. I cannot recall a time when I ever taught a class this way."

"I would never teach a class about drawing this way."

"Teaching art is not as structured as teaching academic subjects."

"Why doesn't she let the students draw what they want to draw using her method?"

"The students will never learn to appreciate the drawing process if this is all they get to do."

"She can't submit this video. The students are not engaged in creative work."

I knew I could not voice these thoughts to the candidate. My biases were shining through brilliantly. At first I did not recognize these thoughts as my own bias. It took a couple of minutes for me to figure out that I had abandoned the teaching standards and was responding with my opinions and background as an art teacher who had been trained to teach in quite a different way from what I had seen in this video. I realized that I had jumped to the conclusion that I was seeing bad teaching rather than using the standards as my analytical framework for looking at the practice or finding out more from the teacher about why she had made the decision she had made. How had this happened? I was an experienced support provider who had worked with several groups of teachers prior to this one. Not only was I now stumped as to what to say to the candidate, I was also questioning my own ability to hold my bias at bay while watching someone else's practice.

I had been completely consumed with my initial negative reaction to the teaching, which went completely against everything that I had been taught to do as a support provider and what I had espoused to the candidate group. Rather than pausing to wonder what her rationale was, I had reached a judgment about this candidate's teaching before knowing more about her teaching context and before giving her an opportunity to tell us about her students' learning needs.

The video ended, and the group prepared to offer their observations and comments. I didn't know where to begin. I had been working with the candidates to help them identify evidence of the standards in teaching, but I was having a hard time getting past my impression that this was not a good example of teaching. I honestly could not think of any evidence of the standards that I saw. If this had been a critique session with my high school art students, I would have had no problem offering supportive comments and plenty of encouragement to strengthen their self-confidence before I began discussing some areas that might be improved or altered. But this was supposed to be an accomplished teacher. What I saw in the video was so far from what I considered good teaching that I couldn't come up with any supportive comments. In the instant of trying to find something to say, I decided to fall back on the questioning strategies that I typically use: encouraging candidates to focus their comments on the standards and helping them bring out the reasons underlying their teaching decisions. On reflection, however, the initial questions that came to my mind (and that I did not voice) did not follow this strategy; instead, they were biased toward my own teaching preferences:

"How does the seating arrangement interfere with student interaction?"

"Does the more direct approach to teaching work better than adding creativity?"

"Would a more flexible class structure encourage greater student enthusiasm about art?"

"Do students learn better in a step-by-step approach?"

I could not find the questions that asked for clarification without suggesting a particular approach. I wanted to start offering suggestions by leading the candidate toward my way of thinking about teaching art, but I know I am not supposed to let my biases interfere with my questions and comments to candidates. I was stymied, unsure of what to say. How can I respond to a candidate's practice spontaneously and yet be neutral of my bias, reflective of the standards, and productive for the candidate?

COMMENTARY

COMMENTARY BY JOAN PETERSON

As a former art teacher, I initially agreed with the assessment of the teaching that Pat described. The classroom environment sounded stiff, precluding the interaction of students with each other. The lesson sounded rote, with predictable results. The interaction with the students sounded routine instead of a free exchange of student responses to the lesson. And there seemed to be preferential treatment to a few students who were repeatedly called on to answer.

Given my experience as the leader of the assessment development team for the Art Certificate, I recognize this support provider's response as a classic example of what—in scoring—is called "jumping the gun" or "sudden death" syndrome. After quickly making an initial judgment, as Pat did, it is very difficult to step back and take a more objective view, regardless of the reason. It is not just holding personal and professional biases at bay, but drawing an immediate conclusion that is so strong it interferes with being open to any other possible viewpoints. Pat recognizes that her own teaching bias or style needs to be "left at the door," but this scenario shows how difficult that is to do, especially when a teacher has honed her practice over many years, is recognized as a leader, and has had her professional expertise validated by becoming a National Board Certified Teacher. She valued a more creative approach than what she was seeing in the video and easily identified areas she thought could be improved. And she readily admitted her bias, stating she has been "trained" a different way.

How do we learn not to jump to an immediate conclusion in such a situation? One technique is to simply write down what you are viewing in the video, from the room arrangement to the interaction between the students and between students and teacher. If you cannot find evidence of a standard, stay occupied with recording observations and then start with general questions based on those observations.

The questions that this support provider wanted to ask the candidate reflected her different point of view. They need to be phrased instead in a way that does not identify her bias. She could ask the candidate to describe the seating arrangement of her classroom and how it contributes to the art lesson. She could ask if the lesson provided enough drawing technique to allow students to progress to other drawing lessons that might be less structured. And most important, she could ask the candidate what standards were being addressed in the lesson.

There are broader unanswered questions here that could also serve as a starting point for a discussion. We do not know the context in which the lesson was presented. Although it would be interesting to know the number of years the candidate had been teaching and more about her background, more important would be to know the expectations of the administration for this course and if she was being asked to follow a prescribed curriculum. Was the candidate expected to teach a step-by-step drawing lesson? Was this art lesson the equivalent of the structured and scripted reading programs that many school districts have adopted where the teacher has no choice but to follow the script? Was the fact that students' desks were in rows the norm of the school or because the candidate was uncertain about her classroom management? Was this the first time the teacher had done a drawing lesson with the students? Was she intending to follow this lesson with an alternative approach to drawing? Was she so nervous about doing a good video for the entry that she relied on a step-by-step approach instead of a lesson with an unknown outcome?

There may be a collision of biases here. The candidate may value a step-by-step approach to the teaching of art or feel confident only when there is a highly structured format to her class to follow or a supposed no-fail approach. The support provider clearly values a more open-ended and creative approach. It is tempting to want to retrain a candidate, but the role of the support provider is only to help the candidates measure their teaching against the National Board standards. This case shows how difficult at times that is to do.

TEACHING NOTE

This case portrays a vivid description of a veteran support provider who experiences difficulty leaving her biases behind as she mentors a teacher whose instructional strategies appear to be much more traditional than her own. She knows that she is supposed to use teaching standards as the framework of her feedback and realizes that her biases are preventing her from raising neutral questions and using the standards as the basis of her feedback. Yet this knowledge doesn't help as she struggles to figure out how to respond appropriately after watching a video of the teacher's lesson.

This brief case and commentary provide an opportunity to explore how to provide feedback that is honest, constructive, and respectful to a teacher whose teaching methods might be different from your own.

ISSUES AND QUESTIONS

Addressing Bias

Reading this case with Joan Peterson's commentary makes us realize how difficult it is to put one's biases aside when providing feedback to another teacher. Both Pat and Joan are art teachers, both appear to share the same perspective on what makes a good art lesson, both are veteran National Board support providers, and both are aware of their biases. Yet coming up with nonjudgmental questions was hard even for Joan, the commentator.

Examine the questions that Pat wanted to ask but did didn't because they would illuminate her bias. Then examine the broader unanswered questions that Joan suggests in her commentary. Note that both sets of questions are generally narrowly construed and reflect a critical stance to the lesson. How might you neutralize some of them to appear less judgmental? Educators who discussed this case suggested alternative questions: "Why did you choose this video?" "What are your goals for the lesson?" "Why are they important for your students?" "At what point does this lesson come in your unit?" "Why did you choose this approach to the lesson?" and "Why did you choose that seating arrangement?" Can you think of others?

Sustaining a Nonjudgmental Stance

Why should a mentor want to appear less judgmental during a feedback session, especially at the beginning? One rationale is the tendency to form an opinion of a teacher's performance without enough information, as Joan eloquently describes in her commentary. Watching either a video or face-to-face lesson represents only a snapshot of a teacher's practice; it's disrespectful and unprofessional to form an opinion without first pursuing more information in a nonjudgmental manner. The generic questions suggested for analyzing videos given in the National Board Certificates provide a useful resource if you are unsure about what kinds of questions to use. When asked, teachers often have quite reasonable responses to such questions, which are invisible unless opportunities are given to react in a considerate manner. (See also Carne Barnett-Clarke's commentary to the case in Chapter Two.)

Providing Constructive Feedback

How should a mentor respond if, after eliciting information about the lesson, she continues to think the lesson is flawed? Although providing critical feedback is difficult in any profession, it may be more challenging among teachers since there is no norm of such activities at the workplace. An increasingly popular strategy is using a set of standards that serves as a framework for the feedback, beginning with those that show evidence from the teaching episode so as to start the critique on a positive note. This was the strategy that Pat intended to use with the National Board standards, but she could not see any evidence of the standards in the video. How should she begin? What would *you* say? What is your responsibility to yourself, the teachers whom you coach, and the teaching profession for being honest with your feedback? (For additional reflections on these questions, see also the case in Chapter One and Lee Shulman's commentary in Chapter Eleven.) Do you have other suggestions for how to proceed?

Recognizing Our Biases

As support providers, we need to consider what biases we bring to mentoring situations. Pat was aware of hers and realized how difficult it was to overcome them and act in a professional manner;

that's why she wrote this case. But too many support providers are not tuned into their biases and are quick to criticize when observing a teacher whose instructional strategies differ from their own. This case rang true with many mentors who discussed it. Where do you fit in?

CHAPTER SIX

THE FACILITATOR, THE CANDIDATE, AND THE MUSHY BRAINS

Working with Biases of a National Board Candidate

How do you support a teacher when you find his or her attitude toward students disturbing? How does this affect your effectiveness as a mentor? In this case, a support provider must delve deeper to find a resolution to this ethical dilemma.

CASE

CASE BY MYRIAM CASIMIR

PART ONE

"The one thing I've realized is that if I want anything done, I have to be very, very explicit," Frank says, nodding at students filing out on their way to their next class. "Everything has to be *very* slow. I have to say, 'Okay, children, write your names at the top of the page, like this. Now make a T-chart, like this.' And I have to show each step on the overhead." Frank looks at me, eyes filled with

---

Pseudonyms have been used to maintain the confidentiality of people and places in the case.

wonder and exasperation. To me, assuming that middle school students cannot draw a T-chart without careful supervision is disrespectful, implying a certain level of stupidity on their part. But I decide not to be hasty. Instead, I probe further to find out what else Frank might mean.

"They won't do it?" I ask. "What grade is this?"

"Seventh grade," Frank answers.

"Is it some of the students, or all the students?"

"Oh, I would say all or most of the students."

"Maybe they come from a boring class," I suggest, "and have difficulty changing gears when you see them."

"No, they come from lunch."

"Well, could it be that they don't understand your English?"

"Oh, they speak English just fine—this is the Mainstream class. (In Frank's district, "mainstream" refers to "regular education," as opposed to English Language Development classes. Students in this district are tracked in ESL 1, 2, 3, transitional, or mainstream classes throughout the year.) It's just been like this as long as I've been in this district—over a decade. The kids just need a lot of guidance to do the simplest tasks. I call them 'my little bananas.'"

"Your 'little bananas?'"

My baffled look leads him to elaborate with a tinge of humor. "Yes, uh-huh. They have mushy brains."

I feel my jaw clench involuntarily. Heat rises from my neck to my ears and temples. I open and shut my mouth a couple of times, attempting to speak, but I am dumbstruck. Trying to quell my anger, I reprocess the conversation, hoping for a different outcome, but there's no mistaking the meaning of this National Board candidate's words. To be sure that I haven't missed something, I ask Frank again: "Are you saying that all your students are like this?" "Yes," he answers, "a *great* majority of them." Given that he is generalizing about all of his students' inability to carry out a simple academic task—without differentiating between students or even offering alternate explanations—this seems to me to be a clear case of bias. Thinking about the potentially damaging effects this bias may have on the children is what leaves me speechless. I wonder what the impact on learning is of Frank's low expectations for his "little bananas." I wonder whether, and how, he communicates to parents that he believes each one of their children can succeed academically.

At the time this conversation took place, I was serving as Frank's National Board support provider as part of an applied research project that aims to bring National Board processes to schoolwide professional development at his middle school. But my role was a bit complicated. I was responsible for helping the school's instructional leadership team plan professional development and for supporting National Board candidates through candidacy meetings, individual conferences, and videotaping entries. At the same time, I was constantly collecting data to document the progress of this project.

Frank's school was selected for participation in this foundation-supported project because of its forward-thinking leadership and its chronically undereducated student population. The middle school serves about a thousand students from some of the lowest-performing elementary schools in California. Nearly all students are from a working-class, Mexican background, and most are learning English as a second language. As part of the school's professional development, the nonprofit I work for aims to equip all teachers with competencies that enable them to know and respect their students and their communities, as well as build their pedagogical content knowledge and collaborative teacher inquiry skills to address their students' need for rigorous, grade-level courses. National Board standards and processes are used to anchor teachers' analyses and reflections on their practice. In addition, this is a research project that aims to have an impact on policy and practice in high-poverty schools.

I have generally found that National Board candidates engage in brutally honest analyses of their teaching. But on occasion I have noticed that an individual's assessment of a situation (in Frank's case, the lack of thinking power among his students) did not match what I saw at the site. When I encounter such discrepancies, I have to rely on what I think is a relatively neutral reading of the situation as I decide how to move forward. I had had plenty of experience observing Frank's students in other settings to know that his perception did not reflect their academic potential. Should I just ignore that knowledge or respond to it?

At the moment when Frank and I were having the "little bananas" exchange, I could not articulate what I really thought. My
indignation left me unable to engage Frank in the kind of questions
that would lead him to compare his viewpoint to the standards for
accomplished teaching. What I really wanted to do was to berate him for not adhering to Core Proposition 1 and Standard 1,
Knowledge of Students. I wanted to be rude and dismissive. As
someone who has taught, I have always been sensitive to the multiple layers of disrespect that teachers must endure as a result of
public opinion. Yet here I was, not affording Frank the professional
respect that I expect everyone to have toward teachers. Since disdain prevented me from fitting my immediate feedback into any
constructive discussion about standards for accomplished teaching, I tried, weakly, to leave Frank with something to ponder: "I
wonder in what setting outside your class your students might perform well." Students were beginning to stream in for the next class
period, so I had to leave the exchange there, and Frank did not
have the opportunity to respond.

My handling of this situation left me dissatisfied on two fronts.
First, I felt that I had let Frank off the hook. Aside from the irritation that had paralyzed me during the exchange, keeping me from
having a rational conversation about the impossible likelihood that
for a decade, hundreds of Frank's students have been "little
bananas," I had felt constrained by the informal setting in which
the issue had arisen. This was a casual conversation, not a candidacy support meeting, so I hadn't felt comfortable pushing Frank
to consider the implications of what he had told me. In the informal context, it might have seemed more a criticism than constructive feedback. But as someone promoting teacher learning
through my broader work, I felt it was imperative that at some
point during the year, I make a dent in Frank's thinking about his
students. Truth be told, I felt that as Frank's support provider, I
would be embarrassed if he gained certification with my support
without changing his understanding of his students' intelligence.

Second, I did not enjoy the self-righteous feeling that my discovery of this bias gave me. It created a conflict between my normal role of facilitating candidates' understanding of National
Board processes and my commitment to educational equity. I was

accustomed to working mostly with candidates who saw and respected their students' differences, and therefore I had had the luxury of remaining neutral as I facilitated their candidacy processes. In this case, my commitment to educational equity was causing me to make a negative assessment of a teacher's perspective, when I knew full well that I was not supposed to make any type of assessment about the candidates with whom I worked. Still, having made the assessment that Frank thought his students arrived at school with an "intellectual deficit," I could not ignore it. Not knowing how to address my own negative attitude, I filed the incident away in my mind and charged myself with developing a strategy for broaching this topic with Frank again.

How should I proceed? Should I let Frank just continue thinking about children in the same ways, with his bias showing through in the assessment? Should I be direct, and explain that his blanket statements about his students' deficits were at odds with Core Proposition 1 and he needed to change his perspective? Or should I guide him to this realization through an inquiry approach? Should I pepper my conversations with hints about noticing and building on the resources that children bring to academic tasks, hoping that he would pick up? Should I give him readings on educational equity? Should I wait for a teachable moment—one that lent itself to discussing the ways in which he classified his students? As a National Board support provider, was I supposed to be doing any of this? I would have to figure out how to address what I perceived as a central issue for Frank as he pursued National Board candidacy.

PART TWO

As I spent time with Frank, I was gratified to learn that he was caring and conscientious in his work with children. This allowed me to understand him as more than just someone who was altogether negative about his students. Although he spoke of all his students as disengaged from academic learning, he genuinely worked to teach them the curriculum. This was an important turning point for me, allowing me to see that sometimes his actions contradicted his words. This disjuncture created a conceptual opening where, with the correct strategy, I might have some impact. So I opted to begin approaching his bias through the candidacy meetings. During these, I highlighted knowledge that other candidates voiced about their students, based on classroom evidence or knowledge of the community. I hoped this would provide Frank with a way of acknowledging students' efforts while still noticing when they were not working at grade level. But I had no way of knowing whether this indirect approach led to any new ways of thinking about students' learning. At the same time, I noted that Frank frequently became defensive whenever peers pointed out areas where his teaching could improve (as when viewing his videos). Frank did not seem to be gaining ground.

I decided to talk to Frank about how he viewed his students individually and in the context of his portfolio Entry One, which requires candidates to justify why they selected different students to highlight various aspects of their curriculum planning. I hoped that by using an inquiry approach to guide the conversation, I could make it easier for Frank to talk honestly about his ways of categorizing the students. Our exchange would be grounded in his teaching context and completion of the National Board portfolio. This, I felt, was much better than my fabricating an occasion for us to "discuss his bias problem," which seemed condescending and might create resistance. Since I was collecting data for the research project, I had the benefit of audiorecording the conversation, which is reproduced in part below.

I began by asking Frank what the entry required, then moved to asking him about the different groups of students in his class. How would he categorize the students? He began by explaining the task: "For Entry One, you have to have two students for each of three assessments in a unit and show evidence of students' understanding. And so I'm going to use some of the science notebooks for that."

"Okay," I said, "so describe to me the—I don't want to use the word *range,* because that implies something linear. But if you can think of a range and then a sort of mosaic, describe to me the different ways in which students grasp chemistry understanding in your class. Like, if you were to see a mosaic, and each tile is somebody different, how are they similar, or how do they differ from one another?"

I was met by a blank look, so I added a sentence starter: "Like, some students are . . . and others are . . . what?"

I hoped this question would allow Frank to elaborate his philosophy of student learning in his classroom. Frank explained: "Some students are at a very basic level. And you're lucky if they know how to spell the word *chemistry,* never mind their knowing what anything in chemistry is."

Frank had begun by saying "some students," which was an improvement over his previous pronouncement about "all" students. I decided to let his flip remark about "spelling the word *chemistry"* go, asking him instead to define his terms. "Okay," I replied, "so describe *basic level.* In this unit you are asking them to do what at the beginning? And then what would constitute a basic level?"

Frank explained: "The kids come in with virtually no experience." I pushed Frank again to use more specific language, rather than speaking in general terms: "In . . . chemistry?" He concurred, "In chemistry." And continued, "They don't know the glassware. The whole concept of the periodic table is foreign to them. They've heard the word *chemical* and they've heard the word *chemistry,* but they don't understand the meaning behind the word."

Noticing that Frank was again using a generalized "they," I probed, "Is this all of them or some of them?" And he replied, "This is a *huge* majority of them." I thought, this could be true, considering the underperforming K–6 schools these children had attended. But then, were elementary school students expected to learn about the periodic table?

I asked, "Are they supposed to know this coming in?"

Frank replied, "You would think that they would have a little bit more of an understanding than they do. I talk to my six year old about chemicals that are under the sink."

So, I thought, this has something to do with the knowledge Frank expects children to gain at home or outside the classroom. I wondered if he thought the homes were inadequate places to gain general knowledge but had no evidence to come to that conclusion. Instead of taking up that issue, I refocused the conversation on the elementary curriculum: "So they came from elementary school. Are they supposed to cover some of this in elementary school?"

"They're not supposed to cover it in elementary school," Frank responded.

"Okay," I said, acknowledging his willingness to consider an alternative analysis.

"So I guess maybe they're coming to me as beginners for a reason," Frank continued.

"Mmhmm?" Progress, I wondered?

But then Frank continued: "I, I guess; but it surprises me every year. . . ."

Unsure about why this would be surprising, I asked, "Even though they're not supposed to have chemistry per se, you feel that they should have had some experience with mixing solutions, and stuff like that, or . . . ?"

"Well, they—it just seems to me like every year, I'm always surprised at what level they come in," Frank reiterated.

I felt some impatience with Frank's surprise given that this happened year in and year out. Yet he had acknowledged that he was expecting all his students to have more "school" knowledge about chemistry, although they were coming from elementary school.

I decided to move on to ask Frank about other ways in which he could categorize students in preparation for Entry One, which required at least two students to compare to one another. I stated as fact something that Frank had not yet articulated as I tried to prompt him to talk about different types of students: "Beyond students' overall lack of exposure to chemistry, you have different students who engage the curriculum at different levels. Describe that variation to me. So, taking that as a given—for most of your students, for some reason, prior to seventh grade, they haven't been exposed to this material—describe the way students' knowledge is nuanced in chemistry. I'm pushing you on this because I want you to select the students now."

Frank responded, "When you start to explain, some kids have . . . an innate grasp of—it's almost as if the framework was there, and the kids say, 'Oh yeah!' And things click into place for these kids. And other kids, you'll explain it [giggles], you'll explain it again [giggles] another way, and you'll try a whole bunch of ways, and they're still looking at you."

I felt myself getting a bit more impatient, because what Frank described was what happens in any class: some kids get it, some don't, and the teacher's job is to find the key to unlock the doors for those who don't understand in the standard ways. Keeping in mind that I needed to maintain my respectful stance toward Frank even when his giggling signaled his disrespect toward students, I tried to model a professional conversation about children's learning: "And the reason for this would be—in your best professional judgment—is this just because they haven't had experience in the past? Or because the language is new to them?"

Frank considered this question for a bit, so I decided to ask him to begin talking about actual children as he thought through the question: "Why don't you think specifically about kids who fit into those two categories, because that might help, as opposed to speaking in generalities. What is one kid who fits into the 'getting it immediately' and another kid who fits in the other category?"

"Okay, Ruby," Frank went on. "Ruby is very quiet, and she is incredibly attentive. She'll be sitting there giving you her full attention even when other kids have decided that it's the end of the day already and they're not paying attention. You can explain something, and Ruby will get it right away. And maybe it's because she's paying more attention. But it's just that it happens so easily for her all the time. . . . And then there's Jeremy. I'm not sure Jeremy has learned anything since the second grade."

Whenever Frank spoke derisively of students like this, I wondered, *Am I getting anywhere at all with this conversation?* I had tried modeling respectful language. This time, I would try challenging Frank to find a "good reason" for Jeremy's lack of success: "What do you mean? Does he have good attendance?"

Frank replied, "He has really great attendance. He's at school almost every single day. But in terms of paying attention, he isn't. He's tuned out. He's drawing pictures, he's staring out the window." This response made me wonder whether Jeremy has special needs that have not been identified, so I asked, "Do you know why? Is there anything in his cumulative folder?"

Frank continued, "Well, we checked last year to see if perhaps he was a special education student. His mother *demanded* that he be tested for special education, because his mother was quite certain that, you know, there *must* be something wrong with her child because he wasn't performing. And she didn't seem to want to accept the fact that Jeremy just . . . [laughs] just didn't see any value in participating or performing academically. So we had to test him for special education and . . . he didn't qualify."

I believed this statement (and the recreating of the mother's words with an ironic tone) meant that I was getting nowhere fast with this approach. Of course, I had to entertain the possibility that Frank could be right about Jeremy and his mother. The trouble was, given the disdain with which Frank spoke about most students (and now at least one parent), I did not trust that he could accurately identify when a parent did not know her own child. It was difficult for me to continue, first, because I was feeling some anger toward Frank and second, because by now I was pressing him on his stance. But replaying the exchange internally, I felt that my position was well supported. In this conversation alone, Frank had expressed in a few different ways his disrespect for students and their parents: "lucky if they can spell *chemistry*"; "you'll try a whole bunch of ways, and they're still looking at you"; "I'm not sure Jeremy has learned anything since the second grade"; and, "his mother demanded that he be tested."

I moved forward, trying to highlight the fact that Ruby appeared, from what Frank said, to be coming to school with more academic resources than Jeremy (not just the will to participate). "So, Jeremy doesn't connect with the material?"

"He doesn't connect with the material," Frank echoed.

"And Ruby does?" I asked.

"And Ruby does," he responded.

"But it's more than that," I suggested, "because Ruby seems to be bringing something special from somewhere in her life that allows her to access that material."

"Right."

I continued: "So my question would be, if you were to pick Ruby and Jeremy, first of all, do they both exhibit learning throughout the unit? Like if you were to look at Jeremy's three assessments and Ruby's three assessments, would you be able to show evidence of growth from one to the next, for each student? Not necessarily in comparison to each other."

With this question, my goal was to get Frank to compare each student to himself or herself at earlier points in time, as is often done with criterion-referenced assessments, as opposed to comparing students to other students, which typically is unhelpful for figuring out how to teach low-achieving students. But Frank's response caused me to drop this line of questioning: "I don't know. I don't think I have enough work from Jeremy. I don't know if he'd be a kid I could actually even use."

I agreed that it would be difficult to track someone who did not turn work in, so although I still had questions about Jeremy, I moved on to ask Frank whether there were other categories of students: "Okay, so then you have students like Ruby, who just seem to have an 'innate grasp,' in your words. And then somebody like Jeremy. Any other kinds of students that you could say exist?"

"Some students are willing to work at it a little longer," he replied, "work at it a little harder, and they're willing to sit down and say, 'Okay, show me again.' And sometimes if you'll sit down with them one on one, they'll get the idea, and they'll say, 'Ah!' And they'll proceed to do everything perfectly. It's just that they missed something somewhere. But they're willing to say, 'Show me.' They're willing to take some of their time."

When discussing this category of students, Frank's tone was quite different from his descriptions of Jeremy and the "little bananas." This time I felt that I was hearing the real reasons behind his frustration with some (or all) of his students. I saw now that he willingly worked with children whom he determined were making an effort to improve, and I tried to prompt Frank to continue articulating this distinction: "They have more initiative?" I asked.

"It's either initiative or willingness to admit the fact that maybe they didn't get it the first time," he replied.

"So, maybe, with Jeremy it's pride; maybe he's embarrassed. Or perhaps he's taking pride in the fact that he knows he's that type of student."

Frank took a minute to think about this and said, "Hmm, it's hard to say without asking him, or, you know, having someone ask him."

I returned to my goal of having Frank elaborate this new category of students: "So, then, what student would fall into the third category [of students who make an effort]?"

"Uhm, that would be Marta," he said. "Marta really struggled last year, and science is not her favorite class. She has a really supportive family. They say, 'Call us any time, call us any time,' and I called quite a bit last year. This year I haven't had to call more than once. . . . She's only running around a C in science."

Here, Frank was providing specific details rather than generalizing, so I continued to probe: "But do you see a change in her work over this year?"

He responded: "She comes and she says, 'Well, show me. Can you show me again? Can I come at lunch?' And she'll make the extra effort to come in and try and get some help. . . . So Marta would be that third type of student who says, 'Help me,' and wants to put some investment into her own education."

At this point, I felt that Frank had made a strong statement about "that third type of student," and this was different from his initial lumping together of all students as incapable of studying. But to me, identifying students like Ruby, who "got it," Jeremy, who was one of the "mushy-brained bananas," and Marta, who was willing to say, "Help me," still was not a very complex way of thinking about students' learning. I was not feeling successful. After what to me had been a grueling conversation, we moved on to selecting individual students he would follow for Entry One of his National Board portfolio.

As I think about my work with Frank during the time he was a candidate, I wonder whether I made any headway in changing the ways in which he perceived his poor, ethnic, and linguistic-minority students and their families. Still, I am not sure that Frank changed any of his initial beliefs. The conversation I have highlighted was just one brief moment in Frank's year as a National Board candidate. How do I know that it made a difference? I am not sure that my efforts to use questions and have a measured conversation about student diversity made a difference at all. I was left wondering whether I should just have let my anger show when I first heard about the "mushy brains." Does Frank need to know that his disrespect makes fellow educators angry? What would that have done to our facilitator-candidate relationship?

I am also led to wonder about my own stance toward Frank. During the months that I worked with him, I feel that I did my best to engage him in honest exchanges about the issue. But as I reread these reflections, I find that I still have not treated him with the professional respect that I give other teachers.

Finally, I am annoyed by my own perennial surprise when I find that teachers are biased against their students' backgrounds. Why am I still surprised? I have encountered it often enough. I expressed impatience when Frank said about his students, "It just seems to me like every year I'm always surprised at what level they come in." In reflecting on this case, I wonder, Why am I still surprised? And I wonder whether this lack of sociocultural sensitivity is something I can change. Should I just let it be, and let whomever certifies certify, without paying attention to their commitment to students and their families? Given my training, I should be able to make a difference, and I believe I do. But given my exchanges with Frank, I am not sure that that is always the case.

COMMENTARY

COMMENTARY BY ANN IFEKWUNIGWE

My first reaction to Frank's treatment of his students was unfettered rage. How dare he treat his middle school students as if they were in kindergarten? How dare he make such sweeping assumptions about the scholastic aptitude of all of his students so casually and summarily? How could he possibly teach with integrity if he viewed his children's mental faculties as akin to that of mushy bananas?

I read and reread this case while wearing many different hats. As a support provider for teachers pursuing National Board Certification, I found Frank's assumptions deplorable and wondered whether he had even taken the time to read the National Board's standards documents. As a National Board Certified Teacher, I found his beliefs to be antithetical to the National Board's five core propositions, and I hoped the assessors would treat his portfolio accordingly. As a woman of color, I took his comments to be racially motivated and was incensed by his abysmal expectations of his students' strengths and abilities. As a concerned citizen, I found myself wanting to do something to protect these students from the devastating racism of low expectations.

After reading the piece several times, I became less enraged but more concerned. I could not help but wonder how many other Franks there were teaching our children. Not only that, considering the special circumstances of Myriam's situation at the school, I realized that these other teachers with beliefs like Frank's were most likely keeping silent. I'm sure many of them harbored the same thoughts and feelings about their students but did not express them, thereby leaving no opportunity for such beliefs to be challenged. So after realizing that Frank's statement was actually a positive thing, in that it gave Myriam an opportunity to challenge—and perhaps reshape—his assumptions about his students, I began to consider how I might have handled the same situation.

My heart went out to Myriam as she struggled with her dilemma. Although I applaud her patient, systematic approach to dealing with Frank's perceptions of his students, I was frustrated that she was so constrained by her clearly defined roles within the school community. I could absolutely relate to her desire to be "rude and dismissive" and fully understood her wanting to upbraid him for his treatment of his students. I also understood Myriam's need to show professional courtesy and engage Frank in a respectful, constructive dialogue about the issue. As a classroom teacher, I know how often teachers are maligned and disrespected.

So what would I have done differently? I know I would have been much more direct in my approach to Frank's treatment of his students. At some point during the initial conversation, after the banana comment was first made, I would have explained to Frank that I was temporarily stepping out of my role as support provider. I would have shared with Frank some of my personal experiences of being a victim of discrimination in an educational setting. I would have made direct reference to his "mushy bananas" epithet, and I would have explained to him the deep and irreparable damage such labels can inflict.

Far too often silence is viewed as acceptance. Absence of criticism is construed as condoning. Perhaps my approach would have caused Frank to shut down. It's quite possible that he would have been loath to share with me after that moment. But in light of the potential outcomes for his students, that is a risk I would have been willing to take. No teacher has the right to belittle his students. No teacher should harbor such negative beliefs about his students, especially not a National Board Certified Teacher.

TEACHING NOTE

This case depicts a mentor struggling to figure out how to deal with a candidate's bias toward his students and her own indignant emotions toward the candidate. The narrative is divided into two sections. In the first part, Myriam questions whether she should ignore the bias. After deciding that wasn't possible, she wonders how she should proceed. In the second part, Myriam provides a detailed description of her inquiry approach with the candidate and speculates about whether her strategies made a difference.

An analysis of the case provides an unusual opportunity to examine closely one mentor's strategy of working with another teacher, because the narrative draws from an examination of a tape-recorded interview. It also raises provocative questions about how one decides whether engaging in a mentoring relationship with a candidate is worthwhile. Since this is a lengthy case, we suggest that the case discussion and analysis be divided into two parts according to the division in the narrative.

ISSUES AND QUESTIONS, PART ONE

Addressing Bias

This case addresses two kinds of bias. The first one is obvious: Frank's bias toward his students. His reference to all students as his "little bananas" with "mushy brains" was shocking and offensive to Myriam, especially since she had observed the students in other settings and knew his perception was faulty. The other one is more subtle: Myriam's potential bias toward Frank. The case vividly portrays her concern about this predisposition throughout the narrative, as she struggled to work with Frank to help him confront his bias and its probable impact on student learning.

How should Myriam have responded when she heard Frank's reference to his students as "little bananas"? She wanted to be "rude and dismissive" and berate him for not adhering to the National Board proposition and standard that dealt with knowledge of students, but decided against this strategy because it would have been unprofessional. Instead, she simply asked, "I wonder in what setting outside your class your students might perform well," and then left the classroom as the students began streaming in.

But she was troubled by the situation and pondered what to do next. Should she be direct, and let him know that his blanket statements about his students' deficits were at odds with the National Board Core Proposition 1? Should she ignore it and let his biases show through on the assessment? Or should she find a teachable moment and use an inquiry approach to help him see his bias? What would you suggest?

Role of the Mentor

Myriam's dilemma was confounded by her dual role as a National Board support provider and applied researcher who enacted professional development activities and documented progress of the project. She heard Frank's derogatory remarks during an informal conversation in his classroom as part of her research, not during a mentoring session for National Board Certification. Some support providers who discussed this case questioned their responsibility as mentors and wondered whether it was appropriate to use such data during a National Board mentoring session. "If Myriam were not a researcher and 'hung around' as part of her job," they suggested, "she might not have learned about his biased perception of students." Others drew a parallel to classroom teachers who knew that some faculty members at their school site had similar biases and wondered whether they should intervene.

As support providers, we all need to consider what biases we bring to mentoring situations. Myriam was aware of her emotional triggers and worked hard to deal with them professionally. Would someone who didn't share her background have focused so strongly on the "mushy brains?" Where do you fit in?

ISSUES AND QUESTIONS, PART TWO

Direct Versus Inquiry Approach to Mentoring

Part Two of the case portrays a detailed account of Myriam's struggles to find windows of opportunity through which to change Frank's perception of his students. She particularly looked for opportunities that would enable him to differentiate among his students and see their individual strengths and challenges. Examine the variety of ways that she selected to work with Frank, beginning with her attempt to raise the issue during a candidate support meeting. What kinds of questions did she pose? Under what circumstances did she probe? How do you think Frank felt during these conversations?

What is clear is that Myriam chose an indirect inquiry approach rather than telling him he was wrong. She didn't think the direct approach would have been as transformative as finding multiple opportunities to help him discover why he should change his perception. Ann Ifekwunigwe advocates a more direct approach in her passionate commentary. Which one would you choose? Why?

Engaging in a Mentoring Relationship

Mentoring is often defined as a "close, intense, mutually beneficial relationship between someone who is older, wiser, more experienced, and more powerful with someone younger or less experienced. It is a complementary relationship . . . built on both the mentor's and protégé's needs" (quoted in Bullough and Draper, 2004, p. 407). It also requires deep commitment and time to allow the mentee to grow and develop. Myriam decided that Frank was worthy of her time, as she began to interact with him more. She saw that he was "actually very caring and conscientious with his students" and worked hard to teach his curriculum. And she was invested in finding a way to change his generalized negative feelings about his students.

Some of the other cases in this book depict teachers whom mentors feel are not worth such an intense relationship (see Chapters Ten and Eleven). What would you do if you had a mentee whom you felt was not worthy of your time?

Reference

Bullough, R. V. Jr., and Draper, R. J. "Making Sense of a Failed Triad: Mentors, University Supervisors, and Positioning Theory." *Journal of Teacher Education*, 2004, 55(5), 407.

CHAPTER SEVEN

FACILITATING THE WRITING PROCESS

How do you help linguistically diverse teachers strengthen their communication skills? Are there different strategies for working with nonnative English speakers, especially with regard to writing analytical prose? How does this change the role of the native-English-speaking mentor?

CASE

CASE BY MARIA HYLER

In 2001, the National Board support program that I worked for began the practice of using a writing coach, knowing that many teachers were overwhelmed with the sheer volume of writing that the process entails. As a former high school English teacher and Adolescence and Young Adulthood English/Language Arts National Board Certified Teacher, I enthusiastically accepted the assignment of writing coach. Many candidates feel unfamiliar with the analytical and reflective writing the National Board calls for in the portfolio. My program believed this kind of support that helped candidates refresh some writing skills, and perhaps reduced distracting anxieties about academic composition, would enable

Pseudonyms have been used to maintain the confidentiality of people and places in the case.

them to fully concentrate on subject area content. I envisioned the task of writing coach as something similar to what I did as a teacher: supporting people in the process of developing their writing, no matter what their struggles might be. I even anticipated some of the people who might come to see me: those who had not written in a while and were concerned about the amount of writing required, teachers who taught in the classes that dealt less extensively in writing, and people for whom English was their second language who felt they needed additional support. Little did I know that this last group might be more than I was able to handle.

The structure of our writing support tutorial was quite simple and has changed little in the three years that we have had a writing coach available for candidates. After candidates met in a large group, they would seek me out and sign up for individual fifteen- to thirty-minute (depending on the demand) sessions with me. These sessions took place while their subject area groups met; by meeting with me, they were missing time with their small groups. During our large-group session, I described the types of services I would be providing. I was particularly clear that the purpose of the writing coach was to provide support for those people who felt that writing was a concern for them. My statement went something like this:

> By popular request, we have added a writing tutorial to the support program. I will be providing extra support for candidates who feel that the writing part of this portfolio is a bit overwhelming. Now this could be because it's been a while since you have written so extensively, or because writing isn't your strongest skill. Perhaps English is your second language and you have anxiety about this undertaking. Whatever your circumstance, we realized the need for writing support, and I'll be happy to sign up candidates for individual sessions after this meeting. Let me stress that this tutorial is for structural and grammatical writing support. If you just want another reader for your portfolio, do not sign up for a session. If you have concerns about your grammar, structure, or clarity of your writing, then this is geared toward you.

We felt it extremely important to make sure that the writing tutorial was used by people who were honestly concerned about their writing structure, not their content. As I stated, I was not going to be reading for content or evidence of standards met. I was solely a resource for people who felt the writing might be an obstacle to the effective presentation of their practice.

The time I spent with candidates was standard. I began the session asking each candidate if there was anything specific he or she wanted me to observe while looking at this person's work. Some did have specific requests: "It's too long. Can you help me cut out extraneous stuff?" "I don't think I am getting across what I mean." "My grammar is awful!!" I would then take the next ten minutes or so to quickly skim over the entries candidates had brought, making notes and jotting questions, focusing primarily on patterns of weaknesses I saw in their writing. The remainder of the time I would talk to the candidates about the strengths and weaknesses of their writing and strategies to improve what they had brought to me.

The first year I also encouraged teachers to e-mail me their work. This soon became too heavy a reading volume, and I limited it to what I could read in the sessions. Under some extreme circumstances, I had candidates send me their work—generally teachers who had a particularly difficult time writing and benefited from constant feedback. The first year I remember a few candidates who came to me for writing support but did not need it. Many of them just needed someone to say that their writing wasn't dismal and they could make it through the process. I read their work and sent them on their way with reassurances about their ability to write in the manner expected by the Board.

For candidates who genuinely needed my support, I found that the types of comments and questions I wrote on their papers centered on issues of clarity and organization rather than usage (though some candidates did need slight support in grammar correction). I worked with some who wrote in a circuitous manner and had difficulty making points in clear, concise ways. These candidates would bring me entries whose pages exceeded the limit. I spent a lot of time marking sections that could be streamlined. Often I pointed out minor strategies such as changing passive to active voice to cut down on wordiness and sharpen focus. In general, candidates' feedback regarding the writing support was positive, and I was pleased to assist them.

Although my introductory remarks to candidates that first year were general and I did mention people for whom English was their second language, I had expected mostly math and science teachers to take advantage of this service. I was proven wrong when two teachers for whom English was their second language signed up for sessions. Both were teachers of languages other than English. Both spoke English fluently, though with heavy accents. I was eager to be able to support them, particularly because I did not want the fact that they were nonnative speakers to hinder them from receiving National Board Certification.

One candidate, Patricia, came to see me a couple of times but was reassured when I read over her work and found few, if any, grammatical mistakes and no problems at all with clarity or structure. After two sessions, she stopped coming to me for support. Another teacher, Veronica, came and shared that she was extremely concerned about the writing and did not feel she had the skills in English to be able to complete the portfolio successfully. She signed up for a session and did so monthly for most of the duration of our support program. We spent from twenty to thirty minutes together monthly, and I received regular e-mails from her between support meetings.

The more we met, the more concerned I became about Veronica. I wanted to ensure that I was able to support her in her efforts to achieve certification. She continued to voice a lack of confidence in her ability to certify. She shared with me her frustration at having to write in English and her belief that her writing skills, particularly in "academic" English, would keep her from certification. I assured her this was not the case and that if her teaching was accomplished, we just had to work together to make sure her writing stated what she wanted to say. At the time, I believed this wholeheartedly. I was especially committed to making sure that Veronica felt connected and a part of the support community. My own experience as a woman of color in an overwhelmingly white support group made me particularly sensitive to candidates who may have felt marginalized for any number of reasons. I did not want her language to isolate her from other candidates in any way.

As Veronica and I met, I saw very few of her completed entries. She would bring in pieces that were quite good in terms of writing mechanics. I sought to reassure her as I did Patricia, but these same strategies were not working. Veronica said the samples she brought me had gone through multiple drafts, with many readings and comments from other people. I failed in all my attempts to get her to bring raw writing to me. Was I doing something to inhibit her ability to trust me? This would have been surprising to me because we had also built a relationship outside the support-candidate roles. We often talked about general education issues and problems of equity surrounding students of color and second language learners and had even met for dinner on one occasion.

About midway through the candidate year, I began wondering if the reason Veronica was having trouble producing work was that her teaching did not meet the standards. Perhaps she was creating a picture of accomplished teaching in her writing that did not reflect what was occurring in her classroom. To follow up on this line of reasoning, I asked if I could visit her classroom. Veronica was excited for me to do so, and I made an appointment to visit her at her school.

What I saw reassured me of her ability to meet the standards in her practice. I observed evidence of many of the teaching standards, such as knowledge of students, fairness, knowledge of language, multiple paths to learning, learning environment, instructional resources, and assessment. And these were the standards I observed in only a forty-five-minute class period. I felt reasonably confident that her teaching was rich with evidence to discuss in her writing. We had a long, fruitful debriefing session, in which I focused on the positives that I saw in her classroom. I also took time to point out the standards I didn't see and mentioned that these were ones that she had to reflect about and make her thinking about them explicit in the writing. Veronica was grateful to me for visiting, and it appeared to be a positive experience for both of us. I thought that the visit might make her more comfortable in sharing her first drafts with me. This proved not to be the case, and I was stumped by her reticence. What else could be keeping Veronica from sharing her raw writing with me?

As the months passed, I became more concerned about Veronica. She continued bringing me bits and pieces of entries. In the sessions, I would carefully read through her work and talk to her primarily about the strengths of her writing. The work she was bringing me was polished. I asked about her writing process. She told me how she worked closely with a friend who was editing her work. I briefly wondered if she was in fact writing the polished entries she brought me or whether someone else was writing for her. Could that be the reason she refused to bring me first cuts? One suggestion I made to help increase her writing volume was to write the initial draft in her primary language to get her thoughts and ideas out on paper, and then to go back and translate the work into English. Although this would be time-consuming, I thought it was a good suggestion for someone who did not seem to be writing much at all. When I shared my concerns about the approaching portfolio deadline, she became agitated and talked about how stressful the process was for her. She was reluctant to write first in her primary language and then translate (she never explained why) and stated that the friend who was helping her edit also helped with her English. Were there any particular strategies to help her work through her language anxiety? I did not know and did not even know where to look to begin to answer this question.

The problem of the portfolio deadline loomed constant. As the due date drew nearer, I became convinced that Veronica would not be able to submit a full portfolio. I had seen about 25 percent of her total portfolio (which was strong) but did not believe she could finish the 75 percent left to do. I shared my fears with her, but saw no more work from her. By the time the portfolio deadline arrived, Veronica had stopped coming to see me as the writing coach, though she continued to attend the support meetings. Had I done something to run her off?

I believe Veronica demonstrated accomplished teaching, but I am not sure that she was able to portray her teaching and thinking in approximately fifty pages of English. Are general strategies for improving writing effective for people for whom English is their second language, or are there specific writing strategies that I missed because of my own lack of knowledge? These are questions I continue to grapple with. I currently support candidates in the same manner and feel that the majority benefit from the support. In the two years since I worked with Veronica, I have had other candidates for whom English is their second language and have not had the challenges I faced with Veronica. Was this an isolated case, or are there qualities about these other candidates that make them better able to manage the writing load? I use no specialized strategies for these teachers; they get the same individualized support that other candidates receive. Maybe I didn't fully understand

Veronica's needs. Perhaps this is where I fell short. There is always the possibility that I did everything I could to support her, and this was more about her than it was about me. Nevertheless, I'll always wonder if there was something more I could have done to better facilitate the writing process for Veronica.

COMMENTARIES

COMMENTARY BY GEORGE BUNCH AND JEROME SHAW

This commentary is the product of a mini case discussion of Maria Hyler's case between two veteran teachers and teacher educators who have experience working with linguistically diverse students and teachers. Our combined experience includes teaching English as a Second Language and subject matter (science and social studies) at both the K–12 and adult education levels, as well as preparing future teachers to do so. One of us has direct personal experience with producing and evaluating the type of writing required for National Board portfolio entries, and the other has researched second-language writing in a variety of contexts.

Maria asked several provocative questions in the final paragraph of the case: "Are there general strategies for improving writing for people for whom English is their second language, or are there specific writing strategies that I missed because of lack of knowledge?" She also suggests, "Maybe I didn't fully understand Veronica's needs," and says, "I'll always wonder if there was something more I could have done to better facilitate the writing process for Veronica." In an effort to respond to Maria's queries, we suggest three preliminary questions that might be helpful for writing coaches and tutors to consider when working with all writers, but especially those who come from linguistic minority backgrounds. While our main point is to argue for the importance of asking these questions, we also provide some preliminary suggestions for how one might go about addressing them.

What Do We Know About a Writer's Literacy Background and Experience in English and Other Languages?

Maria's case centers on her experiences attempting to support writing for, in Maria's words, "people for whom English was their second language." Maria mentions two such candidates, both of whom "spoke English fluently, though with heavy accents." What can be assumed about the language and literacy of teachers who fit these descriptions? Our answer is that not much can be assumed without further information.

Teachers who speak with "accents" come from a wide variety of linguistic backgrounds. They may be native-born and lifelong residents of countries outside the United States, well educated in their countries of origin and exhibiting high levels of literacy in their home language. These teachers have studied English as a foreign language for a number of years in their countries of origin and probably have been required to exhibit English language proficiency in order to teach in the United States. However, because they have not lived in English-speaking communities, they may still be in various stages of learning both oral and written English. Other teachers have immigrated to the United States as adults prior to becoming teachers. Depending on the number of years they have lived in the United States and the opportunities they have had to learn English, these adults exhibit a wide range of language and literacy backgrounds in both their native languages and in English. While some may exhibit few problems in using oral and written English for academic purposes, their interpersonal speech may still sound "foreign," as is normal for the speech of most users of second languages, even those who are highly proficient in the language.

Other teachers either immigrated with their families to the United States at a young age or were born in the United States to immigrant parents. Their parents were either bilingual themselves or were monolingual speakers of languages other than English. After spending their entire childhood and youth in the United States, these teachers are often quite fluent in English for a variety of purposes. However, they may not have had access to a quality education and the opportunity to develop advanced English literacy skills, especially those used commonly in academic settings. And depending on their parents' educational level and their own access to quality bilingual instruction, these teachers may not have had an opportunity to develop advanced literacy skills in their home languages either. Other teachers may have minority surnames and appear to speak "with an accent," yet be highly proficient, near-native-like-speakers of both English and another language, or even monolingual English speakers. Members of this latter group are not learning English as a second language, but rather are highly proficient bilinguals or even native speakers of a minority variety of English. But no matter what their oral fluency in English, speakers of minority varieties of English, like speakers of majority varieties, will exhibit a wide range of literacy skills that may or may not match their oral abilities in the language.

In short, we cannot tell much about language and literacy from the fact that people speak with an accent and appear to be speakers of a language other than English. If Veronica grew up in a family that spoke a language other than English yet did most of her schooling in English, either in the United States or elsewhere, it may be that she writes better in English than in any other language, even if she is struggling to write in English. It therefore may not be helpful for Veronica to first write drafts in her native language and then translate those into English.

We find it helpful, therefore, to determine, as best as possible, people's level of proficiency in academic writing in their different languages and factor that information into assisting with their writing. Some strategies for doing so include:

- Talking with people about their writing experiences and background in the different languages they speak
- Asking to see writing samples they have written in the past in both English and other languages
- Reviewing any available assessment data related to writing proficiency in the different languages

IS A WRITER STRUGGLING MORE WITH INDIVIDUAL ELEMENTS OF WRITING OR THE OVERALL TYPE OF WRITING?

Even if Veronica is a stronger writer in a language other than English, it is possible that she has never encountered, in *any* language, the particular kind of writing required by the National Board process. As Maria puts it, "Many candidates feel unfamiliar with the kind of analytical and reflective writing the Board calls for." We argue that "good writing" is never just "good writing." Expectations for what makes quality writing vary according to audience and purpose and are influenced by historical and cultural traditions as well as local contexts. For those unfamiliar with "the kind of analytical and reflective writing the board calls for," these expectations might be "foreign," even for monolingual English-speaking teachers who have lived their entire lives in the United States. In fact, according to Maria, Veronica's writing in English was "quite good in terms of writing mechanics." Still, Veronica believed that, in Maria's words, "her writing skills, particularly in 'academic English,' would be what kept her from certifying."

How would one go about offering such support? Maria, an experienced high school English teacher, mentions a wide variety of aspects of writing that she has supported candidates with through the years: grammar, organization, clarity and focus, and style (for example, avoiding circuitous writing and changing passive to active voice). These aspects are clearly essential to good writing (as long as it is understood that each of the aspects of good writing will look very different according to the kind of writing being done), and we agree with Maria's decision to focus on them. However, writers who are struggling profoundly may need additional kinds of support. The topics Maria covers can be perfect for those "rusty" writers who, in Maria's words, need to "refresh some skills, perhaps reducing distracting anxieties about 'academic composition.'" They may not, however, be sufficient for students like Veronica, who perhaps have never done the kind of writing called for by the National Board. Here are a few suggestions for additional support:

- Brainstorming and outlining of key ideas that candidates want to be sure to include in their written work, so that such a record exists before candidates get overwhelmed by the writing process
- Examination of model National Board writing and discussions surrounding what candidates notice about how other candidates have structured their arguments
- Examination of weak National Board writing (either real or invented) and discussions about why it might be considered weak
- Use of rubrics or other kinds of guidelines that make explicit some of the expectations for writing for the National Board
- Opportunities for candidates to talk through what they notice

on these models and expectations that is different from other kinds of writing they have done in the past and what they anticipate will be particularly challenging

We make this argument not as a criticism of Maria. It is possible that precisely this kind of support was offered as part of a large-group session, or Maria might have concluded early on that this was not what Veronica needed. We raise the issue in hopes of sparking larger conversations about what kinds of supports struggling writers might benefit from.

In What Ways Do Writers' Beliefs About the Writing Process Match Our Own?

Maria worries repeatedly about the fact that Veronica does not share writing from the early stages of her writing process: the first drafts, first cuts, and raw writing. As American educators who share Maria's belief in the power of the writing process, we are sympathetic with Maria's frustration. But we also know that sharing early drafts of writing can be quite intimidating even for accomplished writers. For struggling writers, especially those who attribute some of their writing problems to their knowledge of English more generally, such intimidation can be overwhelming. Furthermore, many adults, especially but not exclusively those who were schooled in countries other than the United States, have been socialized to believe that they should perfect their writing before showing it to anyone, much less a teacher or tutor. We offer the following suggestions for working with students who seem reluctant to bring in early drafts:

- Talk with students about what kind of writing processes they have used in the past for various kinds of writing and how they feel about the writing process as it is often conceived of in the United States (prewriting, first drafts, revision, editing, "publishing").
- Create easy, quick, and low-stakes prewriting activities for students to do during the tutoring session with the mentor present: quick writes, outlines, graphic representations, and

topic sentences, for example. These sorts of activities are useful for diagnostic purposes and to serve as a basis for conversations about writing.

To aid Maria in her concerns regarding how to provide better support to Veronica and other speakers of languages other than English, we have suggested three starting points, each of which involves getting to know the candidate as a writer in more depth. Although this approach offers no easy solutions for exactly what kind of support to offer, we believe that it will provide a powerful starting point in attempting to meet the needs of struggling writers from a variety of linguistic backgrounds.

COMMENTARY BY SUSAN ELKO

As I read this case, I kept thinking about the same question that Maria raises in her conclusion regarding "if there was something more I [she] could have done to better facilitate the writing process for Veronica." It is this final question that I think merits exploration instead of the continuing controversy around, "Was I doing something to inhibit her ability to trust me?" that is stated midway through the case.

Sometimes when I'm immersed in a dilemma, I repeatedly analyze my existing actions for their flaws (What am I doing to cause this?), instead of trying to identify if the problem arises from what I'm neglecting or omitting. If we flip the problem in this case and consider, "Was I *not* doing something that would better serve Veronica?" perhaps more solutions will emerge.

For example, an idea that might work for a writing coach of adults is to engage the students she coaches in completing a self-assessment of writing skills. At their first coaching session, the students could check off the areas in which they have the most and least difficulty and then respond to a simple prompt to create a baseline writing sample. The match between perceived strengths and actual writing could be useful in charting a course of action for the coaching experience.

In working with preservice teachers who are engaged in student teaching and must capture their experiences in writing for seminar assignments, one of the keys I discovered is to establish a series of prewriting activities that are not graded. I start by observing the student teacher and then ask her or him to write a brief description of the strengths of the lesson to use as a starting point for discussion. This is an easy diagnostic tool to preassess writing skills without the students' thinking that the focus is writing. They focus on the content, not suspecting that I am assessing writing skills as well as their ability to identify and describe their teaching strengths. With a simple exercise like this, Maria could have initiated her coaching with Veronica, and many of Maria's questions about Veronica would have been quickly answered. She would have had the opportunity to observe if Veronica needed to write in her native language, if Veronica was writing with difficulty and taking an extraordinary amount of time to express herself, and if Veronica lacked the skills that her subsequent assignments demonstrated in polished form.

It also seems that there are several options that Maria neglected in her process of assisting Veronica. She states, "Were there any particular strategies to help her work through her language anxiety? I didn't know and didn't know where to look to begin to answer this question." Perhaps consultation with colleagues in education who teach adults learning a second language would be a source of not only strategies, but also ways to understand Veronica's mind-set about the writing assignment. By asking teachers who regularly teach adults the daunting task of learning a new language, perhaps Maria would have gained insight into Veronica's feelings and attitude about creating the portfolio. And independent of the second-language ramifications, there are identified issues unique to coaching adults who have a strong need to maintain their dignity in learning situations that are extremely challenging for them. An additional source of valuable information might be to directly ask adults in the second-language classes how they would react to the task and what coaching strategies would be most helpful to them.

A "put yourself in my place" way of thinking could provide a useful alternative for Maria. I began to think about the kinds of coaching and assistance I would need to undertake the writing of a portfolio in, say, Spanish, French, or German. I projected what preliminary support I would need and what kind of process would need to be in place for me to complete the portfolio. One thought that immediately came to mind was having a coach help me divide and sequence the work into tasks with incrementally increased levels of difficulty. I would need to begin with content that was most comfortable to me so that I could focus primarily on the writing, then begin to test my ability with content as I became more comfortable with the language. Also, establishing a time line for completion of individual pieces would be essential for me to work through the enormity of the task. I think it would be important to collaborate with my coach to develop the time line and establish consequences in advance for not sticking to the schedule. In my experience, adult learners need ongoing opportunities to be actively engaged in establishing the process itself in order to foster ownership of a learning process and make it effective. The relationship between Maria and Veronica reflected more of an expert-novice dynamic than a collegial dynamic that may have emerged with more focus on collaborative planning.

Maria neglected to establish why Veronica "was reluctant to write first in her primary language and then translate." Would it be useful to ask special education colleagues what kinds of assessments are used to identify learners who have specific learning differences related to writing? Codeveloping some writing assessment strategies with special educators or language support teachers to determine if Veronica in fact was experiencing the agitation and stress because of learning differences might be an extremely powerful tool. I would first have her engage in writing assessments in her native language before introducing the tasks in her second language.

If, as a result of writing preassessments, it was apparent that Veronica or any other teacher who requested support from the writing coach needed explicit instruction in basic writing, was the coach equipped to offer that kind of assistance, and was there adequate time to provide more than structural and grammatical help? Although it was clear from the initial statements that the scope of work deemed appropriate for the coach was writing structure, not content, it was not clear what level of writing instruction was appropriate. My sense from the case was that teachers coming in with drafts that needed polishing were the anticipated norm; thus, Veronica's needs exceeded the anticipated workload.

Maria's personal indictment, "Had I done something to run her off?" made me realize the degree to which Maria was personalizing virtually all possibilities for Veronica's behavior relative to completing the total written portfolio. Perhaps Maria would gain some distance and be able to depersonalize the reason for Veronica's behavior by implementing options like administering assessments of writing ability in both Veronica's native language and in English, employing adult learning strategies for facilitating writing in a second language, collaboratively planning an incrementally sequenced process for completing the writing tasks, and simultaneously trying to develop a writing portfolio in a second language to explore the challenges firsthand.

Functioning in the role of adult learner coach in any skill or content area is indeed challenging; serving as a writing coach presents multiple challenges since many adults have not had learning experiences that explicitly teach writing as a skill.

TEACHING NOTE

Maria is a National Board Certified Teacher in English/Language Arts, a veteran candidate support provider, and, most recently, a writing coach for a large support group. Her role is described as a "tutorial for structural and grammatical support." In general, teachers limit their requests to that kind of help. But one teacher, for whom English is a second language, challenges these boundaries and brings in only edited pieces of written entries. After a variety of attempts to develop a trusting relationship and encouraging her to bring in raw pieces of writing failed, Veronica stopped coming for help as the portfolio deadline approached. Maria is left wondering what more she could have done to help and whether she did anything to "run her off."

The case and its commentaries provide opportunities to explore ways of helping linguistically diverse teachers and students with their writing, which might not be so apparent to native English speakers. It also raises questions about appropriate roles for mentors and the trade-offs of going beyond the limitations specified in their job description.

ISSUES AND QUESTIONS

Enacting the Role of Writing Coach

Maria was the writing coach for a large candidate support group. The role was established when the support providers realized how overwhelmed many teachers were with both the volume of the writing required for National Board Certification and their concern with correct mechanics and structure. Examine the role of writing coach as defined by the program and the typical experience of being supported, as described in the narrative. How was Maria's role as writing coach different from that of other mentors in the support program? What were her strategies of working with teachers? What kind of boundaries did she set for herself? If you were in Maria's shoes, would you define your role any differently? Why?

From Veronica's Perspective

Maria often wondered why Veronica was so insecure about her capacity to write in English, especially since the pieces of writing she saw were well constructed. What do we know about Veronica from the narrative? Let's try to imagine the magnitude of the writing requirements of National Board Certification from her perspective. What might be some reasons that she was reluctant to share her writing with Maria? George Bunch and Jerome Shaw focus much of their commentary on this question. They also give us some insight into how little we really know about a nonnative speaker's command of English from listening to the person's accent.

Developing a Relationship of Trust and Integrity

Given Maria's sensitivity to the dynamics of her own candidate experience, she was particularly concerned that Veronica not feel isolated or marginalized because English was her second language. She tried to be encouraging and suggest that if her teaching was accomplished, they would just have to work together to make sure that the writing "stated what she wanted to say." At the same time, Maria was frustrated when Veronica continued to bring pieces of commentaries that others had edited and questioned her capacity to help Veronica portray her teaching in the commentaries.

Many of the cases and teaching notes in this book deal with the risk of sharing one's practice with others (see particularly the case and teaching note for Chapter Eight) and the need for developing a trusting relationship when you you're working with teachers. Examine Maria's strategies for developing trust with Veronica, including Maria's rationale for and the outcome of the visit to her class. Some discussants of this case raised questions about whether the visit, which went beyond Maria's personal boundaries of her role as writing coach, in fact helped or impeded the sense of trust. They wondered whether Veronica might have felt even more uncomfortable sharing writing with someone who was a friend. Others felt that mentoring involves a personal, mutually beneficial relationship; if the visit contributed to developing trust on both sides, it was worthwhile. How would you resolve this dilemma? Why?

Meeting the Needs of Nonnative English-Speaking Teachers

Maria raised several questions about her capacity to support non-native English speakers throughout this narrative. Although she had supported several second language teachers (some after this case was written) with no similar problems, her interactions with Veronica challenged her assumptions about her ability to meet their needs. Examine the strategies that Maria used to help Veronica with her writing, and compare them to the myriad of suggestions offered by George Bunch and Jerome Shaw and by Susan Elko in their commentaries. What more do you think Maria could have done with Veronica? What principles might you generate from this case, other cases, your experience, and any readings about how to work with nonnative English speakers to improve their writing?

Is It Possible to Be Too Personally Invested in a Mentoring Relationship?

As the deadline for the portfolio drew near and Veronica had shown her only about 25 percent of the portfolio entries, Maria began to fear that Veronica couldn't t finish the portfolio on time and shared this concern with her. But this didn't produce any more work. And by the time the deadline had arrived, Veronica had stopped coming for writing support, although she continued to attend the regular candidate meetings. Clearly Maria felt badly about this. She believed that Veronica had shown evidence of accomplished teaching and raised a series of questions about where she might have fallen short. Some discussants of this case wondered whether Maria was too invested in her relationship with Veronica and thought that mentors should have more distance with their mentees. Perhaps Veronica stopped coming for reasons that had nothing to do with Maria. What do you think? Can you develop any principles about mentoring relationships that would fit all cases?

PART FOUR

STRUCTURING GROUP PROCESS

CHAPTER EIGHT

NATIONAL BOARD READINESS
Is There a Right Time?

What is the facilitator's role in establishing group process? How do you help individuals understand their responsibility to themselves and to the group? In this case, a support provider is challenged by a teacher who is chronically unprepared to participate in group activities.

CASE

CASE BY ROSE VILCHEZ

As a support provider of candidates for the past three years, I have found that reluctance and procrastination are often masks for the anxiety that is a natural part of the risk taking required for candidates to videotape and produce written commentaries about their classroom instruction. Sharing and making our teaching visible to others is not part of most teachers' experiences. Even now, as a board-certified teacher, when I demonstrate my own portfolio videotapes as samples with other candidates, I share the sense of risk every teacher must feel when allowing other eyes and opinions into his or her classroom. It takes time to develop the ability to

_____

Pseudonyms have been used to maintain the confidentiality of people and places in the case.

receive and accept criticism and questioning and to value such interaction as a pathway to professional growth.

Many candidates never become completely comfortable with viewing themselves on video. They are often preoccupied with their physical appearance and the merciless honesty with which the video camera captures their classroom environment. But as the focus shifts to substance and they delve more deeply into what is going on in the lesson, they grow increasingly willing to discuss and question their teaching. Becoming more confident, they shift worries about their "rough, rough draft" to the goal of clearly and convincingly answering portfolio entry questions.

Last year, I began work with a newly developed district support network, facilitating a cohort of five candidates in the same certificate area. The district had agreed to pay half their assessment fees on the condition they attend the meetings regularly. This group was unique, as all the teachers knew each other. Elaine, Rosario, Carolina, Alicia, and Lawrence taught different grades but had decided to embark on the National Board journey as a team from the same school site; I knew that they would be able to provide one another with daily support and ongoing collaboration. They all appeared to be friendly and comfortable with one another. I was the newcomer to the group.

As this newly formed group was to begin its work together, I had two priorities. First, I wanted to know the teachers well; I wanted to know their personalities, their approaches to working collaboratively, and their preferred way of giving and receiving criticism. Moreover, I wanted each of the teachers to know that about one another. Their teaching experiences ranged from four to more than twenty years in the district. Second, I knew that time management was crucial; there were only five months until the portfolio due date. The candidates could not know yet how quickly their time would disappear among their planned lessons, units, and assessments, national holidays, and spring break. So it was important to make sure the teachers had a realistic organizational time line for completing their portfolio entries. Even so, realizing that individuals have their own preferred styles for completing work, I knew I must respect their decisions about deadlines.

By the end of our first meeting, the teachers had agreed to set deadlines for themselves. Eager and anxious, they were ready to delve into their portfolios. They agreed to read and familiarize themselves with two portfolio entries and had begun to plan their first excursions into videotaping themselves, arranging to help one another with equipment. I left the meeting feeling satisfied, yet wondering when and how the inevitable difficulties of the required videotaping and writing would emerge among the teachers.

Consequently, four months before the portfolio deadline, I was not surprised to learn that one of the candidates, Lawrence, was not meeting his own personal deadlines, which he had shared with the group just a month and a half earlier. I had designated the first fifteen minutes of our monthly meetings as check-in time, an important way of allowing members to share their progress and difficulties and to preview the materials they would be offering the group for critical feedback. The check-in also let teachers gauge their progress against each other as a gentle spur to continue working until portfolio completion. At the end of our meetings, I asked each teacher to state a portfolio-related goal that they would accomplish by our next meeting. Setting goals in smaller increments this way helps teachers create accountability to themselves and one another. However, I didn't believe that the teachers should be admonished for not meeting their goals. After all, the best plans are bound to go awry. Rather, I stressed that it was more important that the teachers progress toward meeting their stated goals to ensure continued movement toward completion of one or more parts of the portfolio.

At this meeting, the candidates were to share videotapes of classroom environment or instruction. Agitated, Lawrence explained that he had no access to recording equipment; moreover, it had been difficult for him to arrange for someone to tape in his classroom. Elaine and Alicia echoed Lawrence's complaints, but they had managed somehow to videotape one another the same afternoon of our meeting. Aware that equipment was scarce, I provided Lawrence with possible alternatives and recommended calling parent volunteers or having one of his colleagues videotape him. Elaine and Alicia volunteered, and Lawrence eagerly gave his thanks. Carolina and Rosario had also videotaped lessons, so the group began to allocate time for viewing each teacher. I didn't feel overly concerned about Lawrence, because I felt that viewing and discussing the others' videotapes might make him feel less intimidated to show his own. At the end of the meeting, short-term goals were set again. Lawrence promised a videotape in addition to a list of potential units to be featured in the portfolio entries, which was a collective goal agreed on by the group. The group dynamics were positive, and I left this meeting with a growing sense of optimism.

One month later, the group joined to watch videotapes, share the list of potential units, and review any written commentaries. The check-in process made it obvious that Elaine, Alicia, Carolina, and Rosario all came with videos and their lists. Carolina and Rosario had even brought copies of their first rough draft of a written commentary. Lawrence had brought his list of units, which appeared to have been hastily written on a half-sheet of notebook paper. He had tried to videotape on his own, he quickly explained, but had not been successful because his sixth-grade students had acted wildly. He was far too embarrassed to share the videotape and had left it at home; he had not even bothered to watch the video.

"I understand the apprehension you must feel," I began, "but I think it's important that you get a chance to look at the videotape even if it's just to get used to seeing yourself on tape. Just make sure you get a chance to watch it since you don't have it today."

"Of course, of course, I understand," Lawrence answered. "I just couldn't bear to watch my kids go crazy in front of everyone. I know I'll be able to get someone in my class soon, so I'll bring a tape next time. I know I need to get it done."

Lawrence was showing what I considered typical concerns about the technical aspects of certification. I appreciated his frustration in not being able to produce a videotape that seemed adequate to him. Nevertheless, I felt slightly troubled. I disliked presuming that Lawrence was avoiding the inevitable. Shouldn't he feel obligated to share a videotape? After all, it was his choice to participate fully in this group, and sharing work with one another was an assumed responsibility of that participation. I wasn't sure what to do. Was it my job to gently push Lawrence? Or was it his responsibility to push himself? After all, certification was voluntary. Was Lawrence ready to do the work necessary to analyze his classroom instruction, let alone complete the portfolio entries? Or was I being judgmental by even entertaining these thoughts? Perhaps I was jumping to conclusions too quickly. I kept my thoughts to myself.

Another month passed, and now the portfolio deadline was only two and a half months away. This time, everyone but Lawrence showed up with rough drafts of written commentaries, and Carolina wanted help choosing between two videos that she felt might be "the ones." The others in the group refrained from asking Lawrence any questions; he did not offer any explanations. As the candidates began to discuss the specifics of one entry, Lawrence interrupted several times, asking about the nature of the directions. He had not had time to read the directions yet, he explained. Alicia and Rosario patiently explained the purpose of the entry and gave examples from their own teaching to provide context for Lawrence. He listened attentively and took notes.

Although I felt ambivalent about my role in determining Lawrence's progress, I did feel that it was my responsibility to stress to him that he was not participating fully in the support group. At the end of the meeting, I spoke to Lawrence privately as the other teachers prepared to leave.

"I'm glad we have a moment to speak, Lawrence. I'm really concerned that you haven't been able to share any of your videotapes or written work with the other members of the group."

"Oh, yes, well, me too. I've just been overwhelmed with other things." Lawrence sighed deeply and then laughed nervously. "I've been out of my classroom, trying to attend as much professional development as possible. I really haven't kept up on that, you know. The others were willing to help me videotape, but I'm concerned about the tape quality. I finally hired someone to do it for me; that's why it's taking so long. I wish I could have had something today, but I just haven't been able to do it. And I can't do any writing for two of the entries if I don't have my videotapes." Lawrence spoke quickly.

"Well, I'm also concerned about your responsibility to the group. You can bring in the written commentary of the entry without the video. Oh, and have you been reading the entries before you come to this group?" I felt awkward pressing Lawrence to be accountable for his own learning for more than one reason. He was at least twenty years older than I am, an experienced teacher with many more years of teaching. Who was I to question him? Shouldn't he be aware of his responsibilities? Did he truly understand the time commitment that the portfolio required? I started feeling resentful that I was in this situation. "Lawrence," I continued briskly, "what can you definitively bring to the group next time? I really want you to commit this time."

As Lawrence heard my last sentence, his previous slightly embarrassed expression changed to one of cool civility. "Well," he replied in a tight voice, "I definitively will commit to bringing a video."

At that moment, I realized I had gone too far. I had pushed Lawrence into an uncomfortable space where he had been unable to save face. But I tried to be upbeat. "Well, good. I think that will really contribute to the group so we can see what an upper-grade classroom looks like and you can receive some feedback. I just really want you to get feedback from your colleagues, which is supposed to be one of the purposes of this group." I could hear the apology creeping into my last statement.

"Okay, I'll have the video." Lawrence avoided looking at me and quickly left the meeting.

I left the conversation feeling uncomfortable with Lawrence's lack of initiative and lack of knowledge of the portfolio requirements. I also felt that I had not dealt with the situation in the right way. *And what is the right way? But it's not my portfolio,* I silently chided myself. Nevertheless, I was worried. The procrastination that I was seeing signaled something more troubling. Was Lawrence unready to look at his teaching, even on his own, in the in-depth manner required by each portfolio entry? Was his lack of preparedness and familiarity with the portfolio, and to some extent even the certificate standards, a signal that this was not the year for him to try to certify? He seemed scattered in his organization and even in his classroom planning from the little I had heard from him during the meetings.

As I drove home that day, I wondered what I would do if Lawrence came without a video to the next meeting. Should I approach him about waiting another year to attempt certification? Was it beyond my role as a facilitator to suggest this? Should I say nothing and potentially let him fail? What about the resources that the district had assumed for Lawrence to participate in the process? Was it fair to let an unprepared and uncommitted teacher go through the process while the financial resources could benefit future candidates? When I arrived home, I was unsure if I had the right to initiate a discussion with Lawrence about his candidacy readiness.

COMMENTARY

COMMENTARY BY DIANE BARONE

This case is focused on a facilitator and her relationships with National Board candidates. During her fourth year as a support provider, Rose worked with five candidates from the same school. Of these participants, one failed to meet any of his personal or group deadlines for work toward certification. This situation was particularly troubling for Rose, as she wanted him to be successful with this process. In my response to this case, I will share themes that I perceive as running through this case. I will close by sharing how I have come to work with similar procrastinating candidates.

The first theme is centered on being an insider or an outsider as a facilitator and group member. In this situation, Rose is an outsider. All of the teachers have worked together in the school and know each other quite well. They have the advantage of a shared school history and personal and professional relationships. I wanted to learn more about how Rose dealt with this issue. How did she become a part of the group? As I read and reread this case, I wanted to know more about the professional relationships of the teachers. Lawrence appears to be an outsider as well. All four of the women teachers have found ways to support each other, as demonstrated in their willingness to video each other and respond to entries. Lawrence is not a participant in the videotaping process or in peer response. Is his being an outsider based on gender, or is there a history in the school where he has not worked with other teachers or they have elected not to work with him? I believe these to be important questions that if answered would help us to understand the dynamics of this group of teachers, and in particular, Lawrence's relationships with the four women teachers and the facilitator.

The second theme is centered on group and personal norms. The norms in this group were quite public: every member was expected to conform and share his or her work publicly. For example, all of the teachers were expected to share their videos so that they would "develop the ability to receive and accept criticism and questioning, and to value such interaction as a pathway to professional growth." This is a laudable goal, and I believe as well that teachers do grow as professionals through the constructive criticism of each other's videos. However, Rose seems to have left this process quite open. I wondered if Lawrence might have brought a video if he knew the criticism was to be focused on his teaching to National Board standards rather than to his teaching in general. Perhaps even if this had been the case, Lawrence may not have chosen to share a video with this group. Rose believed that he was "intimidated" and "anxious" about sharing. This could certainly have been true, but could there be another interpretation? Perhaps Lawrence did not want to share his work in this public forum with colleagues. I wonder if he would have been willing to share his work privately with Rose. Within this theme is a tension of group versus individual expectations and how they are reconciled by each participant. From what is shared in the case, Lawrence chose not to conform to the group norms.

The third and final theme is authority. I wondered who was in charge. Rose led the group, helped them establish norms, and supported them as they completed entries for their portfolios. Four teachers were compliant and kept pace with all expectations. Lawrence's behavior unsettled this group's work ethic. While the teachers may have dismissed him, Rose consistently reflected on his behavior. She wanted him to fulfill his responsibility to the group. He didn't. She wanted him to be successful, and she believed that he needed to complete work on a schedule and share it with colleagues to accomplish this goal. In addition, she was concerned that Lawrence was a more experienced teacher than she. Did Lawrence respond as he did because he saw himself as a more experienced teacher? Or was this not an issue at all for Lawrence? Perhaps he disliked the nagging and refused to allow the group to see his progress. While his progress was not similar to the other teachers in the group, there was evidence that he was engaged in the process, for he hired a person to videotape. A tension that is evident in this case is centered on pacing in completing the expectations of National Board Certification. As a facilitator, is it reasonable to expect all candidates to be on a similar schedule? How much variability is appropriate among candidates when the facilitator wants each candidate to complete all expectations in a timely fashion? Finally, since this process is voluntary, how much pressure or authority can a facilitator exert over a candidate to complete expectations on a group schedule?

Rose is not the only facilitator to experience a candidate who procrastinates. What is perhaps unique about Lawrence is that he procrastinated and did not become a functioning member of the group. While I have had many candidates who procrastinated, they have been supportive members of the cohort group of National Board candidates that I support. I am a bit different from Rose, however; I believe that each teacher takes responsibility for completing the expectations for National Board Certification. I support each candidate through monthly meetings, e-mail exchanges, and individual meetings. However, I am clear with each of them that the responsibility for this process is theirs. Each teacher, as best as he or she can and on a personal schedule, must complete all of the expectations. I can support them professionally and emotionally, but I am only a facilitator in this process.

Each year, I have several candidates who have a schedule very different from the one I suggest that the group follow. When it is time to share a video, they don't bring one. When we critically respond to written entries, they don't share one. I certainly nudge them through e-mail messages to the whole group, but often they don't respond. What I have found interesting about these candidates is that they are constantly thinking about the process and what is expected, but they just don't write or videotape. Perhaps they are anxious, or perhaps they need more time to process what is expected. What is important is that each of these candidates has completed the process. When the majority of teachers in the cohort have completed their portfolios and are preparing to submit them to the Board, they are still writing and videotaping. Where more task-driven teachers have revised often, they revise less. It appears to me that they have been "writing" all along as they think about their commentary, but they just have not gotten anything down on paper yet. When they do get to the writing task, their cognitive rehearsal expedites the process.

Like Rose, I find these candidates challenging. I always worry that they won't finish or that their entries will not be as rich as they could be. These are my worries, however, not theirs. I am learning, as I continue to support candidates, what a facilitator is. Most times it is challenging, as I must respect each candidate and how he or she personally engages in the National Board Certification process. I have to understand that not all candidates want a public response to their work, even though their teaching may be exemplary. I have to relinquish my expectations for a schedule and follow theirs. I am learning to follow as I gain knowledge of how to better support teachers in this rigorous process.

COMMENTARY BY RAE JEANE WILLIAMS

I identified immediately with Rose. Her issues have been our issues in our support program: reluctance and procrastination. Although her support program was more structured than ours, we also began each session with the candidates reporting their progress. Around the table came excuses: I was attending science workshops, directing the holiday program, creating our professional development series, planning weddings, birthdays, showers. One candidate even said she felt better about not having written anything after listening to the others.

These teachers are part of a research grant we received to support African American educators, so their completing the National Board process was particularly important. Of the seventeen in our first cohort, only half submitted their portfolios. As part of our research, the principal investigator conducted taped interviews with all the candidates, and their responses surprised us. Almost all had wanted more structure and wanted us to be more demanding about their finishing their work. They also felt insecure about their writing and wanted more writing workshops.

In planning our support process for cohort 2 in the second year of our research project, we responded to their suggestions. We developed a time management workshop where the candidates as a whole group brainstormed specific tasks to be accomplished in order to complete each portfolio entry. From there they created individual time lines, entering specific dates on a year calendar that we provided.

Our loose organization became more structured. All of the candidates in the research group are part of our regular National Board support Saturday Academies; in addition, they met with African American National Board mentors for an extra three-hour session. This group also meets an additional Saturday a month.

They meet in mentor-led small groups in the morning. After a working lunch during which they share their progress, each person spends three hours writing on her laptop computer provided by the grant or sharing her drafts in one-on-one writing conferences with writing experts.

We also incorporated writing mini-lessons based on Donald Murray's *The Craft of Revision* (2004), focusing on writing issues that arise in the one-on-one conferences. Part of the goal of these mini-sessions is to help the candidates better understand the writing process and the importance of focusing on content first, convincing them that as accomplished teachers, they have much to share. Refining that content comes later.

We are pleased with our progress. Several of last year's candidates who did not submit their portfolio have joined us this year. They all respond positively to the structure and the additional writing support. This year's candidates are much further ahead in the process than last year's candidates.

Reference

Murray, D. *The Craft of Revision.* (5th ed.) Boston: Heinle, 2004.

TEACHING NOTE

Rose is a National Board Certified Teacher who has three years of experience supporting teachers as National Board candidates. She was hired to work with candidates pursuing National Board Certification in a school district where she did not teach. The members of the group she supported all work at the same school site. When one of the members of her group continually attends group meetings unprepared, she struggles with how hard to push him in keeping up with his responsibilities to the certification process and contributing to the group discussions. She decides to confront him about his commitment to the process. Seeing his response, she raises questions about her own approach in supporting this candidate toward a time line that will help him complete his portfolio and also wonders if she is ready for the certification process.

This case delves into issues of contributions that individuals make to the group analysis of practice and the implications for how a group of teachers can jointly work together toward improving their practice. The case also explores the facilitator's role in establishing the group processes and group members' accountability to one another while engaged in work together.

ISSUES AND QUESTIONS

The Risk of Sharing Your Practice

Rose assumes that part of the reason Lawrence is not bringing videos of his classroom to the group meetings is the risk in sharing his practice with others. Potential critique of teaching practice can be hard for teachers to face, especially if they do not have much experience showing their practice to others, have not talked about their practice with others before, or feel uncertain about what kind of feedback colleagues might offer. Examine Rose's hypotheses about Lawrence and Lawrence's comments about the video that he did make of his teaching. In her commentary to this case, Diane Barone suggests an alternative hypothesis for Lawrence's reluctance to share his classroom videos with the group. What do you think?

One way to mitigate this risk is to create a professional culture and community where sharing practice is safe and educative. Of course, this is a larger systemic professional issue that we continually address in professional development. For a small group of teachers striving to improve practice through analysis and reflection, the issues are the same as in the broader profession. What strategies did Rose use to build trust and develop a shared sense of practice that would allow the group to confront and potentially overcome the risk of showing each other what goes on behind the classroom door? What are some other possible strategies for helping a group of teachers develop safe and supportive processes of sharing and discussing videotape among themselves? What are the advantages and disadvantages of these strategies?

Enabling Versus Nagging

Rose is struggling with how she can enable the members of her group to complete the National Board portfolio while still respecting their decisions about time management and production. For those who are making a continued effort to produce the work of the portfolio (videotapes and written commentaries), her suggestions and advice seem sufficient. She feels uncertain about her approach for Lawrence, who is not producing the work, which leads her to question his readiness for the National Board assessment. Enabling others without stepping in and doing it for them or simply demanding productivity is a delicate balance to find. Examine Rose's strategies to encourage Lawrence to adhere to the deadlines. The two commentaries by Diane Barone and Rae Jeane Williams offer differing perspectives on this issue in two very different contexts. After reading the case commentaries, what is your position? Should a mentor assume responsibility for encouraging teachers to adhere to deadlines, or should she treat the teachers as adults who should assume their own responsibility? What are the trade-offs for your position?

Responsibility to the Group

One of the underlying issues that Rose brings out in the case is her concern about group members' contributing to the group process. She sees four of the five members making regular contributions by bringing in videos to show, sharing written commentary, and keeping up with the reading outside the group meetings. Lawrence is benefiting from the resources of the group, yet he does not seem to be contributing to the group. It might even be interpreted that Lawrence is draining more from the group than he is contributing. Rose suggests that the others, not only Lawrence, will benefit from seeing Lawrence's practice.

To Rose, the lack of Lawrence's participation is an issue of equity and responsibility. The group was designed to help all of the teachers, and if one member chooses not to participate fully, then they all lose to some degree. It is not clear if this sense of group interdependence is an explicit norm for the group or if this is Rose's view of the ideal. What are the advantages and disadvantages of groups such as these having a collective responsibility?

The Readiness Question

Rose closes the case with reflections on her assessment of Lawrence as a National Board candidate based on his behavior and what she knows of his practice. She wonders if she should advise him to wait to attempt National Board Certification in the following year. Or is this even an appropriate subject to address with candidates who have chosen to pursue the certification? She does not know much about his classroom practice given what he has shared, yet she knows the time commitment needed for writing the portfolio entries and can foresee much stress on Lawrence to complete the entire portfolio with such little time remaining. The National Board's policies on ethical support for candidates is clear: support providers should not pass judgment about a candidate's practice, and it is the candidate's sole responsibility to decide whether to pursue the voluntary certification. But with district-sponsored support and candidate fee subsidies, the issue of distributing limited resources would suggest favoring candidates who are not just committed but are most likely to succeed. What are the responsibilities of the support provider when considering the candidate's right to pursue the certification and his or her responsibilities to the district program that is investing resources in a candidate who appears to not be following through on his commitment? What would you do in this situation? (Refer to Chapter One for other views on this issue.)

Many suggest that the process itself is a professionally enriching experience and thus should be open to all teachers, regardless of readiness. If support groups then have a heterogeneous mix of teachers, some who are clearly demonstrating the standards in their classroom practice and some who are not yet meeting the standards, support providers will need to find ways to include all teachers in the conversation about practice. What are some possible strategies for supporting heterogeneous groups of teachers with regard to how aligned their practice is with the teaching standards?

CHAPTER NINE

WHY ARE ALL THE BLACK TEACHERS SITTING TOGETHER?

What happens when organizational dynamics bump up against the dynamics of race? How can you navigate the cultural land mines that are inevitable in a diverse professional landscape? In this case of good intentions gone awry, a veteran support provider is surprised to discover that her usual approach to group structure does not meet the needs of all participants.

CASE

CASE BY RAE JEANE WILLIAMS

It was the second day of our National Board Institute, and I noticed that many of the African American teachers were agitated. After the overwhelming success of our first day, I was confused. We were thrilled that the recruitment efforts for our new research grant to support African American candidates had been so fruitful. There were fourteen African American teachers in our group of forty, all enthusiastic about pursuing National Board Certification. Now

---

Pseudonyms have been used to maintain the confidentiality of people and places in the case.

some of these same teachers seemed angry and hostile. While talking quietly with Ann, the African American codirector of our project, I noticed one of the teachers watching us. Seeing me looking at her, she turned her face away, shielding it with her hand. What had generated this animosity?

Our National Board for Professional Teaching Standards Project begins with an intensive four-day Summer Institute during which teachers deconstruct the certification process, analyze current research, and hear National Board Certified Teachers (NBCTs) share their portfolios. The project continues throughout the school year with monthly Saturday academies facilitated by NBCTs.

During the institute, we plan a series of activities that help the candidates learn about each other and the National Board process. But our initial aim is creating a comfort level that will promote their working together during the institute and subsequent Saturday Academies. On the first day of the institute, we allow the teachers to sit where they want. After that, we group them in differing ways to ensure opportunities for them to work with a variety of people. Sometimes the groupings are heterogeneous, bringing together teachers with as many differences as possible. At other times the teachers could be in groups determined by grade level, geographical location, schools, or certificate area.

Most teachers initially group themselves by school, by school district, or randomly. By contrast, all fourteen African American teachers in this particular institute sat together. Bonding among them seemed instant: teachers who had only met that morning were fast friends by the end of the day. Like all the other self-selected groups, these teachers seemed quite comfortable in their segregated group.

Since one of our goals during the institute is to develop a learning community that values the diversity of group members and encourages them to be resources for one another, I followed my usual practice and decided to mix everyone up on the second day of the institute. I believed that allowing candidates to become acquainted with one another through a variety of heterogeneous groups would better enable them to form the smaller certificate-alike groups they would be meeting with during the following academic year. Moreover, our new grant emphasized that we would provide the African American candidates with supplemental support and not separate them from the rest of the support group.

Before the candidates arrived the next day, I placed their name cards at various tables around the room, deliberately breaking up all the self-selected groups of the previous day. So imagine my surprise to learn from Ann that the very practice I had unquestioningly followed caused the consternation of the African American teachers when they found their name cards dispersed among different tables. The teachers had protested to Ann and also separately to the African American principal investigator of our grant; no one confronted me just then except by scowls. What to me was common practice had become an occasion for dissension among the very group Ann and I would be working with as part of our research.

That night I recorded all these interactions in my field notebook and asked myself several questions: Should I explain why I moved the teachers? It was not just because of ethnicity, but also to break up groups from the same school. I had always moved teachers around during professional development meetings and had never encountered such resistance. Am I being a manipulative white teacher, creating groupings that I like and am most comfortable in? Do I like control? Am I flexible? In our teacher preparation program, we read several articles (in particular, by Lisa Delpit, 1988) about the inadvertent insensitivity of white teachers who teach African American students. I began to wonder if I was also being insensitive to the needs of these teachers.

At the end of the third day, we had our first meeting with the African American grant candidates. As we sat together in a circle—the fourteen teachers, the project principal investigator, Ann, and myself, the only white person—I heard exactly how angry all the teachers were. This homogeneous grouping allowed them the space to be honest. They did not hesitate to tell me how destructive my dividing them up was. Each openly expressed her feelings. One teacher's comment sums up what most of them were saying. She described how wonderful it was to arrive at the first day of our institute to find so many African American teachers. In all her years of attending professional meetings, she was usually the only or one of few African Americans. No wonder they were dismayed by my not understanding the importance of their being together.

I felt so intimidated by their hostility and my lack of sensitivity to group dynamics that I let them sit wherever they wanted on the last day of the institute. Now when I plan any group activities, I wonder if my goal of creating diverse learning communities might threaten or limit group participation and the comfort that comes from self-selected groups. I had witnessed both the power and the hazards of grouping practices; the reaction of the African American teachers I had split up jarred my complacency, forcing me to reexamine my beliefs.

Before establishing groups, I now question the advantages and disadvantages of grouping. Self-selected groups can create space for students of similar interest and background to work together, but they can also result in some students not being selected. Instructor-formed groups can bring together diverse students who can help each other in accomplishing tasks, but deciding who should be in which group can be problematic. Bringing together participants haphazardly in randomly formed groups may not provide the best learning environment for all participants, particularly those who need the most support.

I also approach the creation of groups with a mixture of apprehension and greater understanding, and appreciate that creating groups might work contrary to the goals I wish to accomplish. If I give preference to the comfort of group members and allow them to determine their own groups, how can I accomplish my goal of creating a learning community in which everyone can work together?

My experience has stimulated me to examine more carefully my reasons for grouping in general: Why use groups? Who should be in which group? Who benefits, and how? My standard practice is no longer standard.

Reference

Delpit, L. "The Silenced Dialogue: Power and Pedagogy in Educating Other People's Children." *Harvard Education Review,* 1988, *58*(3), 200–298.

COMMENTARIES

COMMENTARY BY VICKI BAKER

I had an interesting reaction to Rae Jeane's story. As a support provider, I usually relate to the feelings of fellow support providers first. I know how much effort Rae Jeane must put into her work, and so I can imagine how painful it must have been for her to be treated the way she was by the very people she was trying so hard to help. Along with my initial reaction, though, I felt as if I could relate to the African American teachers as well.

Meetings and workshops outside my workplace are always uncomfortable for me at first. I am expected to make small talk (which I'm horrible at) and share thoughts and feelings with strangers. The only thing that makes me feel comfortable and safe is if I am able to sit near people I already know. I feel that I become a much better participant in the group if I am near familiar people. I secretly resent it when the facilitator decides to mix people up. As an adult, I feel that I have earned the right to choose my own seat in a workshop. Yet I never resent it when the facilitator has an activity that forces me out of my comfortable place, as long as I know that I can go back when the activity is over.

So I wonder at the reaction of the African American teachers. How wonderful that they were able to bond so quickly with strangers, due, I assume, to similar cultural backgrounds and experiences. Were they reacting to being taken out of their new comfort zone? Or were they angry because they had already done what the facilitator wanted on their own? They had walked into this meeting and bonded with total strangers. They had made small talk and spoken out even though they had just met the people at their tables, and now they were being told to do that all over again.

I also want to know more about the reaction of the teachers. Why did these teachers feel that they could talk to the two other facilitators and not Rae Jeane? Why did they go along with the new seating arrangements but then behave so overtly angrily? As support providers, we hope that candidates can be honest with us so that we can help them feel more comfortable and safe. How can we help our candidates be more open with their feelings?

COMMENTARY BY YVONNE DIVANS-HUTCHINSON

Fifty years after *Brown* v. *Board of Education* supposedly eliminated the existence of a separate-but-equal society, we remain transfixed and bound by notions of race.

Rae Jeane, a white woman and a long-time colleague since we met in 1978 when I joined the California Writing Project at UCLA, asks, Why are all the black teachers sitting together in the National Board Certification support group? As an African American and an NBCT, I offer an answer to her question.

Admittedly Rae Jeane faced a dilemma. If her case involved a simple matter of grouping, all of her concerns would seem valid, and she would not have to second-guess herself. As teachers, we automatically vary the way we group our students based on our instructional purposes or their needs or desires. Of course, when I allow them to select their own collaborators, my students will choose their familiars—those who look like they do, talk like they do, or have some sort of common ground. On the first day of class at my school, whose student population is mostly black and brown, students invariably enter the room and sit according to race, which leads to a segregated classroom, with African Americans sitting on one side of the room and Hispanics on the other. The same phenomenon occurred years ago when I taught junior high school students, all of whom were African American: the boys sat on one side of the room, girls on the other.

Like Rae Jeane, I place my students in diverse groups in order to establish a unified learning community. Consequently, I am likely to use criteria such as areas of intelligence, skill levels, learning styles, personality, interests, gender, and even race to form diverse groups in which students' talents, abilities, and capabilities provide a complementary context. However, because human nature dictates that people gravitate toward those with whom they feel most comfortable, students may initially resent or resist being grouped according to the teacher's dictates. Because we understand the long-term effect of bonding among diverse groups in our classrooms, we tolerate the initial reluctance to comply with our manipulation.

Unfortunately, in the case of the African American teachers in this NBPTS group, the matter of grouping was not as simple. Rae Jeane found it impossible to transcend the anger and hostility of her group. As I reviewed her case, I readily understood the reason for the hostility. In fact, I identified so strongly with the remark by the woman in the group who declared how "wonderful it was to arrive at the first day of the institute to find so many African American teachers" that I shouted, "Amen!"

Most assuredly, Rae Jeane had the right to expect that directing the NBC candidates to group randomly would be the best way to establish a learning community, but what she did not reckon with were the dynamics of bonding among African Americans who not only find themselves in the minority in the larger population, but often in even smaller numbers in the professional community. There are so few of us that we are just delighted to see each other.

After almost forty years of attending educational conferences, I always search the room for black faces, sensing congeniality when I spot other African Americans. Invariably, we make eye contact, smile, or nod, and if we are close enough in proximity, we speak. Recently I attended a high-powered writing conference in the Bay Area. Of the two hundred or so university, community college, and high school English teachers present, only six of us were black. We made it a point to make eye contact. Two of the people I already knew, and three were new acquaintances. Four of us sat together during meals, reveling in the bond that comes from our being African American, a connection that is often established, albeit temporarily, even among strangers. The joy at finding our "kin" is unbounded because it affirms our place in society, reassuring us, and providing a bulwark against the racism that persists, despite the gains of the civil rights era.

While people who are not black may make facile judgments about how African Americans seem overly sensitive, unfriendly, clannish, or churlish at times, they should understand that being black means facing the specter of race as a constant in our lives. It means that even when we think we have transcended race, something invariably happens to remind us of our blackness. Thus, we continually seek comfort against racism, banding together in our small numbers in joyous recognition whenever we can, continually affirming our humanism and the beauty of our race in the company of our own.

Why are all the black teachers sitting together in the National Board Support group? Dear Rae Jeane, here's my answer: in the words of my African American grandmother, born and raised in the South, God rest her soul, "We just so glad to see each other, we don't know what to do!" Of course, we are not separatists, and we are not impervious to the need to diversify, learn about, and work with others. Might not the NBC candidates in the grant group be willing to join in with the larger group once they have had some time to celebrate their shared identity and racial heritage? Thus fortified, wouldn't they make stronger contributions to the group at large?

TEACHING NOTE

This case depicts a veteran support provider's analysis and reflections on her organization and grouping procedures when the composition of her group changes. The context is a four-day introductory summer institute for National Board candidates in a large urban school district. Typically Rae Jeane used a similar pattern of activities for all of her courses. But when a large group of African American teachers joined this institute as a result of intensive recruiting for a research grant, she was surprised to find that they challenged and resented what she viewed as "tried-and-true" strategies.

While most of the narratives in this book tend to deal with aspects of mentoring teachers, this case helps us focus on the structural organization of working with support groups. It challenges us to consider the needs of participants as we plan activities to develop a learning community.

ISSUES AND QUESTIONS

Structuring Group Activities to Develop a Learning Community

Many of the cases in this book allude to the challenges and risk of sharing one's work with others, and thus the importance of developing a shared professional culture that is both safe and educative. This case is no different. In fact, developing a safe learning community was one of Rae Jeane's primary objectives for her introductory seminar; she hoped to prepare group members for sharing and critiquing their work during subsequent academy meetings. To accomplish this goal, she created a series of activities that purposefully separated groups that came into the seminar with a shared history. Her intent was to maximize learning opportunities from diverse perspectives and foster the probability that group members would be able to share their work in a safe and constructive manner.

Yet the African Americans in this group resented having their seat changed, for reasons described vividly in the narrative. They were so pleased to see such a large group of African Americans in a professional development setting that they wanted to stay together and resented being separated. In deference to their wishes, Rae Jeane changed her plans for the last day and let group members sit wherever they liked. What would you have done in this situation? How might you structure activities to develop a learning community in which group members both felt comfortable and enabled to provide constructive feedback to one another? What are the risks and benefits of each strategy? Yvonne Divans-Hutchinson's and Vicki Baker's commentaries shed light on this dilemma.

Tension Between One's Own Agenda and the Needs of Participants

Rae Jeane noted that this experience "jarred her complacency," forced her to question previous grouping strategies, and stimulated her to reflect on the advantages and disadvantages of different types of groupings (see the description at the end of the case of self-selected groups, instructor-formed groups, and randomly formed groups). If her primary purpose was to create a climate of safety, should she accede to the wishes of group members and let them determine their own groups? But if she did this, might she abrogate her responsibility as an instructor and deny opportunities for learning?

The goal of the National Board candidate process, and any other teacher professional development experience, is to maximize opportunities for individual learning and improve classroom practice. In the case of the National Board process, experience suggests that teachers who work together on similar certificates have the advantage of common content knowledge and classroom experience as they critique one another's videos and provide constructive input on unit plans. Yet if teachers don't feel safe with one another, experience also suggests that they won't risk sharing their work; it is simply too threatening. Given this dichotomy, how might Rae Jeane accommodate both her optimal vision of how working groups should be determined and her candidates' desire to stick together with members of their own kind? Both Vicki's and Yvonne's commentaries address these questions.

When we discussed this case with a group of National Board support providers, we described some candidates' experience of feeling marginalized in their support group and discomfort in sharing their work and then asked: "How important is sensitivity to safety in selecting groups of teachers to work together?" One person responded, "I don't think that's very important. If teachers don't like what we offer, they don't have to attend our support group." How would you respond to this teacher?

Establishing Conditions for Honest Feedback

Vicki raised an important issue in her commentary: she noted that the African American teachers were not comfortable to talk directly to Rae Jeane until they were in their own supplemental group, yet they had been quite comfortable to talk to the African American codirector and research principal investigator. This issue raises a couple of delicate questions that are not often discussed publicly. First, what is it about the safety of groups with similar characteristics (such as race, ethnicity, or gender) that enables group members who may be marginalized in typical professional development settings to be more open with their critical feedback to support providers? And second, "how can we help our candidates be more open with their feelings" (Vicki's question), especially when candidates do not have access to other support groups?

PART FIVE

SETTING BOUNDARIES

CHAPTER TEN

MANAGING THE MENTORING RELATIONSHIP

How do you mentor someone who is eager to improve but unable to translate feedback into action? Does more mentoring make a difference? In this case, we find frustration on both sides when time and effort are not enough to move a teacher closer to her goal of National Board Certification.

CASE

CASE BY DIANE GARFIELD AND AMBER LEWIS-FRANCIS

"Would the group mind watching my video and giving me some feedback?" Suzanne asked bravely at the October National Board support meeting. Everyone was quite impressed that she had a video ready for viewing so early in the school year. She was anxious to move on with this process and get a solid start, if at all possible. This was a highly motivated candidate.

The video opened with fourth-grade students sitting four to a table. Their desks were clear except for a textbook and a paper in front of each child. Suzanne offered clear instructions. "Now open your books to Chapter Thirteen, and answer the questions on your sheet." The students quietly followed directions. Suzanne calmly circulated the room, helping individual children and answering questions as they arose. The group watched for just a few minutes, and then we stopped the video. As experienced support providers and National Board Certified Teachers (NBCTs), we saw immediately that the lesson in the video did not meet the requirements for this portfolio entry: it lacked evidence of both student learning and dynamic interaction between Suzanne and her students. How were the two of us going to support this candidate who was eager but did not seem quite ready for the challenge of National Board Certification?

Our group of twenty-five Middle Childhood Generalist candidates meets monthly as part of a regional support group for National Board candidates. We begin by discussing the board standards, finding examples in classroom practice, and creating outlines of lessons that reflect these standards. We carefully dissect portfolio entry requirements and help candidates develop time lines for completing the National Board portfolio and preparing for the assessment center examinations. A good portion of each session is spent viewing candidate videos, reading portfolio entries, and providing constructive feedback to each other. In the early sessions, we work to foster connections among the group members and establish community guidelines so candidates will feel confident supporting one another without depending solely on us for feedback.

Displaying your own teaching practice in videos can be unnerving for candidates. A high level of trust is necessary to allow others inside a classroom that has been traditionally a teacher's private domain. Before viewing videos, we stress that the aim is to help candidates decide if they have a video that in fact meets the requirements for that entry. We ask them to do this in three ways: looking for technical problems that interfere with viewing and understanding what is occurring in the video, citing examples of clear and convincing evidence of meeting the standards in the entry, and asking clarifying questions when it was not clear if the evidence is there. Through this clarifying process, candidates are often able to see for themselves if their videos are successful in demonstrating the teaching standards in practice.

The feedback discussion about Suzanne's video was awkward. This was the first video we had seen as a group, and we all wanted to offer positive comments, but we could find little to say. The group responded with general comments such as: "You really have a nice manner with the children." "You smile a lot." "Your classroom feels warm and comfortable." We were pleased with the group's positive comments and attitude, but we were not there to tell Suzanne that she is a nice person. We were there to support her in her endeavor to become an NBCT, and our job was to show our group how to provide the type of feedback that would move Suzanne closer to success.

Viewing Suzanne's video provided us an opportunity to model questioning techniques that probe for clear and convincing evidence of standard alignment. We tried to guide her gently by asking questions such as: "How are students actively involved in constructing their learning?" "What do you do to address the learning needs of all of your students?" "What came after this lesson?" Suzanne became quiet and withdrawn as she realized she lacked answers to these questions. Although the group gave her suggestions for how she might proceed in creating a lesson with clearly stated goals, where the children could be actively involved in learning, she left that day feeling badly about her start on this process. It was not clear, however, if she was just discouraged or if she still did not fully understand what was missing and how to go about improving her practice.

At the next meeting, we watched a variety of candidate videos. The more we watched, the better the group became at identifying evidence of standards in practice and the required elements for the portfolio entry. Several videos were outstanding. The children in these lessons were fully involved in their task; they were asked to think, collaborate, come up with their own solution, and, finally, demonstrate their understanding in different modes. Candidates often expressed gratitude when group members pointed out evidence in the videos of meeting the standards in ways that the candidates themselves had not yet noticed. Yet many of these candidates still decided to redo their videos as they gained a deeper understanding of what was being asked of them.

Suzanne also brought a video to show. She said that she was happy with her progress and felt that this one was a great improvement over the last. Our hearts sank, however, as we watched the students in her class talk in groups about how to complete a comprehension worksheet. This video reflected some improvements, but it still fell short of meeting the specifications of the portfolio entry. Had Suzanne not understood our previous comments? Did she not have a clear understanding of the portfolio entry expectations? Or, worse, was she not yet able to internalize the standards well enough to become a board-certified teacher? If that was the case, what could we do?

We knew that this group had become skilled at providing clear and supportive feedback, but in this instance, the other teachers did not want to comment or ask questions. In the awkward silence that followed, Suzanne looked to us, the support providers, for guidance. But we were worried about how to proceed without hurting her feelings. We told her that this video was a big improvement over the previous one, but the lesson was still lacking in clear, articulated goals. We asked questions that would help us to understand if there was more to this lesson than we could see on the video. Were there opportunities for the students to show understanding in ways other than answering questions on a worksheet? What about the students who were unable to adequately read the material? Other members of the group followed our lead by asking questions of their own. What accommodations did she provide for her diverse learners? Why did she feel this curriculum topic was important for her students? These were hard questions to ask, and she did not have answers. We told her that these things were not readily apparent in the video, so it would be difficult to use it as evidence for a written analysis that must address these issues. She left appearing downcast about this process but still not entirely defeated. She said she wanted to take our questions and comments home and try again.

Over the next few months, Suzanne's level of motivation remained high. She regularly arrived with written work and videos and attended all the supplemental meetings we periodically offered. However, now Suzanne would allow only us, not members of the group, to provide her with feedback. When other candidates would offer to read an entry or view her video, she would politely decline and sit to wait for one of us to be free. The time constraints of providing feedback in the group setting did not allow for the in-depth analysis she was seeking. She would ask one of us to view her latest work in private. It seemed that she wanted an NBCT to give her a formula for passing. As difficult as it was for us to accommodate these requests, we understood her reluctance to share her work publicly. When we went through the certification process, we too felt insecure about sharing our work with more than a few trusted individuals.

In the numerous one-on-one sessions we held with Suzanne, she seemed to focus only on the literal interpretation of following directions. In between these meetings, she would e-mail us often for clarification and further instructions. When we tried to address bigger problems, such as the fact that her activities had no clear goals and there was no analysis in her writing, she continued to focus on surface issues. Although the quality of her curriculum choices and writing did show improvement, she remained focused on providing additional description of what was happening in her classroom rather than analysis of why she did what she did as a teacher. The question we continued to ask her was, "Why?" Why did she choose this lesson? Why was this lesson important for her particular students? Why were her stated goals appropriate? Her stock response to these questions was that they were state, district, or school requirements or mandated curriculum.

While continuing to demand our individual time and support, she seemed to react defensively to the feedback we offered by refusing to incorporate many of our suggestions. We were beginning to feel resentful of the excessive amount of time we were spending with Suzanne, yet she commented that she felt we were not giving her enough support. We also felt this was siphoning off attention and feedback other members of our group needed. We were concerned that we were not providing equitable support to the candidates who were not as demanding.

Our natural instinct as teachers was to want to teach all of our candidates how to achieve National Board Certification. We know this is not possible and not what this process is about. National Board Certification is a process of self-reflection and analysis, and each individual has to find his or her own path to completion, growing as a result. The situation with Suzanne forced us to reflect on our role as support providers. Is it possible to "overmentor" a candidate pursuing this certification? How do we as support providers balance the needs of our candidates against the frustration and burnout that result from overcommitting our time? Should we make a policy that we will read and provide feedback for only one entry per candidate? Would that afford an adequate as well as equitable level of support without compromising the success of the group? What are appropriate boundaries for candidates like Suzanne?

COMMENTARIES

COMMENTARY BY RACHEL A. LOTAN

How can support providers resolve the tension between facilitating teacher learning while supporting teachers in their preparations for a high-stakes performance assessment? Bravely and early into the school year, Suzanne was the first in her group to volunteer to share the video of her fourth-grade classroom. Yet within a few minutes, Suzanne's support providers, Diane and Amber, stopped the video. Based on their extensive experience and without much hesitation, they determined that her video did not meet the requirements of the portfolio entry Suzanne was attempting to address. Saddened but with considerable certainty, they cast doubt on Suzanne's readiness for National Board Certification.

I worried for the candidate by the end of the second paragraph. It seemed to me that Diane and Amber did not consider this candidate an accomplished teacher, ready for the National Board. Will this be a case of self-fulfilling prophecy, I wondered?

Diane and Amber rightfully acknowledge that a high level of trust is necessary for "opening the classroom door" to colleagues, coaches and mentors, administrators, or parents. They spend much time and effort building a community for the candidates who view and analyze their videos together, read portfolio entries, and provide feedback to each other. They take time to develop a shared vision of accomplished practice and provide some guidance to candidates for making good choices for a video. However, although she showed two different videos, Suzanne was not able to respond to the questions posed to her regarding her instructional choices in a way that reflected her understanding of the National Board teaching standards. Progressively, she was leaving the sessions feeling badly and appearing depressed. Still, she did not give up and resolved to improve her performance. But trust seemed to be eroding.

Suzanne's routine response to the unrelenting "why" questions of her mentors was that her lessons were based on "state, district, or school requirements or mandated curriculum." While quoting

Suzanne's explanation, the authors fail to comment on it. It struck a chord with me. It is a case of the impact of mandated, scripted, teacher-proof curricula on deskilling the teaching profession, I decided.

Like so many other students who feel exposed, unable to demonstrate success, and whose competence is questioned publicly, Suzanne became quiet and withdrawn. Who wouldn't? Reluctant to continue sharing her work with members of the group and thus risking yet another failure, she requested more personalized and private help from her mentors. Responding generously to Suzanne's needs, Diane and Amber spent a good deal of time in numerous one-on-one sessions, pushing and probing her thinking, urging her to inquire into and reflect on her practice. Suzanne still did not understand what she needed to do.

The genuine concerns and anguished reflections of the final paragraph echoed for me the sentiments of many teachers who have students with special needs in their classrooms. Suzanne was motivated; she wanted to succeed; she did everything that was asked of her. But she needed more. Rather than drawing boundaries and becoming totally dependent on the exclusive interactions with the mentors who do their best to remediate, under what conditions could Suzanne have become a true member of the community of learners in her group? Finally, this is a case of teaching and learning in a heterogeneous setting, I concluded. If so, what are the responsibilities of the teacher-mentor in creating an environment where participants are able to demonstrate what they can rather than what they cannot do, thus increasing the likelihood of improved learning and attainable success?

Reflecting on my many years of working with veteran and novice teachers, I have learned that no effort should be too much when the main purpose is facilitating teacher learning. Just like a classroom full of students with a wide range of previous academic achievement and intellectual strengths and needs, any group of teachers represents a wide range of pedagogical knowledge and great variability in instructional practices. As long as the teacher is willing to keep trying, is open to systematic observations in her classroom, is willing to engage in analysis of the data, and is ready to reflect together on how to make things work better, my instructional team and I devote the time and muster the energy to stand by her and support her in her learning.

However, when helping a teacher develop her practice in the context of a high-stakes performance assessment, it seems to me that the rules change a little. The question of whether there can be overmentoring for a teacher trying to demonstrate the accomplished nature of her practice, as is the case for National Board candidates, is a painful, albeit legitimate, one. Ideally, if support providers had the necessary resources and time to devote to candidates (and most of them would wish to do so), supporting teacher learning would and should be the definitive objective because it will be the students who ultimately benefit. However, within this assessment context, support providers have both personal and professional boundaries to which they need to adhere. Given limited and often nonexistent resources, we do the best we can.

COMMENTARY BY WENDY HACKE

Diane and Amber ask many questions, but they ignored a very important one: Why might this teacher be reluctant to show her work to other candidates? As we read the case, we learn that Diane and Amber had also hesitated to share their work. They write, "We understood her reluctance to share her work publicly. When we went through the certification process, we too felt insecure about sharing our work with more than a few trusted individuals." They do not, however, elaborate on why they acted this way, which could have had a bearing on this case. I would like to focus my commentary on why *I* hesitated to share my work when I was a candidate to give insight into why candidates might behave like this.

I believe, like Diane and Amber, that "National Board Certification is a personal process of self-reflection and analysis, and each individual has to find his or her own path to completion, growing as a result." But I have also come to understand that reluctance can sometimes be a good part of the journey. My unwillingness to share my work in my support group led to three things. First, I did not certify the first year. Second, being an advanced candidate during the next year enabled me to grow in the way that Diane and Amber believe the National Board Certification process is designed.

Finally, it led me to a better understanding of what my current role as a support provider entails.

When I began the certification process, I considered myself to be a highly skilled teacher. All of the feedback I had gotten over my twenty-year career had been that my teaching was above average. Also, my grades in achieving two master's degrees allowed me to graduate with distinction because of a 4.0 grade point average—a fact that led me to believe that National Board Certification would be easy. But when I received my portfolio and began reading the requirements of the entries, my confidence fizzled. Much of what was asked had been neither part of my course work nor what was expected in my current teaching assignment. I became concerned that I might not be ready for certification and might need to learn much more to be the teacher my students deserved. So I joined a local support group that met monthly. But listening to the work of other group members only added to my concern. They were doing things that clearly met the standards, while I was still struggling to learn how I needed to change my practice to meet them.

This realization raised some issues that led directly to my reluctance to share my work and allowed me to use the time I spent at the meetings to learn more about what it meant to be an effective teacher. Like Suzanne, I shared my videos only with the group; I refused to share the commentary. Instead, the support providers let me e-mail my commentary to them, and they e-mailed their suggestions back to me. They did not question my reluctance. Since I had actively participated in the discussions of others' work, they seemed to accept that my interaction style did not follow the norm, and they accommodated to it.

My support providers' willingness to let me begin my journey this way gave me the confidence I needed to share all of my material with my support group during the year of my advanced candidacy. They appeared to understand that my first year focused on building trust with a community that I did not know. When I was a child, my family had moved around a lot because my father was in the air force. This meant that every eighteen months or so, I had to start over, trying to find my place in a new community where friendships had already been established, a task that was made even harder because my appearance was different from other children. I had ptosis—abnormal drooping of the upper eyelid—and was often ostracized and ridiculed by my peers.

Things did not change much as an adult. Twice I was denied employment because of discrimination based on my appearance. This, combined with the fact that a few of my colleagues publicly made snide remarks about my candidacy (such as "National Board Certification amounts to merit pay; anyone who wants to be certified must think they were better than everyone else"), contributed to my wariness of sharing my work with people I saw only once a month, especially since I did not feel that my work measured up to theirs. So while I had always believed that collaboration was the best way to ensure a strong learning environment, it took me a year to realize that I had missed a valuable part of the journey by not sharing my work. It also took that year to reassure myself that I had found a respectful professional community, one that had student learning at the center of evaluating a teacher's efforts.

In hindsight, I know that had I not gone through this experience, I would not be so understanding of candidates who want to navigate an unusual personal journey. I recognize that many who come to my support group are not ready to certify and would be traumatized to show their work to others. But they become ready through the learning that goes on vicariously as they help others examine their practice. As long as candidates contribute something to the group, I believe they should be able to seek the kind of support that meets their unique needs as they grow through their very personal journey toward certification.

As a support provider, I try to meet candidates where they are and accommodate their individual interaction styles. Does this mean I let them sap my time and energy? Of course not! Just as Diane and Amber wondered, you can overmentor and burn out if you do not set boundaries that afford everyone, including yourself, adequate and equitable time for support.

TEACHING NOTE

Diane and Amber are National Board Certified Teachers and veteran support providers of groups of National Board candidates. They are experienced in setting the stage for sharing one's practice by providing a vision of accomplished practice and creating a climate of trust. Generally they appear to be successful in establishing an ethos of inquiry in which teachers learn from and value feedback on their teaching from peers. So they're challenged when one motivated teacher, whose teaching does not yet demonstrate the National Board teaching standards, no longer uses the group process for feedback. Rather, she seeks support solely from them.

This case explores questions of how to provide constructive feedback on practice and what to do when a teacher neither knows how to respond to analytical questions nor shows evidence of incorporating the feedback into her teaching. It also examines issues of equity, personal boundaries, and potential burnout when trying to manage the mentor relationship.

ISSUES AND QUESTIONS

Developing a Vision of Accomplished Practice

One of the biggest issues for support providers who work with National Board candidates is helping the teachers develop a vision of accomplished teaching when their practice does not show evidence of that vision. The National Board teaching standards provide extensive narrative descriptions of what individual standards mean. But unless teachers can operationalize the standards, they will find it difficult to produce and analyze practice in light of these standards.

Examine the ways that Diane and Amber tried to develop the vision of accomplished practice with Suzanne, the candidate in this case, and their support group. If you were using teaching standards to develop a vision of accomplished practice, what kinds of activities would you plan? How could you ensure that group members understood both what was involved in the vision and that there are multiple ways to enact the vision?

Providing Constructive Feedback

Deciding how to respond to a teacher's video of teaching—when failing to see any evidence of standards—is another common challenge for mentors. Diane and Amber want to find some positive comments to make to encourage Suzanne. But they also understand that they must provide constructive feedback so she could improve her practice according to the vision of the teaching standards. Diane and Amber chose to pose the kinds of analytical questions suggested in the portfolio directions to direct Suzanne's attention to the expectations of the portfolio entry. Look at the questions that they and the support group asked Suzanne during the feedback sessions. Do you think these questions were useful to Suzanne? Why or why not? How would you have handled the situation? Would you have done anything differently?

Working with Heterogeneous Groups

A third common problem is facilitating groups in which group members have diverse capacities and learning levels. K–12 teachers regularly work with heterogeneous groups and must make instructional decisions tailored to the needs of their students. So why should working with adult groups be different? Rachel Lotan draws attention to this parallel in her commentary. Suzanne is demonstrating difficulty understanding the assessment expectations based not only on the teaching standards but also the portfolio directions, the support providers' feedback and questions, and the support group's response to her examples of practice. Diane and Amber had hoped that input from the support group could help Suzanne, but Suzanne turned away from the group. Some people who discussed this case during its development wondered if there were ways that the mentors could have supported Suzanne in sharing her work with the group differently—perhaps with more scaffolding or structure. Rachel Lotan advocates for differentiated support for teachers in mentoring relationships similar to differentiated instruction for heterogeneous groups of students. What do you think of this suggestion? How would differentiation work in collaborative group settings that are facilitated? What would be the impact on the mentors' time? Others wondered if it is possible to provide feedback that is both constructive and safe. Put another way, is it possible to learn without feeling pain? How would you respond to this question?

From Suzanne's Perspective

The case is written from the perspective of two teachers who supported Suzanne in a support group setting. Wendy Hacke's commentary illuminates how challenging this situation can be from the candidate's perspective. Rachel Lotan's commentary also reminds us of the possible constraints on Suzanne's practice based on curriculum requirements or school policies. From Suzanne's perspective, can you think of reasons that she may have reacted to the feedback the way she did and the choices she made in seeking support?

How Much Is Enough? What Is Fair?

After spending numerous individual sessions with Suzanne without seeing much evidence of growth, Diane and Amber began to feel frustrated and resentful of spending so much time with her. To make matters worse, Suzanne commented that she was not getting enough support. At the end of the narrative, the authors raise a series of questions about the integrity of their mentoring, equity toward other candidates, and personal boundaries to prevent burnout. Examine the set of questions. What is your position on each of them? Explain your answers.

In her commentary, Rachel Lotan questions how a high-stakes assessment might influence the quality and quantity of mentoring. Lee Shulman also considers this issue in Chapter Eleven. What is your position?

MISSION IMPOSSIBLE
The Exasperating Mentee

How do you mentor someone who just "doesn't get it"?" What if, despite your best efforts, your mentee remains unclear about expectations and unable to work productively either alone or within a group? In this case, both support provider and peer mentor struggle to support a teacher with fundamental performance problems.

CASE

CASE, PART ONE, BY ELIZABETH MATCHETT

"Oh, no," I thought, as I looked around the room at the group and spotted Sophie. It was the first of nine monthly support group meetings that I would facilitate for teachers pursuing National Board Certification. There were about twenty-five teachers around the large table; some I had never seen before, some I knew in passing, and some I knew too well. Sophie was one of those. She had attended several seminars I had directed that focused on learning best practices for teaching world languages. As a participant, Sophie was always a challenge. I knew when I saw her that I was

---

Pseudonyms have been used to maintain the confidentiality of people and places in the case.

going to be in for a long year and a lot of work. Still, I was willing to work with her and do my best.

There were many reasons that I found it difficult to work with her. She skipped meetings, often neglected assignments or turned in work late, interrupted the meetings she *did* come to by asking off-topic questions, and just generally "didn't get it." The one project she did turn in was inadequate because she did not follow directions. In fact, it was apparent when she made her presentation to the large group that she had not understood the material at all. Working with her was like working with a student who needed extra help: you knew you had to put in additional work and time, look for alternate ways to explain things, and be extremely patient. The difference was that Sophie is an adult, and I tend to expect more of adults. Having patience with her was unbelievably taxing because she did not follow advice or react appropriately to suggestions.

My experience with adult learners had taught me that they generally fall into two categories: those who come to the workshop or seminar because they want to be there and learn, and those who come because someone else has directed them to be there or because there is an extrinsic reward. Sophie actually fell into the former category; she wanted to be there. However, she did not react to guidance like the majority of people in that category did. She did not seem to reflect and incorporate; rather, she argued and refused.

Like many of the other candidates I work with, Sophie is not a native speaker of English. She came from Mexico several years ago as an experienced teacher and immediately began to teach Spanish for native speakers at her current school. But unlike the other candidates who sometimes need help with grammar, Sophie needed help with the basics of writing.

I wondered how Sophie would do with National Board Certification. None of my dealings with her had given me the slightest impression that she was "National Board material." "Wait a minute," I said to myself, "that's not fair. You're supposed to be an educator. Educators don't prejudge people and decide who can or can't do something. They educate!" So although my gut told me that this was a mistake, my heart and mind told me that my professional and ethical responsibility was to take her forward from where she was, with the hope that she would learn something from going through the certification process.

But as I feared, Sophie proved to be a challenge at every meeting she attended. Whenever she contributed, she rambled on and on about how important achieving certification was to her rather than talking about the standards or a lesson she was preparing. She said she was being persecuted at her school by her colleagues and administration who didn't understand the special needs of her students, who were predominantly native speakers of Spanish. Teaching them required a different set of skills and norms, she said. The process was hard for her. She had a lot of difficulty writing. No one understood her problems. The rest of us must be geniuses. Could anyone actually help her get her teaching down on paper? Did we truly understand the directions? They made no sense whatsoever to her. She went on and on and on. Sometimes her questions were similar to those of the other candidates, but she asked them at odd times, such as fifteen minutes or so after we had already addressed them. I could not decide if she hadn't been listening, hadn't understood, or needed to process the information by endlessly talking about it. I tried to think of what Sophie needed as a learner and how I could give it to her as an educator.

Every facilitation skill I had ever learned was called on in dealing with Sophie during group meetings. At first, I really wanted to be fair—to give her the opportunity to share, seek advice from her colleagues, and learn from others' experiences. But she rarely listened to what the group had to say. We had set up group norms, but she didn't seem to understand that questions needed to follow along with the topic of discussion. I think she probably didn't realize that when she had a turn to talk, she would go off-topic and labor on for much too long. She didn't bring to the table questions focused on teaching and learning. Rather, it seemed that she just needed a place to vent about her professional and personal frustrations. With other candidates, I was usually able to redirect questions by focusing on the standards or on the portfolio directions. If I tried to do this with her issues, she accused me of not understanding her situation. On more than one occasion she started to cry. I had never encountered an adult learner exactly like her.

To their credit, the other candidates made every effort to support Sophie, at least at first. We had spent a lot of time as a group talking about methods to assist one another and the kinds of behaviors that a productive group member would exhibit. For example, when looking at a colleague's video or reading an entry, a supportive group member will ask questions based on the standards that are designed to get the candidate to reflect and grow in the way she looks at her teaching. The problem was that with Sophie, we were responding to what she said rather than what she showed us; she never brought a video or entry for us to look at. All of our interactions with her centered on her feelings about the process or her school. I noticed that the other candidates attempted to ask reflective questions of Sophie regarding her concerns. After awhile, however, when they noticed that Sophie didn't respond to their support in expected ways, there was often a prolonged silence after she spoke in the group. Looking around the group, I could see some members exchanging impatient glances or looking away to hide their irritation.

After every meeting, I would go home and think about her. I wondered what I could do to help her function better in the group. As much as I tried to avoid it, I felt dislike for her welling up in me like bile. I couldn't help it. Could it be that I felt on some level that she was sabotaging my overall success with the group? Part of me was angry that she was using up valuable group time, and part of me was angry at myself for being unable to meet her individual needs. I hoped that maybe all she really needed was that time to talk things out, to process the information verbally. Maybe she was actually internalizing all we talked about and would be able to use it later in her teaching and writing. Regardless, waiting for her to finish her thoughts was frustrating for me and the rest of the group.

Even then, I wished I could have referred her to another support provider who had no history with her, but there was no one else. I felt that although I was trying to be as fair with her as I could, there was human emotion in the way. I felt frustrated knowing that our group was all she had and my support was not good enough. I felt responsible for her success and inadequate to meet the challenge. Nevertheless, I told myself, not functioning well in a support group really has nothing to do with becoming National Board Certified. It is nice as a support provider when your group members are easy to work with, but all of them are not. I was her support provider, and regardless of how I felt about her, I had the professional obligation to put forth my best effort for her. I hoped that her written entries would allow me to see an aspect of her as a teacher and a professional that I had been unable to discover in group meetings.

But when she finally started writing something, no revelations surfaced. She had reported that she had trouble writing, but the work I received went beyond that. She faxed me sections of lessons with incomplete descriptions and called them a draft. When I faxed back my feedback with specific questions that pertained to the entry directions and standards—typical of the kind of feedback I gave other candidates—she asked for a private meeting so I could better explain things to her. She said she didn't understand what I meant. Other candidates accepted or disregarded my suggestions according to their own professional voice. The conversation during the meeting with her was strained; she just did not seem to understand what I was saying. If I advised her against something, such as describing her students in terms of good or bad, bright or slow, she argued with me. If I asked her why she chose PowerPoint for the topic of a lesson rather than a language theme, she cried. Talking with her sapped my energy and exhausted me. Moreover, I was unsure if we had accomplished anything at all. After this experience, I put her off. There were other candidates with whom I met regularly, but I could not bring myself to do so with Sophie again. Yet the educator in me rebelled. I felt so guilty and sometimes worthless. I was beginning to see that I could not—or would not—be able to meet her needs, and that prospect frightened me. I did not want to accept that I did not possess the skills to meet her needs. We continued to communicate through the fax machine. I would fax her my questions, but she never faxed back any rewrites. In all the time I worked with her, I never saw one complete draft.

About three weeks before the portfolios were due, I sent an e-mail to the group giving a deadline for getting drafts for feedback to me so that I would have enough turnaround time before they had to be sent off. Many members of the group contacted me asking frantically for last-minute help, which I gave. Sophie did not call or fax me during this time. I did not contact her personally, but I wondered how she was doing. I also wondered if my wait-and-see attitude had been the best course of action with her. Ultimately I feel that each candidate has to make his or her own decisions. Although I strongly doubted that she would achieve certification (indeed, I doubted if she would get the portfolio done), I had not expressed any of this to her verbally. Whose responsibility is it to tell a candidate to stop or continue? Through all this inordinate amount of troubled wondering about Sophie, I was reading many entries each day from other candidates, giving comments and encouragement. The deadline I had imposed passed, and I breathed a sigh of relief, knowing that I would not have to look at any more entries until the next certification cycle began. I could rest. I deliberately put Sophie out of my mind, thinking that whatever else had happened, it was too late now for me to do anything else for her.

It was Tuesday night, with portfolios due on Friday, and I was at an evening party at my daughter's preschool, celebrating the end of the school year. I had a glass of wine in my hand and was having a wonderful conversation with a good friend when my cell phone rang. It was Sophie. She asked if she could fax me a "rough draft" of the final entry she was working on. My mouth fell open, and my heart and brain hardened (to match my gut). "No," I said, after a pause, "you can't." And with a perfunctory farewell, I hung up on her. I never heard from her again.

Epilogue

Imagine my surprise when I looked up NBCTs in November and found that Sophie had certified. Maybe she internalized the standards during our support group meetings. Maybe my faxing and conferences made a difference for her. Maybe the whole process coalesced at the last moment for her. She has since moved away from my support area, and I do not know what she is doing now. I continue as a support provider and have never encountered anyone as difficult to mentor as she. Still, I wonder about her.

CASE, PART TWO, BY DAWNE ASHTON

Sophie was a teacher in my school district where I was serving as a consulting teacher to assist teachers with problems or special needs in classroom management, curriculum, and teaching strategies.

When Sophie began working toward her National Board Certification, I had already been working with her for two years as a peer mentor. My assignment had been to assist her in whatever area she wished to improve on. She was a volunteer in this program, so my outcome with her was not evaluated or shared with any administration. This relationship allowed Sophie the opportunity to share with me her frustrations about her unsuccessful peer relationships and problems she was experiencing with parents and students and to ask for advice and support. The school administration was also extremely concerned with the regularity of issues that arose for Sophie. Our relationship did not give me the opportunity to demand or enforce any changes that I thought might be valuable in either her classroom practice or her professional relationships. I could only attempt to provide some helpful ideas and suggest that some changes on her part might make her struggles with students, parents, teachers, and administrators diminish.

In my normal role as a peer mentor and during regular visits to her classroom, we discussed her ideas for how she would pursue the various curricular areas of her National Board portfolio. She trusted me in many things, but since I was a candidate for National Board Certification at the same time that she was and we were working on it during the first year of the World Languages certificate, we both knew that no one was an expert in the process. She had many creative ideas for her portfolio entries, and we settled on several that she decided to follow. As she began to teach to these ideas, I saw more clearly that the greatest weakness in her teaching was the lack of an overarching, cohesive curriculum in her instructional program. Her curriculum was made up of a series of six to eight small, seemingly unrelated units (depending on which course and level) that she stretched into a year of work for her students by teaching them in a computer lab and demanding that they create all results in the form of Web pages before submitting them. For example, she used the concept of learning homophones for a several-months-long unit as the students created alphabetical Web-based dictionaries. Superficially this might seem like a great idea, but the result was that she covered very little of the rich curriculum that was available to teach to the native Spanish-speaking students.

My work with Sophie consisted of putting out small fires and attending to her most pressing needs. Whenever I would begin to ask her to address the broader curriculum questions, the latest problem would take precedence, such as preparing for her classroom evaluations by the school administration. It was no surprise to me that while she was working on her National Board portfolio, it became the focus of all of her teaching.

She changed our regular consultation meetings into reviewing her latest efforts on plans, videos, and understanding the National Board portfolio instructions. Several times my visits that had once been for observing her teaching strategies were changed at the last minute when she asked me to be her videographer. Then during our postobservation conference time, she focused only on the National Board process and her efforts at writing. My consulting time with Sophie averaged two to three visits or e-mails per week all year during her year of candidacy.

Sophie and I both attended the monthly Saturday support group meetings for National Board candidates. It was often unfortunate that she demanded an inordinate amount of the group process time to make her individual pleas, especially when I knew how much assistance she had access to with my regular visits and consultations. It was difficult for me to watch her in the group as she was so "me, me" focused, repeating questions about items we had recently discussed, demanding a focus on her problems or lack of understanding, and rarely, if ever, assisting anyone else. Frequently when she spoke up to voice her questions or misunderstandings, group members would roll their eyes or mutter to neighbors. Her native-speaker status and degrees from a Spanish-speaking university could have made her a resource for others in the group, but that was never the case. I empathized with our group leader and admired her patience and support in her efforts to give equitable assistance to Sophie, especially since I knew how complex Sophie's needs were.

Sophie complained frequently that the process wasn't fair to a non-English native, as she was not allowed to write her portfolios in her native Spanish language. Toward the spring, she told me that an old friend was helping her with her English. Actually, my impression is that her English is quite good, but she makes an occasional error, as most people do in a second language. In March and April she mentioned receiving help from him and several others. When others began working with her, she stopped showing me her portfolios. When the due date came for submitting the portfolios, Sophie called me and said she didn't trust herself to pack the portfolio materials correctly. She came to my home, and together we packed her portfolio to ready it for shipping. She submitted it with several days to spare.

After the school year ended, I spent time preparing for the National Board World Languages exam. Sophie didn't ask for any assistance in preparing for the exam or offer any to anyone else. I received a call from her when the test period was ending. She was very ill and was scheduled for an appendectomy. She could not go to her test. She asked what she could do since she needed to sit for the exam in a few days. I recommended that she call and explain the problem to the National Board. Apparently she did this, but she did not tell me the details of when she was finally able to take the exam.

The following fall she did not volunteer again for the peer mentoring program in our district, so we had less contact. At the end of November, she received word that she had earned her National Board Certification and wrote an e-mail to me saying how proud she was that she, as a nonnative speaker of English who did not attend school in the United States, could achieve this goal when so many others did not.

That winter she had increased interpersonal and professional issues with staff, parents, students, and the school administration. She again called for me to work with her and support her through a difficult time. I attempted to guide her into wise decisions to protect herself professionally and her future as an educator. Her focus stayed on the immediate and not the long-range bigger picture. In April, five months after achieving National Board Certification, the district administration asked her to resign her tenured position, and Sophie left the district.

COMMENTARY

COMMENTARY BY LEE S. SHULMAN

The case of Sophie is a telling tragedy with several plots. It is an account of a courageous, ambitious, perhaps opportunistic experienced teacher who left the comfort and familiarity of her native land to teach Spanish to American high school students and there experienced serious challenges as both a teacher and as a mentee, painfully reported by Elizabeth. It is also a story about "mission impossible": an account of the dilemmas faced by Elizabeth and Dawne when they were asked to mentor a difficult colleague in whom each eventually lost faith, both as a candidate and, apparently, as a teacher. Finally, since Sophie eventually passed the certification process in spite of the severe doubts and criticisms expressed by her two colleagues, I believe these are also narratives associated with an error of measurement, with a flawed assessment. If Elizabeth and Dawne's accounts are credible, it is unlikely that Sophie should have been certified by the National Board, and yet she was. Does this mean that there is something fundamentally wrong with the National Board assessments? Did Elizabeth and Dawne overmentor Sophie and, in some cases, collude in her having inappropriate help in preparing the artifacts to be assessed? Did they behave unethically when they withdrew from their respective mentoring roles, or did they do precisely what they were ethically bound to do?

Zealous Advocacy for the Candidate

Reading these cases reminds me of a basic distinction in the practice of law between the attorney's responsibility to serve as a zealous advocate for his or her client, as against that same attorney's obligation to serve as an officer of the court, responsible to act in a manner that preserves and protects the integrity of the system of justice more generally.

To whom are lawyers more responsible: to the clients (which could be a defendant in a criminal case, the public itself in a criminal case, or either side in a civil case) whom they are hired or called to represent or to the larger system of justice? For example, if a defense attorney gains access to evidence that would incriminate her client, must she reveal the existence of that evidence? If a prosecutor learns that DNA testing proves that the defendant could not have committed the crime but the defense attorney is not sharp enough to mount the appropriate challenge, what should the prosecuting attorney do?

I raise these questions because they may well be germane to the case at hand. If someone is coaching a candidate for college admissions, or National Board Certification, or even the earning of a driver's license, and it is apparent to the coach that the candidate does not meet the appropriate standards, what should the coach do? What if the coach realizes that she can teach the candidate how to perform at a much higher level on the test than the candidate can actually perform in practice? Then what should the coach do? And what if the mentor is coaching someone for a surgery specialty board? Is that different from coaching someone for a spelling bee or a swimming meet? And where, in that range of examples, does mentoring for board certification fall? In all these cases, we ask on behalf of the mentor, To whom do you owe greater responsibility: the well-being of your "student" or the integrity of the larger system? To paraphrase the first-century rabbi Hillel, if you are not working on behalf of your student, who will support and advocate for her? And if you act solely on behalf of your student's success, what harm might you cause to the larger society?

WHAT IS THE GOAL OF MENTORING RELATED TO A HIGH-STAKES ASSESSMENT?

Sophie's two mentors found themselves in difficult positions. When you are mentoring someone, you probably should not be judging or evaluating that person harshly. You should be supportive and should treat him or her with unconditional positive regard and with high and positive expectations. Nevertheless, mentoring or coaching involves a kind of social contract. The relationship should be reciprocal, respectful, and fully collaborative. Sophie repeatedly failed to deliver on her own commitments as part of the mentoring relationship with both Dawne and Elizabeth.

There is an interesting ambiguity about the ways in which National Board support groups function that may well exacerbate some of the problems highlighted in this case. On the one hand, the Board and its support groups take pride in the assertion that in order to improve their performance on the portfolio-intensive board assessments, the candidates must improve their teaching and document those improvements. By using the Board's standards as guidelines, benchmarks, and explicit goals, the quality of the candidate's classroom teaching is itself enhanced.

On the other hand, the support groups clearly encourage candidates to join because participation will increase their chances of success on the assessments. In that sense, they offer inducements similar to those offered by Stanley Kaplan or Princeton Review to those aspiring to score well on the SAT, the LSAT, or the GRE. This places both the candidates and the mentors in a somewhat awkward position. Should mentors coach candidates only in ways that will improve their classroom teaching? Or should they do whatever is needed to help them become test-wise for the NBPTS portfolio exercises and assessment centers, even if that means teaching them things that will never make them better teachers? Or is this, in practice, a meaningless dichotomy?

IS THE BOARD ASSESSMENT FLAWED?

What about the fact that Sophie certified? We know nothing of Sophie's performance as a teacher in Mexico; we cannot presume to know whether her peers in Mexico judged her as highly accomplished or whether she had many of the same problems in her native land and native language as those reported in the two cases before us. Nevertheless, the independent accounts of her work as both a teacher and candidate (from Dawne) and solely as a Board candidate (from Elizabeth) persuade me that she did not meet the standards for National Board Certification. Moreover, she did not seem to meet the standards for responsible colleagueship either. For purposes of this commentary, I will not entertain the possibility that the two case writers erred in their evaluation of Sophie and the Board assessment was accurate, though that could be the case. Instead, let's assume that Sophie is a "false positive," a successful candidate who should not have been certified. Why might that have happened?

False positives happen. So do false negatives. They are inevitable for any test—with the medical boards and the SAT, with the California bar exam as well as the CPA. They occur with blood tests and with MRIs. If we raise the bar for passing the board so high that close calls like Sophie will never certify, we will then risk failing far too many worthy candidates—the problem of "false negatives." And since the first-time pass rate for the board is only in the 30 percent range already, this doesn't seem like a reasonable strategy.

Dawne's case, however, suggests that Sophie's pedagogical gifts were at the lesson or unit level. She could craft an exquisite individual lesson. However, Dawne asserts, Sophie's teaching lacked continuity and coherence from lesson to lesson or unit to unit. The structure of the Board's assessments may be biased toward focusing too much on individual lessons (especially on the all-important video segments) and insufficiently on continuity and coherence over time.

Did Sophie pass because her mentors supported her excessively and crossed the boundary between responsible mentoring and both committing and permitting work on behalf of the candidate that was not really representative of her real competence? A portfolio-based assessment is always vulnerable to that kind of distortion, and yet it may be a danger worth confronting to preserve a highly authentic, empirically valid type of examination whose worth far exceeds that of a traditional objective or essay test.

CLOSING THOUGHTS

When an assessment invites deep mentoring and coaching, which was how the National Board was designed, it needs to provide both mentors and candidates much more explicit guidelines for determining when they are mentoring appropriately and when the mentors and other collaborators must pull back and permit the candidate to work on their own. I sense that these guidelines are currently lacking for National Board support providers. Moreover, this is not a dilemma limited to the National Board. It is an endemic challenge of mentoring. In my many years of mentoring doctoral students during the dissertation process (which resembles coaching for Board Certification in a number of ways), I have often found myself in a similar situation. When are ideas really coming from the student, and when have they come from me? When a student submits the draft of a chapter that is muddled and barely comprehensible, where have I stopped editing and begun to rewrite? Doctoral mentoring is supposed to be a collaborative, supportive relationship, but ultimately the student is responsible for the dissertation and receives credit and substantial recognition for its successful completion. Is there a line that a doctoral mentor should never cross?

At the same time, the coach is also an educator and educational leader writ large. Knowing that any assessment, however sophisticated, is an imperfect measure of someone's "true" ability, the mentor can be confronted with the same dilemma that a good lawyer faces: "I can successfully win this case even though I suspect my client is really guilty." In the law, the guidelines are fairly clear but not perfect. A lawyer is expected to serve as a zealous advocate for her client as long as she does not cross certain procedural boundaries and behave unethically or dishonestly. And there are times and situations when, zealous advocacy notwithstanding, the attorney must act on behalf of the greater good for the society and as an officer of the court, temper advocacy with social responsibility.

TEACHING NOTE

This case consists of two narratives about the challenges of supporting the same teacher. The first, written by Elizabeth Matchett, portrays these challenges from the perspective of Sophie's National Board support group facilitator; the other, by Dawne Ashton, renders her account from the perspective of Sophie's consulting teacher in her district as well as a colleague in Elizabeth's support group. Both authors found Sophie to be manipulative, self-centered, and dysfunctional in group settings and had questions about her capacity to certify. Yet both felt morally and professionally bound to do their best to support Sophie's desire to become a National Board Certified Teacher.

These narratives and the commentary by Lee Shulman provide opportunities to analyze problems and dilemmas relating to mentoring a difficult colleague individually and within groups, as well as ethical and moral issues about supporting teachers who prepare for high-stakes assessments.

ISSUES AND QUESTIONS

Impact of a Common History

In Chapter Twelve, Sandra Dean writes about the trade-offs of mentoring teachers at her school site and raises questions about the challenges of mentoring those whom she knows well. Elizabeth Matchett raises a parallel question, except that the teacher in question, Sophie, and she are not at the same school site. Instead, Elizabeth had Sophie in several previous workshops, and the experience had always been difficult. How does Elizabeth describe Sophie's behavior in previous workshops? How does she prepare herself to work with Sophie? What were her questions? What were her ethical and moral dilemmas? How were her fears realized during the support group meetings? Support your statements with evidence from the case.

Dawne works in the same district as Sophie and is even assigned as her mentor teacher. What is the impact of this other relationship on Dawne's work as one of Sophie's support providers for National Board candidacy?

From Sophie's Perspective

The two narratives that make up this case are written from the perspective of two teachers who supported Sophie in different contexts. Examine both narratives. What do we know about Sophie's background and her commitment to be certified? How did she react during the support group and individually with each of the support providers? From her perspective, can you think of reasons why Sophie acted the way she is described?

Mentoring in Groups

Bringing teachers together to talk about teaching is a challenging endeavor, especially when they are asked to share videos of their teaching, curricula, and student work. For many teachers, making their teaching public in front of others and asking for constructive feedback is risky, sometimes even unnerving. So developing an ethos of inquiry that is also safe is critical if learning is to occur. What were some of Elizabeth's strategies to develop her learning community? What did she do to foster safety and constructive dialogue among group members? If you were the facilitator of a similar group of teachers, how would you develop norms for your learning community? How would you work with a teacher like Sophie, who appears not to have followed the norms of the community?

Mentoring Individually

Mentoring is often described as a close—often intense—mutually beneficial relationship between someone who is more experienced and more powerful with someone less experienced. In the context of supporting veteran teachers or National Board candidates, however, that is not generally the case. Rather, peers typically work together, using the guidelines and standards provided by the National Board certificates, to help one another reflect on and analyze the examples of teaching they have selected for their portfolio entries. Often the mentor is a certified teacher whose authority is based on a metacognitive ability to explain demonstrations of accomplished teaching. Yet there are no issues of power; the "mentees" are not under any obligation to incorporate any of the suggestions made by their mentors or colleagues.

Both Elizabeth and Dawne had individual experiences supporting Sophie—Dawne, more so, since she was Sophie's consulting teacher—and both encountered similar problems. Examine the questions they asked during their interactions with Sophie. Did she respond more constructively to some questions than to others? Why? What might you do if you encounter a person like Sophie in your professional work?

Balancing Personal and Professional Responsibilities

Despite the teachers' many attempts to help Sophie in the group and individually, they continued to question their strategies of mentoring because they rarely saw evidence that they were helpful. Elizabeth wrote poignantly about her angst: "I feel so guilty and sometimes worthless. I was beginning to feel that I couldn't—or wouldn't—be able to meet her needs, and it frightened me." Dawne voiced concern that Sophie wanted to focus only on her portfolio, sabotaging her assignment as a consulting teacher. Clearly both teachers were torn between their professional responsibility as mentors and questions about her capacity to certify, especially since she never showed them completed texts for the portfolio entries.

In his commentary on the two accounts, Lee Shulman draws a parallel to the teachers' dilemma with his distinction between an attorney's responsibility to serve as a zealous advocate for his or her client and the same attorney's obligation to preserve the integrity of the court. To whom is the attorney most responsible? Examine Lee's argument and the comparison to his dilemma while advising doctoral students. As he notes, the problems revealed in these cases are not limited to the National Board: they are "an endemic challenge to mentoring."

We faced a similar dilemma in our National Board network of support providers. In our deliberations we found that participants offer a range of support to candidates; some limit their reading of portfolio entries to the time they spend in their candidate support groups, while others are available almost all the time to read entries. We have discussed this dichotomy in several network meetings but never came to a consensus on the appropriate degree of support. How much assistance do you think is appropriate when supporting teachers for a high-stakes assessment? Should there be a limit on how much help to give any one teacher? Should there be any consequences for a mentee who continually fails to deliver on her commitments (see Chapter Eight for another perspective on this question)? Are there any circumstances under which it is appropriate to abandon a mentee?

Is the Board Assessment Flawed?

To the surprise of her two mentors, Sophie achieved certification. Given the problems they experienced with her, one might raise the question of whether she deserved to certify. Did she certify because of the kind of mentoring that Elizabeth, Dawne, and others in her community provided? Lee Shulman addresses these questions in his comments on the problem of "false positives" and yet provides a solid rationale for the value of preserving this empirically valid type of examination. What are your views on the validity and value of the assessment process? How might you communicate these ideas to others who question the validity and value of the assessment process?

PART SIX

MENTORING ONE'S COLLEAGUES

CHAPTER TWELVE

A CIRCLE OF NATIONAL BOARD CERTIFICATION FRIENDS

Sharing practice and receiving feedback can be difficult even for accomplished teachers. What can mentors do to provide feedback in a way that is constructive, builds trust, and acknowledges the different personalities, backgrounds, and learning styles of their mentees? This issue is key in this case of a veteran educator working with three promising young teachers.

CASE

CASE BY YVONNE DIVANS-HUTCHINSON

"We're going to try out for National Board," my two young colleagues informed me, their eyes alight.

"That's fantastic," I replied. "Congratulations."

"Yeah!" they gushed. "We want to be like you when we grow up." I laughed outright then. Sarah and Sula, both in their mid-twenties with five years of experience as English teachers, had appointed themselves my mentees when I transferred to my high school after teaching junior high and middle school for thirty-three years. I had earned National Board Certification in English Language Arts/Early Adolescence the year before I left.

My friend Rich, the head of our English department, had finally persuaded me to join the staff after three years of cajoling. Apparently he had sung my praises to my young colleagues, for I had scarcely been introduced when they insisted that I become their mentor. Soon after, I accepted an assignment as Sula's field supervisor in the UCLA Teach LA Program. Despite the difference in our ages (my years in teaching exceeded their lifetimes), we shared a passion for learning, teaching, reading, shopping, and laughing.

Sarah, who teaches tenth-grade English and African American literature, is the more easygoing of the two and the daughter of a teacher. She displayed an uncommon classroom presence for a novice and had the makings of an excellent teacher. Sula, my intern, teaches ninth-grade English; she is a bit rougher around the edges but no less promising. She approached her teaching with a gritty intelligence, fiercely determined to eliminate any obstacle that might prevent her from succeeding. She obviously loved teaching and children. What endeared them both to me was their evident passion and the willingness to learn and grow. They fashioned attractive and engaging learning environments in which instruction was student centered. Although they could pass for high school students themselves, they had excellent rapport with their students and held them to rigorous standards.

In the last four years, they have lived up to their promise. Bright, energetic, involved inside and outside the classroom (senior class sponsors, coordinator of the Gifted and Talented Education program, school newspaper adviser), they and their students flourished in attractive, student-centered classroom environments that teemed with excitement. These two were developing into exemplary teachers.

"So, Ms. H., will you be our National Board coach?" They informed me that they had joined a local university-based support group and that they had also been chosen to participate in a supplemental program for African American candidates sponsored by a research grant at the university. The African American support group was established as an effort to better understand reasons for the low rates of African American teachers passing National Board Certification and to consider differentiated support strategies for candidate groups. Sarah and Sula were aware that I had worked as a mentor for the first group associated with this research project the previous year during its inception, but they didn't know at first that I was to be involved with their group. This year's class began with twenty-two candidates, my two colleagues among them. The African American support group met one Saturday a month in addition to the monthly meeting of the larger support group. As a mentor, my duties were to attend the group meetings to help candidates during day-long workshops. One of three mentors, I worked with seven secondary teachers and pledged to make myself available to all of the participants whenever and wherever I was needed.

"So, Ms. H., are you going to coach us?" Little did I know that my "whenever and wherever" would develop into a regular, weekly staff development. Sarah and Sula established their own weekly support group, which met without fail at our school every Wednesday from four o'clock (school ends at 3:09) until nine o'clock at night. We missed only one meeting because of a catastrophic storm of hail and rain in November that flooded our cafeteria, gym, and main office.

Despite the one-time onslaught from the elements, the school is a secure, self-contained, four-story facility with underground parking, which makes it a perfect place to burrow away for an evening of discussion, writing, viewing videos, grading papers, and eating. At first we took turns providing potluck, although it often turned out that I was the only one who prepared or bought food to allow the candidates more time to work. Sarah and Sula invited other members of the grant group to join us. Two of them, Trey and Kenya, attended on a regular basis. Trey, energetic and charismatic, taught middle school social studies and, like Sarah and Sula, is also in his late twenties and a five-year veteran. Kenya is a robust, warmly intelligent woman, who fairly shimmers with enthusiasm. In her mid-thirties, she teaches fifth grade and has eight years in the classroom and two years of administrative experience. Trey and Kenya's participation rounded out an extremely compatible group. In addition, our numbers were occasionally increased by the appearance of one or two of the other grant group candidates and

teachers on our faculty who liked to stay late to catch up on grading or participate in the collegial conversation, and—once or
twice—another NBC coach.

Our Wednesday evening sessions, held in Sula's classroom on
the third floor, began as a love fest, a collegial gathering that called
to mind Alice Walker's statement in her novel *Meridian* (1976): "I
imagine good teaching as a circle of earnest people sitting down
to ask each other meaningful questions. I don't see it as a handing
down of answers." We enjoyed an easygoing, mutually respectful
relationship based on several commonalties in addition to our ethnicity. First, we all taught in urban settings with student popula-
tions that were largely composed of students of color. Our school,
located in south (central) Los Angeles, is a medicine and science
magnet with a 73 percent African American population, 15 percent Latino, and about 2 percent other, including Asian, Middle
Eastern, and Native American. Trey teaches middle school on the
west side of Los Angeles where the population is diverse, consist-
ing of an equal mixture of African American, Latino, Asian, and a
sprinkling of white students. Kenya's elementary school is located
in a middle-class African American neighborhood, and her classroom demographics consists of approximately 95 percent African
American and 5 percent Latino students.

Our first discussion centered on feeling out the process. Naturally the group had plenty of questions about how to get things
done. Sula, a type A personality, had already planned her work
schedule. We pitched ideas about a parent Web site and newsletter
that Sula and Sarah, who often collaborated on classroom projects,
each planned to include as part of Entry Four of the portfolio. Sula
described the family reading night she had scheduled for the late
fall, and Sarah talked about the enthusiastic e-mails she had received from parents in response to the syllabus she had posted on
her Web site. Kenya wondered aloud about a project she was planning for her fifth graders. Trey fretted about his seventh graders
who had never really participated in a freewheeling class discussion before. Joel, a colleague, wandered in, and while he nibbled
on our snacks, he shared ideas about how daunting it was to watch
videotapes of one's own class and offered helpful suggestions for
overcoming technical difficulties. I reminded everyone to distrib-

ute parent permission forms to all of their classes and start to videotape soon and often.

One aspect of our first evening meeting concerned me. My youthful colleagues expressed trepidation about sharing their work, especially drafts of their writing. Sula, the most outspoken of the group, fairly trembled at the prospect of my scrutiny, saying that I probably wouldn't find it up to my standards. Sarah too showed some reluctance, refusing to share her written commentary because, she demurred, "It's not good enough yet." Although I understood their anxiety, given the gap in our age and experience and my deep involvement in teacher education, I sought to allay their fears by gently reminding them that I had been privy to their practice for several years at their instigation. "Yeah, we know," Sula admitted, "but Hutch, we still get so nervous when you scrutinize us and this is National Board!"

"Yes," Sarah chimed in. "Ms. Hutchinson, you are our idol. We still get nervous every time you come into our rooms. It's scary, but we do want you to help us pass National Board." Trey smiled, "That's true, Hutch, we watched your NBC video and have heard so much about you." "Yeah," Kenya added. "You're a legend." I looked around at my circle of "earnest friends," delighting in the praise, savoring their awe, but thinking what a wonderful learning opportunity this was for all of us: they, the novices to the profession, and I, the grizzled veteran whose teaching career exceeded the length of their lives. I smoothed away their anxieties by assuring them that I would learn as much from them as they would from me. I regaled them with tales of my missteps and woes as I worked on my National Boards. That settled, we continued our sessions, which developed into a wonderful, challenging learning community and the best kind of staff development, sitting down to ask each other meaningful questions about teaching.

One of the first problems to come up was what to do about classroom discourse—whole-group and small-group discussions. Because I had observed them, I knew Sarah and Sula were adept at involving their students in authentic learning conversations. Trey, expressing some envy about the engagement of the students in my NBC video, volunteered that he had never involved his students in discussion beyond question-and-answer sessions. Kenya, a great talker herself, had already regaled us with stories of her students' oral skills. Perhaps because they were proficient, Kenya and Sula were the first to experiment with videotaping. Kenya's first showing of an articulate and gifted group of fifth graders, who pondered ways to provide shelter for a group of homeless people, inspired a conversation about how much or how little the teacher should do, especially during small-group interaction. Kenya's students' precocious exchange of ideas demonstrated clear and consistent evidence that she had taught them to engage in literate discourse independent of her. While she was justly proud of them, it was obvious that she would have to intervene so that evaluators would be able to assess *her* effectiveness as a facilitator and learner with her students.

Sula's first whole-class video had technical problems, stemming from the lighting and seating in the room. Trey brought a video that showed him interrogating a classroom full of mostly petrified seventh graders about the qualities of a leader as demonstrated in ancient culture. It was evident that these students were not accustomed to engaging in discussion. During this session, we focused on three issues: ways to engage students in oral discourse, how to honor students' home language, and culturally relevant teaching. I shared my protocol for literate discourse with Trey, a strategy shown on Sarah's tape that required students to call on one another and ensured everyone would have a chance to speak. During our discussion of Sarah's and Kenya's lessons, questions about the students' use of language emerged. "What do we do if a student is making brilliant points but not necessarily speaking standard [mainstream American] English?" We agreed that the issue of "Ebonics" or African American speech (dialect) should be addressed in their written commentary to provide assessors a context in which to fairly evaluate speakers who communicate in their "home language" or so-called nonstandard American (mainstream) English.

To help them frame their comments, I advised them to read pedagogy, among them books by Gloria Ladson-Billings and Lisa Delpit, whereupon I was met by blank stares from Trey and Kenya. Kenya confessed after a slight hesitation, "I don't know who those people are." Sheepishly, Trey chimed in: "I have to admit, I don't know either." Sula brought out a copy of *The Dreamkeepers* (1994) by Ladson-Billings that I had loaned her, and Sarah showed her copy of *The Real Ebonics Debate* edited by Theresa Perry and Lisa Delpit (1998). I went upstairs to my classroom and retrieved copies of *Talkin' and Testifyin'* (1986) and *Black Talk: Words and Phrases from the Hood to the Amen Corner* (1994), both by Geneva Smitherman. We talked about the necessity of honoring the language and culture that students bring to the classroom and how to capitalize on their prior knowledge, something aptly demonstrated by Kenya's video, in which one pigtailed fifth grader remarked emphatically, "He a single father with a little baby. You know how these men are; they need help. He should be the first one to get a room in the homeless shelter."

While most of our Saturday and Wednesday support sessions were congenial, helping two of the candidates, Trey and Sula, with their class discussion entries proved to be especially problematic. Given all of our discussions and examples of classroom discourse, Trey's inability to facilitate discussion among his students troubled me. His classroom management skills, the level of respect and involvement of his students, as well as his evident competence and knowledge of subject matter showed that he had the potential to do well in this aspect of his practice, but I was worried nevertheless. Despite at least two sessions in which the group and I had shared strategies for engaging students orally, his videotapes continued to show his students responding stiffly to questions from their teacher, punctuated by awkward silences. It is evident that his students adore him and that they are learning, but their reticence is overwhelming. A few loquacious students responded brilliantly, but his whole-class and small-group discussions would not earn him high marks. What else could I do for him? Would it help if I went to his school and conducted a demonstration lesson? Would that undermine his authority with his students? Should he participate in classroom observations or watch more videos of exemplary discussions?

Surprisingly, the toughest challenge, also with facilitation of class discussion, came from Sula, the most driven and emotionally tense of the group, who was given to stormy outbursts. Big on control, when fate (or some inept person in her view) threatened to wreck her plans, something did not make sense, or something was missing, she collapsed in tears of anger and frustration, treating everyone to a rant.

During one of her outbursts, she railed against the two coordinators of the program because she felt that a writing workshop on Entry Four, conducted several months into the process, had come too late to be of much help. "Why didn't you show us this sooner?" she raged. "Why now? This is too little, too late!" Despite one coordinator's assurances that the group had gotten adequate instructions at the beginning of the process and that this was assistance for those who "hadn't quite gotten it," she persisted in her tearful denunciation, proclaiming that the group had not been well served in this instance.

Sula is a perfectionist. She plans meticulously, establishing time lines and adhering strictly to her own personal deadlines. Perhaps because of a difficult upbringing and the inspiration of a beloved teacher, she is almost obsessive in her desire to become an exceptional teacher. She does not suffer perceived inefficiency, incompetence, or neglect kindly. Plus, she seems to have a fragile ego and desperately craves approval; the latter trait often led to her loss of self-control and perspective. To her credit, she is a dedicated, passionate teacher whose talent is finding ways to help students construct their own learning by using creative and innovative classroom strategies. When in good humor, she is funny, witty, and down-to-earth, beloved by students and respected by her colleagues.

On one particular night, her ill-tempered side appeared with a vengeance. One of her early videos showed students in small groups participating in a writing workshop on peer editing. Each group stood with their backs to the camera discussing a paper that had been copied on a poster and adhered to the wall. After watching the tape, I began with a positive comment, a commendation—standard operating procedure for all presentations by adults and students. I remarked that her students were obviously engaged in a meaningful process. The reality was that although they seemed intent, all we saw were their backs; consequently, we could not hear their discussion. Whenever Sula approached a group and asked them questions, they gave hesitant, inaudible responses. After the others in the support group chimed in with commendations on the level of student involvement, I suggested that perhaps she should tape another of her ninth-grade classes and seat them in circles so their faces would be visible. I also suggested that she sit on a stool or chair at eye level with each group.

The next session she did bring in another videotape. Alas, the only thing that was different this time was that everyone was now seated. Sula did most of the talking, asking question after question. The students answered questions woodenly, responding in mono-syllables and phrases and lapsing into silence. There was no real conversation among them or with their teacher. When the tape ended, I began what I thought was a gentle probe and asked her to tell me how the task was described in the NBC prompt. Obviously irate, Sula answered defensively, "It says to engage students in a conversation. . . . It didn't say the teacher couldn't talk!" As I tried to help her to see that the conversation had been one-sided, she became very angry and accused me of suggesting that she was "a bad teacher." Then she refused to talk any more, saying only in response to my query about what discussion strategies she had taught, "My kids don't discuss. None of them know how to discuss." When I asked why, she snapped out a petulant, "I don't know!"

Temporarily defeated, I declined to remonstrate with her further. Instead I accompanied Teresa, also an elementary school teacher and an occasional guest from the grant group, and Sarah upstairs to my classroom to watch Teresa's fourth-grade small-group discussion videos. She wanted to show two tapes, she said, and because of the conversation we just had with Sula, she admitted that one of them was more of a question-and-answer session rather than a discussion. We watched both videos; one provoked a rich discussion about how to expose students to rigor, knowledge of students, meeting the standards, literate discourse, and, most significant, the teacher's role in small-group discussion.

What a marvelous learning opportunity, I thought. This is just what Sula needs. I called on my room phone, told her that we were having a session that might be helpful to her, and invited her to join us. Sula arrived and sat staring sullenly as we replicated our session, viewing the tapes and discussing them. She refused to join our conversation. An angry scowl on her face, she sat half-turned away from us and tapped with her keys on the desk. My attempts to involve her met with hostile grunts or terse declarations of "I don't know!" Abruptly, she headed for the door, tears streaming down her face. As she left, she threw over her shoulder, "I just know I'm the only one who gets to look like a bad teacher. I don't get any commendations. All I get is put down!"

Stunned, we followed Sula back to her classroom, our head-quarters. After an interval of some minutes, I confronted her about her petulant and, in my opinion, selfish behavior. Without replicating the argument, suffice it to say that the air was finally cleared. She ranted; I raved. She cried. I cried. She denounced us all for not "commending" her. She expressed her anxiety that I and the others seemed to be negating her teaching skills; Sarah and I found her guilty of selfishness; we felt that she was merely interested in receiving approval rather than honest, constructive criticism and that she seemed largely insensitive to the needs of the other candidates when it did not square with her own personal agenda. Because we had forged strong bonds, we were able to go away and lick our respective wounds.

My mind whirled in a mix of emotions: sadness, anger, amazement, dismay. How is it that this volatile young woman did not realize that I have the utmost respect for her intelligence and talent? How could I make her understand that she sometimes gets so caught up in wanting to be at the top of her craft that she loses perspective? Could I have been more sensitive? What about my own approach contributed to the breakdown in communication? Would I be able to restore her faith in me, in us, her colleagues, in herself? What should I do to cut through the anger, hostility, and disappointment in time to bring her back to the job of preparing her entry?

What can I do to show the way to Sula and Trey? How do I validate them as the excellent teachers they already are? Alice Walker was right: "Good teaching is a circle of earnest people sitting down to ask meaningful questions." In my efforts to help my young charges to successfully complete the NBPTS process, I hope to arrive at some meaningful answers.

References

Ladson-Billings, G. *The Dreamkeepers: Successful Teachers of African American Children.* San Francisco: Jossey-Bass, 1994.

Perry, T., and Delpit, L. (eds.). *The Real Ebonics Debate: Power, Language, and the Education of African American Children*. Boston: Beacon Press, 1998.

Smitherman, G. *Talkin' and Testifyin'*. Boston: Houghton Mifflin, 1986.

Smitherman, G. *Black Talk: Words and Phrases from the Hood to the Amen Corner*. Boston: Houghton Mifflin, 1994.

Walker, A. *Meridian*. New York: Pocket, 1976.

COMMENTARIES

COMMENTARY BY GLORIA LADSON-BILLINGS

I must admit I feel a bit like Yvonne Divans-Hutchinson's young colleagues when I think about writing a commentary on her work. Having seen her portfolio and shared a conference session with her I know just how impressive she is. I also know that like almost every other outstanding teacher I have studied or observed, she is always looking for ways to grow professionally. Mentoring young teachers toward excellence is a powerful way to improve one's own practice.

The case is beautifully written. The reader gets an almost palpable sense of the camaraderie and collegiality that developed during the sessions. Yvonne's willingness to meet with her young colleagues every week reflects her incredible generosity and investment in these young people. Yvonne describes the early meetings as "a love fest, a collegial gathering," and I imagine that they were places where the candidates felt comfortable and supported. It would be hard to believe that any other coaches worked harder than Yvonne.

As the weekly meetings proceed, Yvonne begins to express concerns about two of the candidates—Trey and Sula. In Trey's case it is not clear that he fully understands what constitutes a discussion or if, after having spent so much time honing his management skills, he feels prepared to allow the students to assume responsibility for their own learning through discussion. To some degree, we could argue that this is developmental. As Trey becomes more confident, he will relax enough to allow the students to take on more. The question is whether this maturation will occur soon enough for him to produce an adequate entry for the National Board.

In Sula's case, what Yvonne describes seems to be a personality issue. Sula is trying to be perfect, and such a desire is self-defeating. I am unsure whether anything Yvonne does can alleviate Sula's anxiety about the National Board process. However, there may be some strategies that Yvonne can employ that take the onus off her and create more of a shared sense of responsibility and accomplishment.

Evaluating people is always difficult. It requires the evaluator to be honest yet kind, and the person being evaluated must be vulnerable yet receptive. One of the things that Yvonne and her group had going for them was that they were a group. Too often, one-on-one evaluation disintegrates into a battle of wills. The principal who evaluates a teacher may already be cast as the "bad guy or gal." The teacher may already be cast as incompetent. These unequal power relationships are fraught with tensions, and it is difficult to move back and forth across the roles.

Yvonne was cast in the role of the expert (which she is), but her younger colleagues also seemed to make her the standard. One strategy that Yvonne might have employed to mitigate some of that thinking is the process of self and group critique. When Trey showed his video, Yvonne might have started out with, "Trey, tell us what you think about the video. What aspects of it do you think meet your expectations, and what aspects of it do you think need work?" My experience working with groups of novice teachers in this way has been helpful in moving them away from believing that I have the answer and toward the kind of self-reflective practice they must develop if they are going to continually improve.

Typically people are harder on themselves than anyone else. Yvonne's young colleagues are likely to nitpick every aspect of their practice (for example, "I said 'umm' too many times," "I can't believe how loudly I am speaking"), but they also are likely to identify some of the real problems in their practice. Next, Yvonne should encourage the other participants to share what they thought were the strengths of the video and offer suggestions for improvement. These comments tend to be gentler. Peers are reluctant to criticize peers. So you have a process where the individual starts out tearing herself down, but the peers quickly build her back up. Finally, Yvonne, as the most knowledgeable coach, can choose to add more positive comments and more suggestions, or she can comment on how thorough the candidates were in their assessments and decline to add anything else.

The unavoidable trap that Yvonne and most other experienced teachers fall into is being seen as the "mother." While she acknowledges that she has been a professional longer than her colleagues have been alive, her biggest challenge is keeping this a professional relationship. Sula was having a classic mother-daughter struggle with Yvonne, and these are unwinnable. However, Yvonne realizes that she took on a responsibility with these young people and wants to see it through. My suggestion is to get back into professional mode as quickly as possible. Lay out the ground rules for participation (for example, everyone is going to hear critical comments about his or her work; as much as I like you, we're here to accomplish a task; always remember this is professional, not personal), remind the participants often of the shared responsibilities this task requires, and don't lose sight of the larger goal.

I cannot think of anything that Yvonne did "wrong" in this case. The problem with people is that they are unpredictable. Just when we think we know what to do with them, they are likely to display a new twist. Like the consummate professional she is with her high school students, Yvonne began problem solving rather than hand wringing. Of course, Yvonne holds only half of the solution. Sula and Trey hold the other.

COMMENTARY BY SANDRA DEAN

When I read Yvonne's case, my first response was a feeling of intense longing to be part of one of those circles "of earnest people sitting down to ask each other meaningful questions." I have been in those circles and hope I will be again. Living and working with colleagues within that circle is both a great joy ("a love fest," as Yvonne called it) and a great challenge. In our training and in most of our practice, few of us learn to talk about teaching in the way that pursuing National Board Certification requires that we do. Teaching is a demanding job accomplished largely in isolation from other practitioners. Learning to be affirming and, at the same time, to ask one another the hard questions that help move us toward exemplary teaching is a delicate balancing act. Yvonne's commitment to creating that balance shines through in her case. But as I read her story, I conjured several questions that arose from her case as well as from my own experience.

My first question is one that Yvonne identified early in her narrative: her young colleagues were in awe of her. She truly is a legend, as anyone who has seen even a small snapshot of her work will attest. The belief that there are hard and fast answers to nearly all the dilemmas that arise in the classroom is a common pitfall of our early teaching years. Teachers like Yvonne, who make the work look effortless and brilliant, affirm the belief that after awhile, it all becomes easy and uncomplicated. The task for Yvonne became helping her young colleagues by asking the right questions of them and by making her own questions about teaching episodes transparent. Otherwise she is left to struggle with Sula's rage as she confronts the shortcomings in her work and with Trey's confusion about the nature of accomplished teaching.

When Yvonne wonders about strategies for helping Trey learn to create authentic dialogue in his classroom, I found myself thinking right along with her. Of course, I thought, go model those techniques that will get students to talk and discuss together in really powerful ways. When she invites an angry Sula to watch a video of a teacher who has gotten it right, I thought it made sense. A compelling model would help Sula see what needed to be done and help her over a tough spot at that moment. There is, however, a part of the process of National Board Certification that is not immediately obvious when we first begin to pursue it. I refer to the transformational aspect of the process. As I considered Sula, whose passion seems both blessing and curse, I was most acutely conscious of the need to be mindful of this. For some, like Sula, the quest to become better at anything evokes a powerful range of emotions that arise in recognition not only of the ways in which one's practice must change but also the ways that one must change as a person in order to become an accomplished teacher.

I recognized that challenge from my own experience coaching a colleague who spent three years learning how to accommodate personality traits rooted in a sad childhood. For her, becoming the teacher described in the standards meant learning to recognize the behaviors she had cultivated to deal with her past and the ways that those behaviors compromised her tremendous potential as a teacher. She taught me that my role needed to be very different than it was with other candidates. I needed to help her see her strengths in a new light and to help her identify the ways she had of unconsciously setting herself up for failure. She had to learn for herself that these were serious roadblocks toward her pursuit of becoming a better teacher.

I do not know if this can ever be done easily and without a lot of struggle. I would guess not. As I read about Sula, I wondered if the trait that would keep her from coming to the circle was that of earnestness. She needed to want to come into that circle with the honesty and humility essential to being a true learner. Ultimately Yvonne's offer of a shoulder to cry on and a firm insistence that she keep on working were exactly what were most likely to bring Sula into the circle.

Although Trey's case was less dramatic, his need to be in control of the interactions in his classroom presented some of the same challenges. Yvonne considered taking a "show, don't tell" approach with him. I wondered about what ways could be used to help Trey generate for himself the kinds of questions that were needed to transform his teaching. Trey was definitely in the right place to begin to do this. Leveraging the talents of people like Sarah and Kenya who already knew how to ask those provocative questions might have been the most promising strategy.

In the end, Yvonne had to rely on her instincts. When teachers fall back on instinct, the biggest questions emerge. There is only one way to know, then. Did the student learn as a result of the teacher's responses, and did the teacher learn from the student's? The conversations in our circles of earnest people are often likely to be about just that.

TEACHING NOTE

A small group of teachers who decide to pursue National Board Certification enlist the help of a well-respected veteran National Board Certified Teacher. Regular meetings of the group, who share common teaching experiences and are all African American, result in a learning community that is supportive and motivating for all. However, when the National Board candidates begin sharing videos of their lessons that are supposed to demonstrate students engaged in class discussions, Yvonne feels that at least two of the candidates need some coaching on how to enable their students to participate in classroom discourse. She struggles with the approach she should take with each of the candidates, and we see one of the candidates become offended, defensive, then nonresponsive after a group discussion about her video.

This case helps us think about the individualized nature of the mentoring process: each teacher brings to the mentoring situation a unique life history and a trajectory of where he or she would like to go in seeking to become better teachers—as well as the role that community plays in sustaining the learning process.

ISSUES AND QUESTIONS

Can There Be Too Much Respect?

When the younger teachers first approached Yvonne to be their support provider for National Board Certification, she immediately felt that they were holding her in reverence. While this high degree of respect for her and what she had accomplished during her career of teaching was flattering, she almost immediately realized the downside. The teachers openly expressed their sense of intimidation in having Yvonne read their entries and see their practice. They eagerly wanted to learn from Yvonne and benefit from her wisdom and experience, but at what risk to themselves? Would the master find fault in their practice? Would their novice attempt be found worthy in the eyes of one who was already so accomplished?

With this knowledge, Yvonne had to think carefully about her role as a support provider. She made overt statements about learning from the candidates, and she valued the collegial nature of their work together. What kinds of preparation do you do to foster not only the respect of your mentees but also the trust that you will be fair, sensitive, and understanding of their practice?

Preparing for Honest, Critical Feedback in Group Sessions

This case reveals the camaraderie that the group shared while they were meeting regularly around their National Board portfolio work. We know that the group was purposeful in its conversations, the participants were eager to learn from one another, and they were eventually comfortable in sharing their classroom work with each other. However, the case does not precisely outline the routines or structures of how the group talked to one another when they were discussing and analyzing their classroom together. Given Sula's reaction to the group comments about her classroom video and Yvonne's uncertainty about how to reengage her in the conversation, one of the underlying issues in this case is how Sula and the others were prepared to hear honest and critical feedback from Yvonne and the group.

Consider what group processes might be helpful in a group mentoring situation. Refer to the suggestions made by Gloria Ladson-Billings in her commentary. What ground rules or protocols do you or would you use to examine others' classroom practice? What routines or procedures for providing feedback to each other do you suggest or would you use?

Pushing Practice

Preparing for National Board Certification takes on many faces. For some teachers, the process is a confirmation; for others, it is a tweaking of practice; and for still others, it is a reinventing. In her commentary, Sandra Dean speaks of the transformational aspect of the assessment process. In mentoring environments, the work of the group sometimes focuses on the logistics of the assessment process. Yvonne describes how the group initially took up questions of time lines and permission slips and video technicalities. As the group engages more deeply with the process, the potential for those transformative experiences increases.

It is important to remember that the National Board does not expect all teachers' practice to look the same. When pushing someone to reconsider a teaching practice, support providers must be careful not to lead candidates to think there is a right way to teach (the National Board way) and a wrong way to teach. With that said, it is also the case that there are expectations for classroom practice such as seeing students actively engaged in a classroom discussion that is more than a question-and-answer session between teacher and students. The balance that the support provider must negotiate is when and how to push another teacher to promote change in his or her practice that better aligns with the National Board teaching standards. Yvonne and her group took on this challenge in this case. What did she do to suggest alternative approaches to leading classroom discussions? What would you have done?

CHAPTER THIRTEEN

CAN WE REALLY TEACH LIKE THIS?

How does the process of intense professional development change your professional identity, your relationship to your colleagues, and the larger school culture? This case examines some of the unexpected consequences, both positive and negative, when a group of teachers from one school embarks on the quest for National Board Certification.

CASE

CASE BY SANDRA DEAN

"Can we really teach like this?" colleagues at my school asked when we first met to talk about pursuing National Board Certification. The 450 children in our primary school, like those in many other large metropolitan areas, are mostly from poor families, largely immigrant, and few speak English at home. The neighborhood has a high crime rate. Many of our children live in shelters for battered women or recovering substance abusers. For us, the role of teacher often includes being counselor, translator, liaison to community legal and health resources, and sometime "parent" along with usual classroom responsibilities. It is not surprising, then, to hear

---

Pseudonyms have been used to maintain the confidentiality of people and places in the case.

concerns voiced about the ability to teach at levels the National Board calls for.

We had been encouraged to examine the idea of National Board Certification through an initiative of the Bay Area School Reform Collaborative (BASRC), an organization that had sponsored and worked with our school for several years to help us meet the challenges of improving school for some of the neediest children in the Bay Area. Their idea was to use National Board Certification as a vehicle to improve teaching, basically the heart of school reform. It was one of several initiatives they presented to schools in the collaborative during the fall of 1999. The collaborative had hired a single coach who would work with school teams to help them begin the certification process.

By the time we met to consider the idea, it was already October. The ten to twelve teachers at that first meeting felt a mixture of excitement and dismay. It was not news to us that good teaching was the essential ingredient in creating more effective schools. Nonetheless, the National Board standards described something that none of us was sure we could even aspire to. The course we finally chose was to learn as much as we could and to study the standards for a while. Two of the group's veteran teachers decided to apply for candidacy that year. I was one of them. The others would learn from us and support us in whatever ways they could.

Shortly after filing for candidacy, we learned that BASRC had shifted its focus to other areas. This meant we would not have a coach. My colleague and I decided to pursue certification on our own. In retrospect, it was nothing short of miraculous that either of us finished a portfolio. We tried to collaborate, but our classroom commitments along with responsibilities outside school seriously limited what we could do for each other. Neither of us had enough knowledge about what we were really being asked to demonstrate and document. Our colleagues continued discussions about the standards and their implications for developing as accomplished teachers. They even began to study and suggest ways they wanted to change their practice. It was a year of learning.

For the two of us pursuing certification, it was intense and exhausting. We both submitted portfolios with an attitude of resignation. We had done the best we could but were prepared for more work. We had truly been steering without a compass, so it was not a surprise when both of us failed to achieve certification that first year. We were prepared for that, and we saw continuing candidacy as a way to learn more. Our colleagues decided to wait a year to see what happened. I admit that failure is exceedingly difficult for me. I was determined to succeed not just for myself but also for my colleagues, who had been so excited about this undertaking a year earlier.

I was lucky enough the second year to find a regional support group that was well able to offer help to a slightly discouraged advanced candidate. My colleague and I soon saw ways to approach our second year differently. At year's end, I was glad I had chosen to continue the work. I had resubmitted the entries I thought displayed my greatest strengths. I felt they now reflected a dimension of my teaching that I had previously not fully explored. While I had always loved the inquiry aspect of teaching, that year I became highly systematic about being a student of my own teaching. I became more aware of being sure there was a clear rationale for every instructional decision I made. (That is, happily, one of the habits that has endured and flourished since certification.) I shared my feelings and perspectives about what I had learned with the other teachers at my school, and I had begun to imagine what it might be like to be part of a school culture where classroom practice was routinely analyzed, studied, and refined. We finally understood what real collegial work might become in a school where teaching was truly guided by the kinds of standards that exemplify those of the National Board. We all reinvested in our original vision of establishing a cadre of accomplished teachers.

My achieving certification in the fall of 2001 was an event significant not just for me but for my school as well. Six of my colleagues elected to pursue certification that year. One of these was the colleague who had still not certified after a difficult year as an advanced candidate. I encouraged all my colleagues to become part of the support group at Stanford University. I offered to help with videotapes, listen to questions, and encourage their efforts in any way I could.

Although their lives were being consumed by their work on certification, I was at times envious of the new group of candidates. Their support for each other was impressive. They worked on critiquing one another's lessons, videotapes, and selections of artifacts.

They dedicated afternoons and evenings to work together. They traded entries to read, and carpooled to the support program one Saturday each month to work with the support group there.

By February they were giving me entries to read and asking for comments. I confess that I was not sure how to respond. It is exceedingly difficult to learn to give one's colleagues the kind of feedback that helps them analyze their own teaching more critically. I had learned a lot through my own failures about clearly representing and analyzing my teaching, but that did not automatically qualify me to do this for anyone else, least of all my own colleagues. I knew they were all good teachers. I also knew a great deal about their teaching, which, unfortunately, I could read into their entries even when it was not there.

When they completed their portfolios and shipped them off, I was so excited for them I came very close to ordering NBCT lapel pins to present when they received their congratulatory letters the following November. It was a good thing I held off. Not one of them achieved certification. They all came close, but none certified. We were devastated and, I confess, angry. It was a blow to each of the teachers and a blow to our collective self-esteem.

Those weeks from late November until winter break were gloomy indeed. I found myself thinking we had all made a serious mistake. A whole group of deeply disheartened teachers in one highly challenging teaching environment could not possibly be good for the children who needed those teachers to bring their best, most confident selves to school each day. I had no idea what to do or what to say to any of them. I elected to let them come to their own decisions, but I let them know as well that I would be there to help if they chose to try again. The discouraged teachers raised many questions: Was the process of certification flawed and perhaps biased? Who passed and why? Could "teachers like us" ever pass?

It is a hard thing for anyone to acknowledge and accept that failure is an integral part of learning. But that is what each of these six teachers ultimately came to do. They each did it in different ways.

As teachers we first look at the work of our students with an eye on their strengths. In their role as learners, each of my colleagues began looking at their own work for evidence of their weaknesses as well as for the strengths on which they could build.

As January arrived, all the candidates had selected the work they would do. One of them, Suzanne, had even begun to write the professional accomplishment section of her entry again. Suzanne is a highly organized young woman, an expert at multitasking, and determined to succeed. She is an excellent teacher, a fact none of her supervisors or colleagues would dispute, who believes in the power of studying one's own teaching. Spurred partly by lingering anger over not earning certification, she had strong feelings about what she would and would not do to earn it. More than the other teachers, she was convinced that she would not learn much more by doing any of her entries again. Yet while eager to move on, she was meticulous, selecting aspects of her professional work that would make a coherent statement about her contributions to teaching. She made sure that she presented the dimensions of her work with parents and the community.

Suzanne talked to me about the selections she made and let me preview the way she planned to write about each of her accomplishments. I worried not about the quality of her work but about the worth of it to her personally. I wanted her to learn something. Her written analysis seemed to demonstrate that she was actually seeing some things differently, but when I asked her if she was learning, there was a tone in her voice that caused me to question. After months of agonizing, I finally decided to accept that maybe for some candidates, like Suzanne, the real learning had happened in the first year and this second stage was chiefly about making her work and its meaning more visible to others.

All of the teachers in this group had done badly on the science and math entry. Working from two of their own entries, the teachers were helped by a science education specialist to uncover what became an essential piece of learning for all of us. The "big ideas" about science had been badly underdeveloped in all the entries. It wasn't enough to see well-executed lessons; the teachers needed to be sure that the concepts they were teaching were important and helped children develop the skill and knowledge needed as a foundation for learning about the scientific principles governing their world. Equally important, the math incorporated in these lessons needed to be useful tools for helping children make sense of their observations of scientific phenomena. Two teachers in the group had done interesting lessons with kindergartners studying the properties of magnets. Their videos were filled with children happily finding out how magnetic materials behave and sorting and classifying what they discovered. Missing was the rationale for the lessons presented and clear articulation about why students were doing what they were doing. As a group we came up hard against the great peril of primary teaching: the all-too-frequent temptation to make sure children were engaged in activities at school without asking whether the activity is really leading to important learning.

The teachers pursuing the science and math entries were eager to get it right and to bring to their teaching the crucial missing element. Jackie, Margot, and Inga all began planning their science lessons after considerable background reading. Each made sure that the work they were asking children to do was important in developing conceptual and procedural knowledge and that they could help children master it at a level matching their development. Jackie had chosen her topic from an event that had happened in her classroom. Margot and Inga chose topics that they had presented before, but this time they constructed the learning events in very different ways. Our conversations preceding the actual planning and teaching focused on helping children acquire important scientific concepts in ways that were considerate of their developmental levels. The question that surfaced over and over was, "What will it look like if kids are really understanding and using what I am trying to teach?"

I actually felt that providing support to my own colleagues held a strong advantage over supporting teachers from other schools. Our discussions epitomized what I think collegiality ought to mean. We talked about the shared context of our work and the performance of all of our students along the continuum of the primary years. Our shared work became making sure that teaching important ideas in science and math was connected to the high standards of teaching and learning defined by the National Board.

The transformational potential of having several teachers on a staff pursue board certification was clear here. We had heard a lot during the previous eight years about paradigm shifts being key to successful reform. Here was one that seemed to happen before my eyes. It changed a lot of the classroom work of these teachers during those science investigations. Being part of that learning was a time of selfish pleasure for me personally. I was not paid for coaching my colleagues in dollars, but what I received in learning currency was far more valuable.

Three of the teachers were resubmitting the literacy development entry. They were all strong teachers of reading and writing. They understood how reading develops in children, and they knew about ways to intervene to help struggling readers. They had demonstrated success in their classrooms. You wouldn't think any of them would have difficulty documenting the literacy development of their students and reflecting on their instructional processes and decisions. In fact, the amount of their knowledge seemed to be part of their problem. We began meeting to talk about this entry, the standards, and the work they were doing. We included a teacher I was coaching from another school.

Those meetings became extremely interesting and useful professional development sessions for all of us. Literacy instruction for all four teachers took the major chunk of their teaching time. Interestingly, none of them was particularly good at talking about what they did to produce certain outcomes. They seemed to be on automatic pilot. As these teachers searched for evidence of the standards in their work and tried out ways of talking about the literacy development of their students, they started to reflect again on why they made certain choices and to reconsider alternative strategies. They shared insights and helped one another discover perspectives about the teaching standards they had not seen before. I had worried that this entry would not occasion much deep learning. In the end, I was completely wrong.

Doing this kind of thing with one's colleagues is, in some respects, easy. We do, after all, understand our shared challenges. But in other ways it is very hard. My emotional investment in the work and success of my colleagues was very high. I know them as colleagues, and I know them as friends. I worried excessively about one of the teachers whom I began to think was afraid to succeed. Using the National Board process to improve her teaching meant learning to believe in her own efficacy, something she had struggled with a long time. Would I have known that about a teacher I coached if she were not my colleague, I wonder? Would I worry so much that each of these teachers learn from their work if I hadn't been so invested in what happens for the children we teach together? Could I more easily give constructive criticism about a videotaped teaching vignette if I did not know so much about the teacher from many other episodes not featured in the video?

I coached other candidates not at my school site and was highly invested in their success as well. I know I care as much about what their learning means for the children they teach. I do not know if my distance from their classrooms made supporting their work easier or more effective. I do know that the two experiences were different and that I find myself wishing I could have combined aspects of the support I brought to each of these situations.

The teachers involved in National Board Certification have taken leadership in changing the school climate to better serve the needs of young children. They have coordinated professional development activities for the whole staff. They have found ways to increase the amount of time spent working in each other's classrooms and planning instruction together.

While our values, beliefs about the ethics of teaching, and desire to live a professional life in teaching have defined us as a community, we have also experienced a sense of separation from colleagues on our staff, a result none of us would have anticipated. None of us is completely sure why this is true. We began to expect more of ourselves and of each other in the process of pursuing board certification. Could it be that our expectations affected our relationships with our peers in subtle ways we did not recognize? Did our desire to build on the kinds of collaborative experiences we had shared make us too eager to want more from our work with our colleagues than they were ready or able to give? Were we reacting to feelings from a few of our fellow staff members that we were engaged in a pursuit of a kind of elitism not welcome in the teaching profession? Or is it that striving to attune one's teaching to the standards set by the National Board simply changes the way we think and act as teachers in ways that truly do separate us from many others in our profession?

COMMENTARIES

COMMENTARY BY ANN-MARIE WIESE

This case tells the story of a journey, of a group of teachers at one elementary school striving for self-improvement through the National Board Certification process. These teachers looked to the certification process as a way to improve their own teaching, as a vehicle for professional growth, "to establish a cadre of accomplished teachers." I respond to this case by illuminating what I see as three distinct phases in the journey, highlighting particular themes and unresolved issues. In my response, I draw on my work on a national study of National Board Certified Teachers (NBCTs) in low-performing schools, as well as my work on a project that leverages the National Board Certification process for schoolwide reform in two high-priority schools.

The first phase of the journey was one of discerning whether this was a journey to be undertaken. Key to this decision was the question of whether the teachers were prepared for such a journey and whether they could "really teach like this." As I read the case, I wondered whether this uncertainty came from their sense that certification posed an additional task, one that seemed burdensome given that they taught in a high-priority (that is, low-performing) school. Other alternatives might be that they viewed their particular students as a barrier to their own success as teachers, or even that they felt their own preparation as teachers and the opportunities they had in professional development limited their experience to the point of feeling unprepared for such an endeavor. Whatever the reason, it is important to recognize that teachers face a difficult decision in choosing whether to pursue National Board Certification, regardless of the particular context in which they teach. While only two teachers pursued certification that first year, the rest of the group decided to learn more about National Board standards. Since the certification process looks at teaching as responsive to the context of students and school, it would be particularly interesting to explore the teachers' concerns, especially since they were at a high-priority school.

The second phase of the journey involved the pursuit of certification over a span of three years for a total of eight teachers and the challenges they faced in the pursuit of self-improvement. Of all eight teachers, only one certified, the author of this case, in her second year of candidacy. Six new candidates undertook the challenge the following year, and although they all came close, none certified. Still, they came to accept that "failure is an integral part of learning." Sandra Dean talks about how all the teachers became students of their own teaching in very personal ways. All this learning was truly a form of professional growth for these teachers, and it happened in the context of authentic collegiality, as opposed to "contrived collegiality" (Hargreaves, 1994). The teachers at Sandra Dean's school "talked about the shared context of our work . . . and making sure that teaching . . . was connected to the high standards of teaching and learning defined by the National Board." Her description was one of "collaborative cultures" where teachers came together voluntarily, spontaneously, establishing a community that was pervasive across time and space. It was not contrived in any way.

Furthermore, not only the form of professional community but the content as well supported their efforts to improve teaching and learning. The guiding framework of the National Board for Professional Teaching Standards has at its core the crucial element of critical reflection. In reading about this phase of the journey, I wondered what it takes for such a professional community to be established. Still, while the transformative power of the National Board Certification process has come to the light through these teachers' experiences, it has also had an impact on their relationships with others in the school.

This brings me to the third phase of the journey. As this group of teachers worked together around the National Board Certification process, they began to experience a sense of separation from the rest of the staff. Through a series of questions, Sandra raises some interesting possibilities for why this came to be, including issues of student expectations, norms of collaboration, and perceptions of the National Board and, in particular, National Board Certification. As I read this section, I kept thinking about one school in particular from my work, where the NBCTs and National

Board candidates are recognized for their incredible achievement and their contributions to the school through leadership roles. At the same time, as the principal talks about the NBCTs, he describes how they are still "part of the family." In other words, board certification is a wonderful achievement, and NBCTs should share their expertise with others, but they are not the only experts.

I was also reminded of our work at WestEd with two high-priority schools that draws on the National Board Certification process for schoolwide improvement. In this project, teachers engage with the National Board for Professional Teaching Standards (NBPTS) with increasing depth as they participate at different levels. Throughout our work, a key factor is whether the NBPTS is viewed as a vehicle for professional growth for all teachers, as opposed to just accomplished teachers. When implemented most successfully, the standards become a vehicle for professional growth for all teachers, and engaging with the standards at any level is valued. The model provides multiple points of entry for teachers, depending on their readiness and willingness to engage with the NBPTS. Most broadly, all teachers participate at the schoolwide level where the NBPTS serves as the framework for all professional development activities. At the candidacy preparation level, teachers can learn a bit more about the certification process and begin to prepare for the challenge ahead. Then there is the candidacy level, and finally the NBCTs who take on leadership roles for both schoolwide efforts and in supporting Board candidates.

Thus far, our collaboration with rural middle schools has been more successful than with the urban high schools. Despite differences across the contexts, we have found key factors that play a significant role in how the model plays out in action in both schools. First, the broad educational context, including both state and district initiatives, is a powerful force shaping the broader landscape of our work. At the district level, Los Ríos Middle School has complete autonomy in deciding how to use professional development days, while Grant High School has had its number of professional development days reduced each year and even taken over by mandatory district meetings for certain teachers. As one can imagine, this has resulted in regular, consistent schoolwide work with Los Ríos and a very limited scope of work with Grant. While both schools are under significant pressure to increase student achievement, as measured by the state's accountability system, how each administration responds dramatically affects the day-to-day operations of the school.

This leads to the second key factor, the school context, including the nature of leadership in the school, the institutional structures, and the nature of the professional community. Grant High School is characterized by leadership that is always in crisis mode, schoolwide professional development scheduled for one hour per month, and divisive relationships among the staff. Los Ríos Middle School serves as a dramatic contrast to Grant High School. Shared leadership is central to the school's operation. In fact, all professional development is planned by a leadership team comprising teachers (both NBCTs and non-NBCTs) and administration. Every Wednesday, one and a half hours are set aside for schoolwide professional development. Overall, the staff engages productively around conflicts of ideas, teaching philosophy, and other areas. Again, given these descriptions of school context, it makes sense that our collaboration with Los Ríos Middle School has been more successful than that with Grant High School.

The final key factor is the role the National Board Certification process plays in professional growth and, in particular, whether it is viewed as a vehicle for all teachers or just some. At Grant High School, the administration has viewed the certification process as a minor part of professional development, but it is not the guiding force. So it is not surprising that in a recent survey, teachers on average reported that the National Board Certification was peripheral to professional development for all teachers. In contrast, at Los Ríos, the principal made it very clear that it "all directly relates to the National Board" for all teachers, whether they are pursuing certification or not. This comes across in interviews with teachers and administrators, as well as teacher survey responses. However, distinctions still continue to be drawn between NBCTs and other teachers, in particular those who have pursued certification but did not certify after the first year. So even in such a promising context, it is important to acknowledge that no model serves as a magical solution.

Overall, this case tells the story of a group of teachers striving for self-improvement through the National Board Certification process. Throughout their journey, they faced personal challenges around their own teaching and also built a professional community where they could work, reflect on, and analyze their practice in productive ways. Still, while the teachers in the case experienced the transformative power of the certification process for themselves, perhaps a cohesive schoolwide effort, with multiple entry points for all teachers, might have tempered the sense of alienation from the rest of the school community.

COMMENTARY BY HECTOR VIVEROS LEE

I appreciated reading Sandra Dean's case of teachers pursuing National Board Certification at her school. As a National Board Certified Teacher (NBCT) who has taught in a high-priority elementary school for over ten years, coached candidates in the district for four years, and is currently released full time to coach teachers at my site, I identified with Sandra's challenges. The narrative also made me reflect on how much the National Board candidate process has affected my work. The two issues that I focus on in this commentary are: how the unique nature of high-priority schools (HPS) can diminish a teacher's desire to become certified, and how one learns to coach teachers on-site to incorporate the National Board standards into their teaching practice.

The difficulties of working in an HPS cannot be overstated. Simply classifying HPS as "low performing" adds constant stress to the staff. Teachers are often perceived to work within a "deficit model," where students and teachers are viewed largely as what they have failed to achieve and not by what they are able to do. This image compels teachers to work constantly to overcome this view, either at an unreasonable pace or in incoherent directions, and the anxiety of failing—yet again—must be overcome if HPS teachers are to attempt National Board Certification. Other obstacles include the socioeconomic challenges that require teachers to address the nonacademic needs of students, which take time away from closing the achievement gap; the instability of the teaching corps and administration; the high percentage of noncertified teachers; and the tendency to adopt new reform initiatives without coherence or long-term commitment. I was not surprised to read that the Bay Area School Reform Collaborative decided to shift its focus on reform from National Board Certification to other areas at Sandra's school.

So how does one effect changes in a school culture so it becomes collaborative, inquiry based, aligned to professional standards, and with an impact on student learning? Sandra's strategy was to work with a cohort of teachers to become certified. She imagined "what it might be like to be part of a school culture where classroom practice was routinely analyzed, studied, and refined" and supported six other candidates to enact that vision. But while work with these teachers was wonderful and defined them as a professional community, they sensed a separation from other colleagues, a result none had anticipated.

My story is a bit different. I was one of five teachers at my site who elected to pursue National Board Certification. A couple of years earlier, I had been invigorated by the discussions of teaching in a Bay Area Writing Project Summer Institute and viewed candidacy as an opportunity to continue the conversation. When I initially read the standards for Early Childhood Generalist, I felt that I fell short in many areas. But with encouragement from my colleagues, I was challenged to redesign my teaching to achieve those standards. Although I attended two local support groups, I think that being part of a small on-site cadre of teachers seeking certification was pivotal to a successful experience. During our weekly meetings, we provided support and feedback in selecting our videotapes and rewriting our entries, and we critically examined our practice, challenged each other, and reflected on how to improve our teaching. Four of us submitted portfolios, and all four of us achieved certification.

This was definitely a high point. Many of the teachers at my site were proud of our accomplishment, and we gained district recognition as the only school with four NBCTs. I became involved in the district's candidate support group and was one of a few people invited to participate in a meeting to promote accomplished teaching sponsored by NBPTS. Most important, however, was belonging to a group of teachers who supported and challenged my teaching practice. It stimulated me to think about how I might engage other teachers in conversations about their practice.

Things changed the following year. One NBCT left the school, and although several teachers appeared interested in becoming candidates, none applied after realizing the amount of work it entailed. I wondered how I was going to continue the on-site discussions about practice, when a new opportunity opened up. I was asked by several teachers to take on the role of an instructional reform facilitator, which had remained vacant that year. In discussing my goals for the position with the principal—to implement elements of National Board Certification into the job description—I was assured that the position was flexible enough to allow this. I envisioned creating a school that lived up to what it meant to be an accomplished teacher—no easy task. This would be the standard of teaching that would be expected at our school. In hindsight, I realize it was my way of bringing in teaching standards through the back door.

Since sharing my videotapes with colleagues was such a positive experience for me—pushing me to think and rethink my practice—I have brought the video camera into the classroom in my role as instructional reform facilitator. I want to address issues of poor teaching, demonstrate specific practices, look at student engagement, and provide a mirror to teachers who want to look at their practice. But I also recognize that the video camera can be invasive, so I have approached teachers cautiously. It has been a slow process. Some are open to being videotaped, and others are very resistant. I am trying to build trust so teachers can value the use of a video camera to improve their practice.

One strategy that has been somewhat successful is to invite a couple of grade-level teams to study teaching together in monthly meetings. The meetings entailed discussing professional readings, analyzing appropriate assessments, and demonstrating a best practice. Then, with my encouragement, a few teachers took the risk of videotaping themselves demonstrating a best practice and sharing their videos at our meetings. Discussions generally centered on explaining the lesson, setting the context, and answering questions. The deliberations were not always as deep or as challenging as I would like them to be, partly because of the group's effort to make teachers feel safe and partly because we are all learning how to speak critically of a colleague's practice. But it is a start. Our next step is to focus on a particular standard and to look for evidence in the videotape.

I am beginning my third year as an instructional reform facilitator. Like Sandra, I am honing my skills as a coach and continue to find it challenging to give my colleagues the kind of feedback that helps them analyze their teaching more critically. Since these kinds of conversations are usually not the norm for teachers, they must be developed over time. But if teaching is to become a true profession, we must learn to speak frankly to each other about the standard of educational practice expected at schools. I have learned how to look for evidence of standards in teachers' practice and help teachers explain their practice. But as mentors, we must also learn to establish trust, encourage, challenge, guide, scaffold, and, at times, withhold feedback. Sometimes we do this successfully and sometimes less so. This is the learning curve that describes our growth and understanding as we coach teachers.

Sandra raised another challenge that I also face: speaking the truth among colleagues who are also friends. How do I approach a colleague and friend whose practice is substandard? Will he be defensive? Will it affect our relationship? Will she welcome the professional appraisal? And will looking critically at colleagues' practice be welcome at a school with so many other pressures? There is a culture among teachers that we must get along with our colleagues; if anyone is to challenge subpar teaching, it should be an administrator, not a fellow teacher. But as coaches and accomplished teachers, I think teachers must learn to hold each other accountable for the standard of care in educational practice. Accomplished teachers know their students and the subject matter they teach; they engage and differentiate instruction for their students; they address fairness and equity in the classroom, and they are a part of learning communities. We must expect our colleagues to do likewise. I envision a time when the one-lesson evaluations by principals will be replaced by ongoing communities of teachers who watch one another's videotapes, examine student work, and challenge each other to reach a standard of excellence in their practice.

This will not be easy. I'm trying to introduce a paradigm shift: making teaching public instead of hidden behind a closed door and measuring teaching according to a standard, which is difficult for some teachers to accept. A few teachers have already questioned whether, in my role as a quasi-administrator, I have forgotten how difficult it is to be a classroom teacher. I wonder if it would have been more effective to implement change by unilaterally adopting National Board standards as the school's benchmark rather than introducing the standards in individual small groups, as I have done. Put another way, would an above-board adoption of National Board standards have been more effective? Will the factors prevalent at HPS derail the process I'm trying to establish? I am also currently working with Partners in School Innovations where we are learning to use data to address instruction in order to have an impact on student achievement. I am being challenged to relook at how I work with teachers: Are there more focused ways I can use my time to improve the teaching practice and student learning at my site? Or is it just another element of school reform in the work that I do? One thing is certain: I must continue to build up allies from within to implement the changes, and I must seek professionals from without to verify that these changes are, in fact, affecting the practice and learning at my site.

Reference

Hargreaves, A. *Changing Teachers, Changing Times: Teachers' Work and Culture in the Postmodern Age.* New York: Teachers College Press, 1994.

TEACHING NOTE

This case portrays the journey of a group of eight teachers from a low-performing elementary school that worked together on National Board Certification over a four-year period. None of the teachers achieved certification on their first try. When the first one certified, she worked with the others on their portfolios. One result of this endeavor was the development of a strong learning community of teachers who worked together to improve their teaching and took on leadership roles to help others "better serve the needs of young children." But they also experienced a schism from the rest of the faculty, a result none of them had anticipated.

Analysis of this case and its commentaries provides an opportunity to explore how National Board Certification (NBC) can provide a framework for developing a learning community for teachers at a school site, engaged in trying their best to serve the needs of their students. It also examines some of the thorny issues that can arise when working with one's colleagues.

ISSUES AND QUESTIONS

Can We Really Teach Like This?

This is one of the common refrains we hear from teachers who teach in high-priority/low-performing schools when they see the National Board standards. Granted, teaching in these schools presents challenges that schools with higher-achieving students do not have; case author Sandra Dean and commentators Ann-Marie Wiese and Hector Lee enumerate several of these challenges. But they also portray numerous examples of strategies that teachers draw on to raise the bar in their teaching and in their schools, using the standards as a framework for their work together. Examine the variety of strategies that were used in both the case and commentaries. Which ones might have relevance for your practice?

Need for Appropriate Mentoring

Initially, Sandra worked on her National Board portfolio with a colleague and had no structured mentoring. When she failed to certify, she joined a regional support group. There she learned that there's a big difference between the inquiry aspect of teaching and being systematic during her reflections. The coaches and other candidates taught her to look for evidence of standards as she analyzed her teaching, and she used similar strategies when she mentored her colleagues. Examine the variety of strategies that she used as she worked with her colleagues on their portfolios. Also look at how Hector Lee used some of these methods with the teachers in his school, even though they were not National Board candidates. Can you think of other methods that they may have used? What are the risks and benefits of each one? Sandra also learned that mentoring needed to be different for new candidates than for advanced candidates (those who did not certify the first time). How did she tailor her mentoring to each group of candidates?

Mentors who discussed this case were particularly taken with Sandra's invitation of a science specialist to work with the teachers on their math/science entry. They noted that they often worked with candidates from a variety of disciplines and age groups and were often limited in their capacity to judge the merits of a particular lesson or unit. Others discussed the advantages of being a generalist. What are the advantages and limitations of being a generalist when mentoring other teachers? Under what circumstances might it be useful to bring in—or suggest talking to—an outside resource?

Providing Constructive Feedback to One's Colleagues

Many of the cases in this book deal with the difficulty of providing constructive feedback; this one is no exception. Both Sandra and Hector describe positive and challenging aspects of providing feedback to their colleagues. What are some of these trade-offs? Sandra and both commentators also describe the potential impact of learning how to analyze teaching systematically and give and receive constructive feedback to one another on a school site. What are the risks and benefits of using these strategies with teachers at a particular school?

"Failure Is an Integral Part of Learning"

One of the most challenging aspects of supporting National Board candidates is helping those who don't certify work through their hurt, humiliation, and, sometimes, anger. National Board Certification is a rigorous process; as of 2004, fewer than 40 percent of the candidates achieve certification on their first attempt. So mentors must anticipate that some of the teachers they support will become advanced candidates. For Sandra, this was particularly difficult, since none of her colleague teachers achieved certification on their first try. Yet she was able to get all of them to accept that "failure is an integral part of learning." As a result, they dug deeper into their analyses of their teaching and continued to learn together. How was she able to accomplish this? Can you think of other strategies she might have used?

The Importance of Context

Ann-Marie Wiese's commentary focuses on the influence of context in determining whether a school-based professional development initiative—such as using National Board Certification to raise the quality of teaching and learning—has the potential to draw in an entire faculty. One of the disappointing results of Sandra's endeavor was that the teachers noticed a schism that developed between their learning community and the rest of the faculty. What are some of the obstacles that might prevent a professional development initiative to be successful at a school site? What are some features that might make it more likely that such an initiative could be successful?

CHAPTER FOURTEEN

CONCLUSION
Making the Most of Case Discussions
Judith H. Shulman

During the past twenty years, educators have come to view case-based teaching as one of the most promising ways to reform teacher education and staff development (for a selected bibliography on case methods, see www.wested.org/icd). Staff at WestEd have been active participants in this reform effort, publishing a dozen casebooks, leading case discussions, conducting facilitator seminars, and coordinating national conferences. Our experience and research show that skillfully conducted case discussions can help participants bridge theory and practice, spot issues and frame problems in ambiguous situations, interpret predicaments from multiple perspectives, identify crucial decision points and possibilities for action, recognize potential risks and benefits inherent in any course of action, and test teaching principles in classrooms. In short, cases and case discussions can help teachers develop flexibly powerful pedagogical understanding and judgment (L. Shulman, 1996).

We are also aware of the pitfalls of poor discussions (J. Shulman, 1996). It is possible, for example, to participate in an animated case discussion and learn nothing new. This chapter is focused on increasing the possibilities that learning will occur. Our

---

Some parts of this chapter were drawn from J. H. Shulman, A. Whittaker, and M. Lew, *Facilitators' Guide: Using Assessments to Teach for Understanding.* New York: Teachers College Press, 2002.

experience and research suggest that the more knowledgeable a facilitator is about the issues depicted in a case and the more she can anticipate the variety of participant responses in a case discussion, the greater the likelihood is that useful learning will occur as a result of the discussion.

If you are using cases in a program of study, Misty Sato, my colleagues at WestEd who develop and use case discussions, and I recommend that you incorporate several in your curriculum. This will prevent a tendency to overgeneralize from a single case and provide opportunities to discuss issues from several perspectives. For example, one of the thorny issues that several case authors in this book explore is how to meet the needs of challenging mentees. Examining several accounts about how authors deal with this dilemma should enable you to make better judgments when you are faced with needy mentees than if you were only to examine one case (see Table I.1).

PREPARING THE DISCUSSION

Both the quality and the outcome of a discussion depend on what facilitators do to prepare for it. Consider how you would respond to questions such as: What is your purpose for using the case? Where in your curriculum will you use it? Will you have supplementary readings with the case, or will your case discussion stand alone? If you are using more than one case in your program, which ones will you select? How will you sequence them?

Just like novice teachers realize—sometimes too late—that they need to carefully plan their instruction, such preparation is also critical to the success of case discussion. You will need a thorough knowledge of the case as well as clear ideas about how best to use the teaching notes to guide the sessions. This means that you should read the cases several times. As often as I have used individual cases, I never cease to learn something new each time I prepare for a case discussion. The following suggestions can help guide your reading:

• On your initial reading, take note of your first impression. What excites you? What bothers you? With whom did you relate? Subsequent readings may influence your answers to these questions, so it is important to jot down your initial reactions to use as diagnostic tools. These responses should help you recognize any biases you may have about the case and later help you understand the participants' reactions.

• Since each case has many layers of meaning, each reading yields more information and understanding. Ask yourself questions—such as: "What is this a case of?" "What are different ways to interpret this case?" and "How would the various characters in the account interpret what's happening?" Also note the descriptive words, key phrases, and dialogue used, especially early in the case, as the author introduces the characters and set of events.

• Look for trouble spots in the case—instances when a mentor is confronted by angry or perplexed colleagues or puzzled by a dilemma. These events can serve as teachable moments in the discussion. For example, in "National Board Readiness: Is There a Right Time?" (Chapter Eight), the case author is perplexed by a teacher who continually made excuses about why he didn't bring a video to share with the support group and wondered whether she used the appropriate approach with him. Ask yourself—and later participants in a case discussion—"What might prevent this teacher from wanting to share his video with other teachers?" You and the group might come up with some reasons the author never considered, thereby providing opportunities to make better decisions in similar circumstances.

• Look for subtle cues. Cases like "The Facilitator, the Candidate, and the Mushy Brains" (Chapter Six) raise ethical questions about how to work with a teacher who has biases about what his students can learn. An understanding of the teacher's faulty preconception and the various ways his mentor tried to help him inductively recognize his bias may require examining the narrative's details, perhaps making paragraph-by-paragraph notations.

USING THE COMMENTARIES

The commentaries that follow each case add information, expert testimonies, and analyses from various perspectives to the dilemmas embedded in the narrative. They are meant to enrich the study of the case, not to provide the "best" interpretation. Many instructors in teacher education programs have asked their students to add their own commentaries.

USING THE TEACHING NOTES

The teaching notes that accompany each case are designed to help you plan your discussion. As analytical interpretations, they alert you in advance to potential problem areas and provide sample probing questions. They are *not* designed to give you a particular pathway for moving a group through the case. You can use the notes to identify stages of discussion and select questions that enable participants to view the case through different lenses. They might also help you anticipate responses from the group members, which will help during the discussion. Just as you customize case selection and sequence, you will want to tailor questions to suit the profile of your particular group.

PLANNING THE PHYSICAL SPACE

The arrangement of the physical space for discussions can either encourage intimate participation or discourage it. We have used two kinds of room arrangements, again depending on our purpose for the case discussion. If we plan on using small-group discussions, we arrange the tables for four or five people in each group, and periodically ask people to talk among themselves before coming together in a larger group. This plan works particularly well when trying to facilitate a discussion with a large number of participants. If we don't plan on using small groups, we have found that the U-shaped arrangement, with participants sitting at tables on the outside of the U, works best. This arrangement enables group members to maintain eye contact with one another during a discussion and allows the facilitator to move within the circle at will; it is also conducive to asking participants to share ideas in pairs. We usually ask participants to write their first names on the front of a folded index card and place it in front of them on the table so we can use first names during the discussion. We also place either a board or easel with chart paper in the front of the room for recording major points made during the discussion. This enables participants to see how the discussion is progressing.

Planning the Time

It takes time to peel away the surface layers of the cases and get to the underlying problems. Allowing two hours for a case discussion should give you plenty of time to delve deeply into most of the case. But what if you have only ninety minutes or an hour? This doesn't mean you shouldn't try to discuss a case, but you will have to plan your time accordingly. Just note that you may not get through all the segments of the discussion as thoroughly as you would like. It is often helpful to distribute the case before the discussion and ask participants to read it carefully, jotting down questions and noting issues before class. If you are pressed for time, keep one eye on the clock. It is easy to become caught up in one section of the discussion and run out of time before you complete all the parts you had planned. Stopping a discussion before you can bring it to closure can be more harmful than cutting short a particular section midway through the discussion (see Table 14.1 below).

Creating Your Plan

After you have established your purpose for the case, major issues you want to address, questions you may want to pose, and the amount of time you have for the discussion, you are ready to develop a plan. Table 14.1 illustrates the major segments of a case discussion that we use.

Although this pathway appears to be linear, discussions rarely follow such a straight path. We recommend, however, that you adequately analyze the issues in the cases from a variety of perspectives before generating alternative strategies that a teacher may pursue. Our experience suggests that educators are quick to make judgments and begin making suggestions for the teacher-author before adequately analyzing the problems.

In a typical discussion, the initial focus is on the particularities of the case and an examination of what happened. The effectiveness of the analysis depends on your repertoire of questions that encourage reflection. As facilitator, you should be prepared to follow participants' responses with probing questions that deepen their reflection. The teaching notes are a resource for questions. Another is the typology of questions in Table 14.2.

Table 14.1. Structure of a Case Discussion

Part One: What's going on?	What are the facts?
Part Two: Analysis (usually half of the discussion)	Identify issues and questions Analyze the problems from multiple perspectives Evaluate solutions proposed in the case
Part Three: Action and principles of practice	Propose alternative solutions Consider trade-offs—risks and benefits—of each potential solution Consider long-term and short-term options Formulate generalizations about practices based on case discussion, prior discussions, experience, and theoretical understanding
Part Four: "What is this a case of?"	Moving up the ladder of abstraction, link this case to more general categories Rich cases are, by nature, "of" many things

These questions serve different purposes. Some act to pull more information from participants (for example, the open-ended, diagnostic, and information-seeking questions), while others push the discussion (for example, the challenge, prediction, and hypothetical questions). Each discussion should have a balance of both kinds of questions. It often helps to jot down some questions that you want to be sure to use. Our research and experience suggest that participants learn more when the facilitator pushes the discussion in a variety of ways.

Beginning a New Group

If you are starting a new group, it is important that group members have an opportunity to get acquainted with one another, especially if they will work together for a period of time. Then start with your goals for the seminar and a general introduction to case methods: defining what cases are (how they differ from individual

TABLE 14.2. TYPOLOGY OF QUESTIONS

Type of Question	Example
Information-seeking questions	What are the support structures for mentors in your district?
Open-ended questions	What do you think about the mentor's strategies with his mentee?
Diagnostic questions	What is your analysis of the problem? What conclusions can you draw from the data?
Challenge (testing) questions	What evidence supports your conclusion? What arguments can be developed to counter that hypothesis?
Action questions	What strategies would you use to help this teacher?
Prediction questions	How do you think your students will react?
Hypothetical questions	What would have happened if the teacher had not asked her mentor for help?
Questions of extension	What are the implications of the mentor's strategies of helping this neophyte?
Questions of generalization	Based on this discussion and your experience, what principles would you use to help challenging teachers?

stories), explaining why we use them in teacher education and professional development, and foreshadowing a typical case discussion (see Table 14.1). Emphasize that your aim is to establish an ethos of critical inquiry that encourages multiple interpretations, conflicting views, and equitable participation, and not to come up with a consensus on the one best way to analyze the case. This is not always easy and demands that you create a climate of safety that allows differences of opinion. Often it helps to develop some norms of discussion such as these:

- Respect each person's contribution and point of view by listening carefully to each person's contribution.
- Do not interrupt! Wait for speakers to finish before responding.

It is also important to reiterate that the authors wrote the cases because they hoped that others would learn from their experience, as they did while presenting their cases to other case writers.

FACILITATING THE DISCUSSION

Before beginning any discussion, we suggest that you set a context and purpose for using the case, so participants have an advance organizer for reading the case and the ensuing discussion. This helps to encourage people to focus on your goals and discourages off-track discussion. Then we ask participants to read the case, if they have not done so already, and highlight or make notes on important questions and issues. When they have finished, we usually ask participants for a literal description of the case, either by stating the facts that are important to understanding the narrative or describing what happened in the story. These are both comfortable ways to enter the discussion and enable everyone to begin with a shared sense of what happened.

We have multiple entry points for the next stage of the discussion and select one based on our purpose for using the case. One strategy is to break the group into pairs or trios to identify key issues and questions from the case. This gets everyone talking and is especially important for those who hesitate to participate in a large group. After about ten minutes, we record their questions on a board or chart paper, usually taking a question from each group and then opening the conversation to all if there are questions that were not noted. This strategy provides an immediate barometer of where the group is in relation to important issues, so you can gauge how you might want to direct the discussion. It also makes it clear that there are many ways to examine a case and should help prevent any tendency to becoming fixated on one point of view. After completing the list of issues and questions, we often ask the group to decide where *they* wish to start the discussion. To gain consensus, sometimes we ask the group to vote on where they want to begin. This technique sends a subtle message that we respect the group's agenda and will not impose our own. It works particularly well when there is flexibility about how the discussion proceeds.

If you have a particular reason for using the case and may have only one opportunity to analyze a particular problem, however, you may want to choose a more focused opening by asking a specific question. If you decide on this strategy, consider the opening question carefully, because it will set the tone for the entire discussion. You can get at the facts during the discussion by periodically referring to details in the case. Another option is to give small groups study questions to discuss among themselves before examining the case as a large group. We have found that if you are working with a group for a period of time, using multiple approaches to vary the discussion experience is helpful.

One of the intriguing challenges of using case methods is that each discussion is different and takes on a life of its own. At times the discussion may appear at an impasse, or participants may be ignoring information you believe is key to understanding the case's problems or dilemmas. At such times, you can shift the topic or perspective by saying something like, "We have been talking about this topic [provide example] for awhile; have you thought about how [give example] might view the situation?" Another tactic is to play devil's advocate and introduce an ignored problem or quotation from the narrative to push the conversation in different directions. A third strategy is to incorporate activities such as role playing or small-group discussions, which can offer a change of pace. Occasionally you may feel the need to provide some additional information based on the teaching notes or other scholarly sources. If you choose this tactic, be careful to keep it brief; participants may feel you know the answers you are looking for and may be reluctant to offer contrary opinions.

Be sensitive to the possibility that there may be tension between your agenda for a case discussion and that of the group. This requires a delicate balance. If you stick to your discussion plan without letting participants move in a direction they prefer, you communicate that you are in control and they might hesitate to bring up their issues and concerns. But if you merely follow where the participants want to take the discussion, you abrogate your role as a teacher. One way to get around this dilemma is to look for opportunities to build on participants' ideas rather than raising new ideas yourself. Remind them that your role as facilitator is to challenge their ideas and push them to defend their views, regardless of their position. Ultimately you are trying to move participants from reflection to problem solving and a willingness to investigate their own practice.

CLOSING THE DISCUSSION

Another challenge is making sure that participants have opportunities to synthesize what they learned and connect it to other case discussions and their experience before the discussion concludes. One approach that we often use is to ask participants to reflect on the case and respond to the question, "What is this a case of?" This question, which began as a suggestion from Lee Shulman, is a theme that weaves through all our casework. It asks teachers to characterize a particular case in relation to other cases, their own experience, and the conceptual or abstract categories with which they are familiar. Lee Shulman suggests that it is a way of encouraging participants to move between "the memorable particularities of cases and the powerful simplifications of principles and theories" (1996, p. 201). In our experience, this technique has been extremely valuable in helping participants connect the particular narrative to the variety of categories it represents.

We also ask participants to give us written feedback about what they learned, responding to such questions as these: What mentoring dilemmas embedded in this case have relevance for you and your practice? What questions about mentoring did this case raise for you? What insights, if any, did you gain from this case discussion on how to solve the dilemmas? Do you have any lingering questions that have to be resolved? Many people appreciate the opportunity to synthesize their thoughts in writing before sharing them in the larger group.

ROLE OF THE FACILITATOR

Although you may have more expertise than the group you are working with, as facilitator you should take a neutral stance, like that of an active listener, reflecting by your words and body language that you heard, understood, and accepted what the speaker communicated. Your responsibility is to help participants analyze the issues in each case by directing them to pertinent information and eliciting alternative perspectives. It is best to have at your disposal a set of probing questions that helps to expose, clarify, and challenge assumptions and proposed strategies that participants raise during the discussion.

If members in your group appear to accept or reject ideas too quickly, play devil's advocate and offer other perspectives for their consideration. Your goal is not to tell them what to believe or do, but to help them come to their own conclusions about the best course of action. One of the most difficult aspects of leading case discussions, especially for new discussion leaders, is the possibility that participants may leave a meeting with what appears to you to be the wrong point of view. You may feel compelled to give the "correct" answers, as if there is one best solution. Instead, be patient. Changing beliefs takes time, and being told what to believe is rarely effective. Individuals come with their own set of experiences that help shape their beliefs. They need time to evaluate these during case discussions and later in their work as a mentor. The cases in this book are constructed and sequenced so that participants and facilitators have numerous opportunities to revisit the same issues.

Your challenge as a facilitator is to build an ample world of ideas for the group to explore and then to move the discussion up and down the ladder of abstraction—up to principles, back down to discrete practices, then up again. Put another way, the challenge is to move the discussion from the level of opinion swap to the desired level of applied knowledge. Here are some suggestions on how to do this:

- Try not to become emotionally involved in what's being said. You will be more effective if you keep some distance and appear impartial.
- Periodically synthesize issues of disagreement and summarize what has been learned. This keeps group members from repeatedly coming back to the same point or digressing so far that their conversation no longer relates to the case. When

there are questions about what happened, it is helpful to read excerpts of the case aloud.

- At opportune moments, ask participants to come up with generalizations or principles based on this and previous case discussions and their experience. This develops their capacity to transfer what they learn from the analysis of a particular case to similar situations they may encounter in their own work.
- Remember that you are teaching the skills of case analysis. Our goal is that participants will apply these skills when they are faced with problems in their own practice.

When you have finished conducting a discussion, reflect on what transpired, individually or with a partner, and examine any feedback that you have collected. Make notes to yourself so the next time you conduct a discussion, you can benefit from your own learning.

If you have questions or comments about the cases or facilitation guides or want to share what you have learned, please contact us at jshulma@wested.org or msato@umn.edu; we would love to hear from you. We hope that you and your stakeholders will learn as much from discussing these cases as we did while working with the case writers and putting this book together. It can be an exciting and rewarding professional development journey.

References

Institute for Case Development. "Selected Bibliography." www.wested.org/icd.

Shulman, J. H. "Tender Feelings, Hidden Thoughts: Confronting Bias, Innocence, and Racism Through Case Discussions." In J. Colbert, P. Desberg, and K. Trimble (eds.), *The Case for Education: Contemporary Approaches for Using Case Methods*. Needham Heights, Mass.: Allyn & Bacon, 1996.

Shulman, L. S. "Just in Case: Reflections on Learning from Experience." In J. Colbert, P. Desberg, and K. Trimble (eds.), *The Case for Education: Contemporary Approaches for Using Case Methods*. Needham Heights, Mass.: Allyn & Bacon, 1996.

WORKING WITH CASE WRITERS: A METHODOLOGICAL NOTE

Judith H. Shulman and Mistilina Sato

This book is the legacy of a network of National Board candidate support providers, who met regularly over a five-year period at WestEd to share experiences, get technical assistance, and discuss the celebrations and challenges of mentoring veteran teachers toward a high-stakes, standards-based assessment. Participants in this learning community included teacher educators, staff developers, administrators, and National Board Certified Teachers (NBCTs), as they increasingly began to assume mentoring roles for novices and veterans in their school districts. As we worked together and as newcomers joined the group, we became convinced that the practical and moral issues that were discussed during the meetings were worthy of developing into teaching cases about teachers mentoring their peers. They represented a class of dilemmas that most mentors face, whether they work with teachers, graduate students, or persons outside the profession of education.

Just as in a case discussion where we seek multiple perspectives on issues embedded in the narrative, the same is true during case development. For this book, Shulman served as the

---

Some parts of this chapter were drawn from J. Shulman, "A Methodological Note," in J. Shulman, A. Whitaker, and M. Lew, *Using Assessments to Teach for Understanding: A Casebook for Educators.* New York: Teachers College Press, 2002.

expert on case development, and Sato, a scholar in science education and teacher development and former coordinator of the largest National Board candidate support group in the San Francisco Bay Area, served as the expert on mentoring. We had collaborated on several network programs, including designing and conducting a seminar for new National Board support providers, and felt that we could learn from one another's expertise.

As collaborators, our first task was to conceptualize this book. To help with this endeavor, we used part of a network meeting to describe our project and asked group members, "What challenges and/or dilemmas should this casebook illustrate?" Put another way, what would these narratives be cases of? Using the network members' feedback, we designed a set of topic descriptors and writing prompts for case writers. These topics were meant to provide a trigger for thinking about potential cases, but we were also open to the idea that some experiences of support providers would have multiple facets that overlap into more than one topic. The initial list of topics included:

Balancing Professional Development and Assessment
    Support for Candidates

Supporting a Vision of Accomplished Teaching

The Role of the Support Provider

Boundaries for the Support Provider

Complexities of Effective Coaching

Sustaining Effective Groups

Structuring Support

Determining Candidate Groups

Next, we selected a group of case writers. For this task, we identified people who were active in both of our organizations—the National Board Support Group at WestEd and the National Board Resource Center at Stanford University—and whom we thought would be good writers. We did not recruit indiscriminately for interested case writers. The one stipulated requirement was that they attend a two-day introductory case writing seminar held during the summer and two follow-up sessions during the fall. (This two-day seminar can also be used as an excellent professional development activity for educators who want to grapple substantively with pertinent issues through lively discussion and dialogue, whether or not their narratives will end up as published cases.)

DRAFTING THE CASES

This section describes our process of developing a publishable case. The process is rigorous and time-consuming. It portrays a collaborative endeavor among case writers and editors that seeks input from potential readers and users when drafts are complete. We also examine our methods of conceptualizing cross-cutting themes among cases.

INTRODUCTORY SEMINAR

The goals of this two-day seminar were to introduce the authors to our conception of dilemma-based cases and help them begin drafting their narratives. We took care to sequence a set of activities that introduced case writing in a safe and supportive environment for writing. Shulman has used a similar seminar to introduce each of the six previous casebooks that she has coedited (see www.wested. org/icd for information on these books).

After preliminary introductions, which set the stage for a supportive learning community, we engaged the teachers in a case discussion using a narrative from a published casebook. Our purpose was to introduce the process and value of cases and case discussion as tools for professional development. During a debrief after the discussion, we analyzed both the structure and content of the case as narrative so that the writers understood the genre of teaching cases.

Next, we examined topics to consider and deliberated about the kinds of episodes that would illustrate the themes in each topic. When case writers began to describe what they might want to write about, we asked, "Would this be a good case?" By that we meant whether the particular story would make a theoretical claim that it was a case of something or an instance of a larger class. For instance, after one teacher described a variety of problems she encountered with a teacher whose instructional strategies looked more like those belonging to a beginning teacher than to a veteran applying for National Board Certification, we asked questions such as, "Does this story ring true?" "Will other mentors identify with it?" When the answer was yes, we said that this story, or "case seed," could potentially develop into a good teaching case. As noted in the Preface, to be valuable as a case, the narrative should represent the type of class or dilemma, problem, or quandary that arises with some frequency in teaching situations.

When we felt that participants had an idea of what they wanted to write about, we engaged them in a ten-minute freewriting activity, suggesting that they write nonstop about their chosen topic without being concerned about the quality of their writing. We then asked them to read what they had written, underline key ideas, and take three more minutes to elaborate on one idea. Then we divided the group into pairs, asking one person to present his or her case seed and the other to take the role of active listener and raise questions. After both partners had the opportunity to discuss their respective ideas, we debriefed again as a group. We asked participants to spend the next few hours writing on their own, elaborating on their "seeds" using feedback from their partner. Ideally, when participants leave this first day, they have a clear idea of the episode on which their cases will hinge. Nevertheless, some do change their minds during the drafting process.

The following morning, they returned to the group and shared their narratives in groups of three or four according to a list of questions intended to scaffold the conversation. Each person had approximately thirty minutes to discuss his or her draft. During these discussions, we participated in the group discussion and raised questions that helped authors identify essential information for the case or uncover their own unexplored assumptions. In the afternoon, we debriefed the process, listed the themes of their cases on chart paper, and discussed how the themes related to one another. We also discussed how to craft their narratives into a teaching case and used one of the participant's case seeds as an example. When we adjourned, most participants had a good idea of how to write their first draft. Nevertheless, telephone calls and e-mail messages often went back and forth between authors and editors in response to questions.

FIRST DRAFTS

When the drafts were completed, the editors met to discuss each one and agreed on the kind of feedback we wanted to provide, based on a review form with questions such as:

- What was effective about the case?
- What needs clarification or elaboration?
- Do you have suggestions about the style or structure of this piece?
- Are there ways to improve the beginning or ending of the case?
- Do you think the beginning draws someone into the case quickly?
- Does the ending spark discussion naturally?
- What is this a case of?

We gathered for two follow-up sessions with the authors, during which much of the time was spent working within the same small groups used during the introductory seminar. To prepare for these sessions, we sent copies of the drafts and the case review form to each group member, asked that they read the drafts in advance, and come prepared to provide their thoughts. We also assigned one person from each group to write comments using the review form and to lead off the small-group discussion. In the feedback collected at the end of these sessions, most participants found the discussions useful for both their own learning and their ability to craft a case that would serve as a professional development opportunity for users.

During the last session, we dealt with some of the ethical issues in case development: first, the use of pseudonyms to maintain confidentiality of people and places in the cases. In two of the most sensitive cases, the authors decided to mask some of the characteristics of people to further protect identities. We also discussed whether they wanted to be identified by name as the author, which can be a delicate topic. In the past, some people wanted to have their names associated with their case; others preferred anonymity if they were concerned that confidentiality for persons in their narrative was at risk. This group decided to have their names associated with the cases they wrote.

FINAL DRAFTS

The writers made their final revisions based on feedback from the meeting and, in most cases, ongoing e-mail or telephone conversations with the editors. When we received the final drafts, we examined them once again, asking ourselves, Are the cases compelling? Are the mentors' dilemmas clear? Will the cases stimulate analysis and rich discussion? If we still had questions, we made these queries by telephone or e-mail and incorporated any changes into the text. We took liberal editing license with some cases, reorganizing and paring down text or inserting transitions to help with narrative flow. We always sought to maintain the voice and text of the author, and we always sent the final narrative to the author for approval; sometimes this process took several iterations.

In two of the cases written for this book, the narratives had resolutions that tied everything together at the end. The cases were wonderfully crafted stories drawn directly from each author's experience, but they left no dilemma or point of uncertainty about the mentoring episode. Although the mentor had choices to make, everything worked out in the end with a proverbial happy ending. In both of these cases, we worked with the authors to find the point at which they found themselves faced with a decision or a choice. The authors both described their situations as difficult to manage and that they were uncertain about their course of action. We encouraged them to end their cases after they described their dilemma or course of action rather than telling the reader how the situation resolved. We thought this technique would provide a better opportunity for reflection and thought on the part of the reader.

When all of the narratives met our final draft criteria, we entered the last stage of the process: sending the cases to an outside editor and returning them to the authors with the editor's notations and questions. Authors always had the final word on suggested revisions.

COMMENTARIES

When the final drafts were complete, we again asked ourselves, "What are these cases of?" and solicited commentaries from other educators. The purpose of these additional viewpoints was not to provide the right answer to the dilemmas in the narratives but rather to enrich potential analyses. The commentaries added information about a particular topic, alternate analyses of the challenges and dilemmas in the case, and suggestions about courses of action. Typically two commentaries follow each narrative, each from a different perspective—either a researcher and a practitioner or two practitioners. Occasionally we had conversations with the commentators to ensure that they focused on the issues in the case rather than a critique of the author.

FIELD TEST

The field test represents the final step of the case development process. We piloted the cases with other educators who assume the role of mentoring—teacher educators, staff developers, administrators, and National Board Certified Teachers—to see what kind of discussion ensued. While one of us conducted the discussion, the other took notes. At times these sessions were videotaped for further reference.

The field test had several purposes. First, we used the notes and written feedback from participants as grist for developing the teaching notes that follow each case. We were also interested to see if any parts of the discussion were problematic and could be resolved by a simple addition to the text. For example, in one case discussion, when participants were given one additional piece of background information about the case author, their perspective on the case shifted. Along with the author, we chose to incorporate this information into the case in an effort to circumvent an unproductive line of reasoning during a case discussion.

Finally, we wanted to confirm our hypothesis that although these cases were situated in the context of supporting National

Board candidates, the dilemmas represented in the narratives were relevant to other educators who mentor teachers. So we selected the annual meeting of the American Association of Colleges of Teacher Education as one of our field test sites. In two separate sessions, we received unanimous agreement from the deans of colleges of education and teacher educators who participated that the cases were indeed applicable to their mentoring practice and their program design decisions.

TEACHING NOTES

Each case in this book is followed by a teaching note, geared to both potential discussion leaders and independent readers with no access to group analyses. The notes were written after the commentaries and field test for each case were completed. They analyze key issues, offer sample probing questions for analysis, and often include insights and questions from participants in the field test. Data from the field test and discussions among case writers were extremely valuable for this endeavor.

TABLE OF CROSS-CUTTING ISSUES

The development of Table I.1 began at the end of the introductory case writing seminar when we asked the authors, "Let's go up the ladder of abstraction: What are your cases of? What big ideas are represented in your narratives?" We began with the initial list of topics to consider. The table went through numerous iterations as we tested our conceptual categories during each phase of the development—drafting the topics to consider, crafting the narratives, soliciting commentaries, field-testing the cases, and creating the teaching notes. Some categories were deleted after we realized that some topics encompassed all cases and others were added; many titles were changed; and identification in individual cells sometimes shifted as a result of comments during the field test. During one session, a few people differed with our analysis of which topics were selected for a particular case. At this point, all we can say is that the table represents our best effort to identify the cross-cutting issues of each case. Perhaps our analyses will change as we continue to use the cases. We never cease to learn something new each time we lead a case discussion.

SUMMARY

We have focused in this methodological note primarily on our methods of guiding authors to progress from creating case seeds to crafting teaching cases. The development process was both time-consuming and rigorous, with multiple opportunities for collegial input from the community of case writers and editors. We felt the need for this degree of rigor given our goal to publish cases that were both authentic to the authors and powerful enough to stimulate rich analysis and discussion among others. Such rigor may not be necessary for groups that want to use case writing as a constructive tool to stimulate substantive discussion among students in a university course or within a community of practitioners. Indeed, the most important feature of our method is the creation of a safe and active teacher learning community in which individual experiences become shared narratives. These stories are then both interrogated and appreciated until they are transformed into teaching cases. They remain personal, but they emerge as community property, a source of learning for all.

SELECTED ANNOTATED BIBLIOGRAPHY

Gloria I. Miller

In education research and professional publications, the term *mentoring* is used typically to describe the relationship between an experienced teacher and a novice teacher. The settings in association with mentoring are usually in either teacher preparation (preservice education) or induction into the profession. Rarely does the literature refer to mentoring as an indicator of a peer or near-peer relationship. The near-peer relationships under discussion in this book are also referred to as *coach–teacher, critical friends, community of learners, support network, collaboration,* and *study group* terminology.

Bambino, D. "Critical Friends: Redesigning Professional Development." *Educational Leadership,* 2002, *59*(6), 25–27. In this short article, Bambino provides a personal account of using a critical friends group structure to improve teaching. Critical friends are defined as colleagues meeting to examine student work and the teacher work that promoted it. The training for participating in a critical friends group focused on building the trust needed for engaging in direct and productive conversations with colleagues about the complex art of teaching. Bambino describes the functional aspects of a critical friends group and provides examples for each of the four elements: feedback, collaboration, solution finding, and community creating.

Beasley, K., Corbin, D., Feiman-Nemser, S., and Shank, C. "'Making It Happen': Teachers Mentoring One Another." *Theory into Practice,* 1996, *35*(3), 158–164. The authors describe, through journal entry reflections, a year-long mentoring project among two elementary teachers and a university professor. They reflect on the power of focused observation, writing, and practice-centered talk to promote teacher learning. They also discuss the concerns of learning to work together.

Bey, T. M., and Holmes, C. T. (eds.). *Mentoring: Contemporary Principles and Issues.* Reston, Va.: Association of Teacher Educators, and Athens, Ga.: University of Georgia, 1992. This monograph, commissioned by the Association of Teacher Educators Commission on the Role and Preparation of Mentor Teachers, articulates key ideas that could be used to guide the development and implementation of mentoring efforts. Mentoring in this monograph is conceived as a support system for beginning teachers. Among the ten principles of mentoring are these: mentoring is a complex process and function; mentoring involves support, assistance, and guidance, but not evaluation; mentoring requires time and communication; mentoring should facilitate self-reliance in protégés; and mentors should be trained and offered incentives for their work. Of particular interest for this casebook are the first three chapters, which address the complexity of mentoring, the need for psychological support for both mentor and protégé, and avoiding formal evaluation of the protégé.

Cohen, N. H. "The Principles of Adult Mentoring Scale." In M. W. Galbraith and N. H. Cohen (eds.), *Mentoring: New Strategies and Challenges.* San Francisco: Jossey-Bass, 1995. This chapter describes the mentor role in terms of six behavioral functions defined from data collected in academic settings, which, the author suggests, ought to be incorporated into preparation and ongoing professional development programs for mentors:

- Relationship focus. To what extent does the mentor convey through active, emphatic listening a genuine understanding and acceptance of mentees' feelings?
- Information emphasis. To what extent does the mentor directly request detailed information from and offer specific suggestions to mentees about their current plans and progress in achieving personal, educational, and career goals?
- Facilitative focus. To what extent does the mentor guide mentees through reasonably in-depth review and exploration of their interests, abilities, ideas, and beliefs?

- Confrontive focus. To what extent does the mentor respectfully challenge mentees' explanations for or avoidance of decisions and actions relevant to their development as adult learners?
- Mentor model. To what extent does the mentor share life experiences and feelings as a role model to mentees in order to personalize and enrich the relationship?
- Student vision. To what extent does the mentor stimulate mentees' critical thinking with regard to envisioning their own future and developing their personal and professional potential?

Feiman-Nemser, S. "Teachers as Teacher Educators." *European Journal of Teacher Education,* 1998, *21*(1). Teachers who work as mentors for novice teachers rarely see themselves as teacher educators. Feiman-Nemser explores this issue from epistemological and sociocultural views. Two personal anecdotes and findings from a comparative, cross-cultural study of mentored learning to teach are used to investigate what educative mentoring looks like and what it entails. Feiman-Nemser adopts a theoretical perspective to explore two aspects of the mentoring act: joint work and thinking aloud. A case for seeing mentoring rooted in the contexts of teaching is presented.

Feiman-Nemser, S., and Parker, M. B. "Making Subject Matter Part of the Conversation in Learning to Teach." *Journal of Teacher Education,* 1990, *41*(3), 32–43. Feiman-Nemser and Parker studied conversations between mentors and their novice teachers to reveal whether or how subject matter was being addressed. They present four case studies to illustrate the striking differences in how the mentors treated subject matter concerns. While the authors make no claims about which style of conversation is more productive, they suggest that more explicit attention to subject matter is needed to help bring together knowledge of subjects with knowledge of students, contexts, curriculum, and pedagogy for the novice teachers.

Little, J. W. "The Mentor Phenomenon." In C. Cazden (ed.), *Review of Research in Education.* Washington, D.C.: American Educational Research Association, 1990. This classic review focuses on the organizational and occupational significance of mentoring among practicing teachers, with particular emphasis on issues related to school organization, occupational socialization, and the structure of the teaching career. Little traces the history of adopting mentoring structures for the induction of new teachers through the use of case studies that chronicle the emergence of the mentor role. Highlighted issues include mentor role ambiguity and role conflict, the selection of mentors, the training of mentors, time spent mentoring, and the substance of the mentoring. Little also discusses the recurrent problem of recognizing expertise in teaching and the relationship between the mentor's role and the debate on an agreed-on body of knowledge confounded with the accessibility of teachers' knowledge.

Lord, B. "Teacher's Professional Development: Critical Colleagueship and the Role of Professional Communities." In N. Cobb (ed.), *The Future of Education: Perspectives on National Standards in America.* New York: College Board, 1994. Lord discusses various content standards and asks the following questions: In what ways might professional development contribute to a more reflective stance toward instruction? How will teachers be helped to move beyond relatively superficial interpretations of national content standards? From whom might teachers get critical feedback on their teaching, and how might constructive criticism be built into the very fabric of professional development? Lord provides an overview of current professional development practices and highlights the main contradictions. To combat these contradictions, Lord suggests developing a network of support that provides "critical colleagueship."

Marsh, M. "The Influence of Discourses on the Precarious Nature of Mentoring." *Reflective Practice,* 2002, *3*(1), 103–115. This article presents a personal account of mentoring episodes between a university professor and two first-year teachers. Marsh discusses how a mentor's stance—or point of view—can interfere with a conversation between a mentor and mentee by portraying two contrasting cases that highlight the importance of clarity in communication and co-constructed concepts of good practice. Marsh concludes that alignment about beliefs in relation to what counts as good practice is important to understand and share in establishing a working relationship.

Neufeld, B., and Roper, D. *Coaching: A Strategy for Developing Instructional Capacity.* Cambridge, Mass.: Education Matters, 2003. Retrieved April 10, 2004, from http://www.edmatters.org/webreports/Coaching Paperfinal.pdf. Based on a six-year qualitative study of coaching as professional development in Boston, Corpus Christi, Louisville, and San Diego, the authors make a distinction between "change coaches," who focus on leadership for whole-school improvement, and "content coaches," who focus on discipline-based instructional improvement. Activities of coaching and conditions that support coaching as development are described. Of particular interest is the discussion on the challenges of coaching that includes finding the time to do the work, measuring the quality and impact of coaches' work, and changing teachers' practices.

Orland, L. "Reading a Mentoring Situation: One Aspect of Learning to Mentor." *Teaching and Teacher Education,* 2001, *17*(1), 75–88. This article presents a single case of an experienced teacher and her learning trajectory as a novice mentor. Orland uses reading as a metaphor for the mentor's evolving understanding of the context of mentoring as "learning to read a text interactively." The study reveals that learning to become a mentor is a conscious process of induction into a different teaching context and does not emerge naturally from being a good teacher.

Schaverien, L., and Cosgrove, M. "Learning to Teach Generatively: Mentor-Supported Professional Development and Research in Technology-and-Science." *Journal of the Learning Sciences,* 1997, *6*(3), 317–346. Using a constructivist viewpoint, Schaverien and Cosgrove investigate Australian primary teachers' learning over a year-long professional development engagement with a mentor. Teachers learned technology and science in workshops where teaching approaches aligned with generative learning (generating ideas, testing them, and regenerating improvements) were modeled with additional support during classroom teaching. One teacher's learning trajectory is illustrated to make a case for this particular style of mentoring conversation. With a generative view of learning, the authors suggest that mentors could both perceive and select those aspects of learning events that were likely to help teachers appreciate and develop generative teaching approaches.

Wang, J., and O'Dell, S. "Mentored Learning to Teach According to Standards-Based Reform: A Critical Review." *Review of Educational Research,* 2001, *72*(3), 481–546. The authors review the literature dealing with mentoring issues within the context of relationships among experienced teachers and preservice or novice teachers. They analyze three mentoring program perspectives—humanistic, situated apprentice, and critical constructivist assumptions—that typify and address the dynamics of learning to teach aligned with standards. The authors provide a comprehensive review of studies about the expectations that novice and experienced teachers bring to the mentoring process and present four case studies that illustrate the necessary content and processes that help mentors move novices toward the kind of teaching envisioned by the reform standards.

Wildman, T. M., Magrialo, S. G., and Niles, R. A. "Teacher Mentoring: An Analysis of Roles, Activities, and Conditions." *Journal of Teacher Education,* 1992, *43*, 205–213. This article reports the results of a qualitative analysis of 150 mentor teachers who work in dyads with novices about their activities as mentors and the conditions that promote or hinder their success. The authors also provide suggestions for conceptualizing the mentor's role. Of particular interest is the discussion of conditions that influence mentoring relationships.

THEMATIC ISSUES OF JOURNALS

European Journal of Teacher Education, 1998, *21*(1). This thematic issue on mentoring responds to the idea of mentoring as a hot topic in educational reform and a favored strategy in policies for teacher preparation and beginning teacher induction. All of the authors work in teacher preparation programs where they are directly involved with mentor teachers. This may explain why the authors primarily address issues of definition, practice, and impact and make few attempts to place mentoring in a broader sociopolitical context. The authors represent perspectives of their home countries: the United Kingdom, Norway, Israel, and the United States.

Journal of Teacher Education, 1992, *43*(3), 162–226. This issue on induction and mentoring presents a reformulation of induction as a preplanned, short-term, structured assistance program for new teachers. These ideas were in their infancy in 1992, and the addition of a mentoring framework was innovative. The articles in this issue provide good background reading for those interested in the roots of mentoring, initial definitions, challenges, and constructions.

INDEX

Reading for Understanding
*A Guide to Improving Reading in
Middle and High School Classrooms*

Ruth Schoenbach, Cynthia Greenleaf,
Christine Cziko, and Lori Hurwitz

Paper / 240 pages
ISBN: 0-7879-5045-9

This book introduces the nationally recognized Reading Apprenticeship™ instructional framework, a research-based model with a proven record of success in increasing the engagement and achievement of adolescent readers, including many considered "struggling" or disengaged students. Filled with vivid classroom lessons and exercises, the book shows teachers how to "apprentice" students to reading in the disciplines. This is an approach that demystifies the reading process for students so they can acquire the necessary motivational, cognitive, and knowledge-building strategies for comprehending diverse and challenging types of texts. The book also presents a detailed description of the pilot "Academic Literacy" curriculum, a year-long course in which a group of urban ninth-grade students made an average of two years' gain in reading comprehension. In addition it shows how Reading Apprenticeship™ strategies can be embedded in science, math, English, and social studies classrooms, thus serving as a useful guide for teachers working across the curricula in grades 6–12.

Ruth Schoenbach is project director for the Strategic Literacy Initiative at WestEd. For the past twenty-five years, she has worked as a classroom teacher, curriculum developer, and program innovator with a focus on literacy in diverse settings from preschool to adult education.

Cynthia Greenleaf is director of research for the Strategic Literacy Initiative at WestEd. For the past fifteen years, she has provided professional support to secondary teachers and studied the impact of classroom innovations on student learning and achievement.

Christine Cziko is codirector of the CLLAD program at UC Berkeley's School of Education, where she works in teacher education. She taught English for twenty-five years in New York City and San Francisco public schools and worked as a teacher consultant for the New York City Writing Project.

Lori Hurwitz is a teacher in the English department at Thurgood Marshall Academic High School in San Francisco and a teacher consultant with the Strategic Literacy Initiative. She teaches Academic Literacy and assists other schools in implementing Academic Literacy courses.

Building Academic Literacy

Lessons from Reading Apprenticeship Classrooms, Grades 6–12

Audrey Fielding, Ruth Schoenbach, and Marean Jordan, Editors

Paper / 192 pages
ISBN: 0-7879-6556-1

Featuring pieces by five practicing teachers, this book shows how the Reading Apprenticeship™ instructional framework can be adopted to diverse classrooms and teaching styles. The book includes extensive resources and tools for implementing Academic Literacy course units, as well as examples of classroom practices using selections from *Building Academic Literacy: An Anthology for Reading Apprenticeship* (Fielding and Schoenbach, 0-7879-6555-3), making this an invaluable teacher companion to the related student reader.

Building Academic Literacy

An Anthology for Reading Apprenticeship

Audrey Fielding and Ruth Schoenbach

Paper / 304 pages
ISBN: 0-7879-6555-3

Building Academic Literacy: An Anthology for Reading Apprenticeship is a volume for middle and high school students addressing the topic of literacy and the important role it plays in our lives. Contributors include such writers as Maxine Hong Kingston, Richard Wright, Sherman Alexie, and Richard Rodriguez, and the anthology is thematically organized to invite students to explore the questions of why and how we read, and the connections between literacy, self-empowerment, academic success, and life achievement. Featuring lively and provocative essays, journalistic writings, and poetry as well as inspiring personal stories.

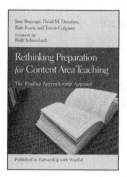

Rethinking Preparation for Content Area Teaching
The Reading Apprenticeship Approach

Jane Braunger, David M. Donahue, Kate Evans, and Tomás Galguera

Cloth / 290 pages
ISBN: 0-7879-7166-9

The Reading Apprenticeship™ (RA) framework has received national recognition as an effective, research-based instructional approach that supports all students, including underachievers, in successfully engaging with and learning from academic texts. First introduced in *Reading for Understanding* by Ruth Schoenbach et al., the approach is based on a program with a proven record of success in boosting the reading levels of urban high school students. Emphasizing social, personal, cognitive, and knowledge-building tools, the Reading Apprenticeship™ approach can be useful to teachers in any content area classroom.

In *Rethinking Preparation for Content Area Teaching,* Jane Braunger and her co-authors make the case for incorporating the Reading Apprenticeship instructional model into secondary teacher preparation programs. Arguing that teacher education programs need to foster a broader understanding of adolescent literacy, especially if teachers are to help their students read in discipline-specific ways, the authors show how RA can serve to strengthen content-based instruction, how elements of the model can be embedded in teacher preparation curricula, and what types of course activities enable new teachers to understand and practice this approach.

Jane Braunger is senior research associate for the Strategic Literacy Initiative at WestEd.

David M. Donahue is assistant professor of education at Mills College, Oakland, California.

Kate Evans, formerly assistant professor of education at San Jose State University, now teaches at the University of California, Santa Cruz.

Tomás Galguera, is associate professor of education at Mills College, Oakland, California.

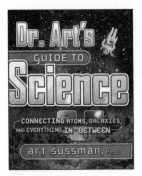

Dr. Art's Guide to Science
Connecting Atoms, Galaxies, and Everything in Between

Art Sussman, Ph.D.

Cloth / 256 pages
ISBN: 0-7879-8326-8

Richly illustrated with four-color graphics, *Dr. Art's Guide to Science* offers a captivating "big picture" view of science to excite young and older readers alike. Presenting science as an adventure, the book takes an awesome journey through atoms, energy forces, and the universe, and on the way it helps readers understand the guiding ideas of science, what they mean, and how they fit together. Challenging concepts such as photosynthesis, the greenhouse effect, and the mysterious connections between energy and matter are explained in ways that are brilliantly clear and engaging.

Venturing into the vastness of space, the book peers into the depths of time to describe the role of gravity and fusion in the birthing of galaxies, how the elements were formed, and why ancient stardust infuses our planet to this day. The book also explains how our planet works, from the tectonic forces that shake us up to the deadly and delightful partnerships that keep ecosystems in balance. Delving inside the cells of living organisms, the book describes the vital roles of protein along with the amazing DNA molecule that carries the genetic code of life. Finally, we learn about evolution and the history of life on our planet, including crucial questions about our future.

Thoroughly grounded in science standards, this book can be used as a primary or supplemental text in any science classroom. Related activities are available on the author's Web site.

Art Sussman, Ph.D., is a science educator and the author of the award-winning book, *Dr. Art's Guide to Planet Earth.* He received his doctorate in biochemistry from Princeton University and did scientific research at Oxford University, Harvard Medical School, and the University of California. Dr. Art works at WestEd in San Francisco. He assists states with their science education programs and presents "Dr. Art's Planet Earth Show" at conferences and museum science centers.